THE CHACO HANDBOOK

An Encyclopedic Guide

Second Edition

R. GWINN VIVIAN

BRUCE HILPERT

The University of Utah Press

Salt Lake City

The Defiance House Man colophon is a registered trademark of
The University of Utah Press. It is based on a four-foot-tall Ancient Puebloan
pictograph (late PIII) near Glen Canyon, Utah.

Library of Congress Cataloging-in-Publication Data
Vivian, R. Gwinn.
The Chaco handbook : an encyclopedic guide / R. Gwinn Vivian,
Bruce Hilpert.
p. cm. — (The Chaco Canyon series)
Includes bibliographical references (p.) and index.
ISBN 978-1-60781-195-4   (pbk. : alk. paper)
1. Pueblo Indians—New Mexico—Chaco
Canyon—Antiquities—Encyclopedias. 2. Chaco Culture National
Historical Park (N.M.)—Encyclopedias. 3. Pueblo Indians—San Juan
River Watershed (Colo.-Utah)—Antiquities—Encyclopedias. 4. Chaco
Canyon (N.M.)—Antiquities—Encyclopedias. 5. San Juan River Watershed
(Colo.-N.M.)—Antiquities—Encyclopedias. I. Hilpert, Bruce, 1950-
II. Title. III. Series.
E99.P9 V574 2002
978.9'82—dc21
2001006784

THE CHACO HANDBOOK

Drawing of Pueblo Bonito in 1896, by Patricia Vivian

For Florence Lister and Tom Windes—treasured friends
and master interpreters of the Chaco story.
—R. G. V.

To my daughter, Morgan
—B. H.

CONTENTS

ENTRIES

ILLUSTRATIONS

Figures

Maps

Time Lines

Much has happened in Chacoan archaeology since the first edition of *The Chaco Handbook* was published ten years ago. The period of intense Chaco Project fieldwork in Chaco Culture National Historical Park was followed in the 1990s by an almost complete cessation of research involving excavation or testing. The most significant work in the Park, reopening Neil Judd's three trenches in the Pueblo Bonito trash mounds, was conducted by Wirt "Chip" Wills and Patricia Crown with students from the University of New Mexico. Investigations at two major Chacoan great houses outside the Park also were carried out at the Salmon Ruin and the Bluff Great House.

At the same time, in addition to continued publication of technical volumes in the National Park Service Chaco Series, the literature on Chacoan history and prehistory increased significantly. In particular, the long-planned synthesis of Chaco Project research in the Park resulted in two landmark publications. Stephen Lekson edited *The Archaeology of Chaco Canyon: An Eleventh-Century Pueblo Regional Center* and Joan Mathien authored *Culture and Ecology of Chaco Canyon and the San Juan Basin* (see Selected Annotated References). Complementing these publications on new research are archival data now made available through the Chaco Research Archive.

Abundant new data underscored the need for an updated Chaco handbook. In reviewing this information it became clear that Chacoan scholars were devoting considerable time and pages in scholarly publications to debating the function of great houses and ultimately the reason for a Chacoan Phenomenon. Whereas many archaeological site clusters such as those in Mesa Verde National Park have been "interpreted" for the public, Chaco for both the archaeological community and the public has tended to foster "explanation" rather than interpretation. This process has been underway for close to a century and though we have far more data today than Neil Judd had in the 1920s, we are in some respects no closer to explaining Chaco than he was. A review of this effort was deemed sufficiently important to add a new chapter, "Explaining Chaco," to the handbook.

Bruce wrote the introductory chapters in the first edition of the handbook and has authored the new chapter, with Gwinn editing his work for accuracy and perspective. After reviewing all existing entries we determined that thirty-one required some updating and revision. We then compiled a list of twenty-one new entries. Gwinn drafted the text for these and Bruce edited them for clarity. Of the twenty-one new entries, ten are Chacoan scholars and half of those entries are women. These figures reflect both the burgeoning number of professionals working in Chaco and, more importantly, the valued contributions made by women.

As in the first edition, the text benefited immensely from review by a number of individuals. Russell Bodnar, Chief of Interpretation, and G. B. Cornucopia, Interpretive Ranger, at the Park provided critical comments that improved the new material. Douglas Palmer of Albuquerque, New Mexico, thoroughly reviewed the text of the original handbook and rose to the occasion again. From our initial meeting at the Great Kiva in Chetro Ketl many years ago, Doug has contributed his time and skills to numerous Chaco projects including detailed study of the Kin Bineola water control system. We sincerely appreciate his dedication to "things Chacoan." And we acknowledge with thanks Pat Vivian's careful review of all new material and note that her frontispiece drawing of Pueblo Bonito in 1896 was from a photograph and not, as some have asked, sketched in the field in 1896.

The University of Utah Press once again provided skilled assistance throughout the process of preparing this new edition. We thank Glenda Cotter, managing editor, and Ginny Hoffman, copy editor, for good advice and skilled help. We particularly thank Reba Rauch, acquisitions editor, for consistent and careful oversight of this project.

—R. Gwinn Vivian
Bruce Hilpert

There is no other place like Chaco. Some who go there find it remote, harsh, oppressive, and they leave quickly. Others return, pulled by a subtle yet unmistakable power captured within the canyon walls. Most acknowledge sensing the echo of those who once created a "Center Place" before time silenced their voices.

We want to help you know Chaco a little better. There are multiple ways of knowing, and discoveries can be made on many levels. We hope this handbook will become a tool for making discoveries about Chaco Canyon, the larger Chacoan World, and its prehistoric inhabitants. It is also intended as a reference volume on Chacoan culture that provides accurate, concise, and up-to-date information that is not too technical for the casual reader but still has value for the professional archaeologist.

To facilitate its use as a handy guide at home, at Chaco, or elsewhere in the field, we chose an encyclopedic format as the best way to provide information about words and topics used in trail guides and books or mentioned during site tours and evening campfire lectures. The first four chapters offer a brief overview of the Chaco Phenomenon, a general culture history of Chaco Canyon, the history of archaeological research over the past century, and a summary of more than a century of attempts to "explain Chaco." Time lines help to bring order to that information.

The alphabetic list of entries, "Chaco: A to Z," offers information about important Chacoan sites, major place names in the region, archaeological terms, and prehistoric objects and architectural features. Several people who played significant roles in Chacoan studies or the Chaco area are also included.

To assist the reader, terms that are defined in the handbook are shown in **bold** when they appear in other entries. We also provide a number of synonymous entry titles (for example, *tree-ring dating* and *dendrochronology*; *corn* and *maize*). Selected annotated references provide leads to more detailed information.

There are hundreds of prehistoric Chacoan sites in the San Juan Basin, but only a small number are commonly known. Our entries include the great houses of Chaco Canyon, major great houses in the Chaco Core, and some of the better-known great house outlier communities. We also have cited a number of smaller sites that have been interpreted in the park or that are significant in Chacoan research. In the interest of protecting sites outside the Chaco Culture National Historical Park, the text and maps give only general locations, which we believe are sufficient for most readers. A number of these sites (for example, Lowry Ruin) are open to the public. Others are not, and tribal or government agencies that protect these sites on lands they administer should be contacted for permission prior to visiting. Ground plans of many of the prehistoric buildings are included to make comparison of different structures easier.

The Chacoan landscape is marked by many topographic features that were undoubtedly important to the prehistoric inhabitants. We will never know the names they gave them, so we have used the place names used by later Navajo residents and others who passed through this country during historic times. Where possible, we have explained the derivation of these names.

We believe it is important to include basic archaeological and professional terms that are commonly used but often not fully understood by non-archaeologists. Defining these terms will help to explain the importance of certain techniques, shed light on the process of archaeological work, and clarify some of the more mysterious scientific techniques.

Chacoan peoples are best known for their architecture and the unique objects that they produced. In selecting handbook entries, we chose items that are distinctly Chacoan (for example, cylinder jars and stone discs) and also included a number of general items (for example, maize and pithouses) that were foundations of Puebloan culture.

More than a century of research has been conducted at Chacoan sites, often by rather colorful characters. The early archaeological investigations were sometimes marked by intense rivalries and personal tragedy, as well as dramatic discoveries. We have cited some of the prominent early archaeologists and a few of the institutions that played important roles in the evolving process of exploration and investigation. We also included entries on a number of local Navajo residents who made contributions to Chacoan research and ruins stabilization.

In 1971 a new era of Chacoan research began when the National Park Service and the University of New Mexico joined to create the Chaco Center, a facility for administering an extensive program of survey, excavation, analysis, and report writing centered on Chaco Canyon but including areas beyond the canyon. The work of the Center, known generally as the Chaco Project, lasted for more than a decade and in many respects significantly revised views of Chacoan culture. The quantity of data produced by the Project was so great that a final synthesis was only begun in the late 1990s.

The Chaco Project coincided with an enormous number of regional contract archaeology studies and mandated federal agency investigations in the San Juan Basin, work that continues today. This combined research produced valuable information and new approaches regarding the nature of the Chaco Phenomenon. We have attempted to cite the major results of this work in appropriate entries throughout the handbook. However, the volume of work in the past few decades is so great that we have not cited all of the programs and personnel. Our aim is to provide a historical balance in presenting the past hundred years, while recognizing that research momentum accelerated dramatically after 1970.

THE CHACO HANDBOOK

THE CHACO PHENOMENON

The view from the headwaters of the **Chaco Wash** in northwestern New Mexico is of an empty landscape that seems to stretch forever. Grassy hills fade into miles of an unbroken expanse that ends in the faint blue curtain of the **Chuska Mountains** sixty miles to the west. The sandy, yellow ridges are marked only by a sprinkling of low, gray-green sagebrush and an occasional outcropping of sandstone.

But one apparent sandstone formation in the foreground is different from those in the distance. Its towering silhouette stands out on the horizon like a cultural exclamation point. Square windows pierce the flat, dark brown rectangles stretched across the ridge, and slowly the realization sinks in. This is not a work of nature, but rather the work of humans. It is the remains of **Pueblo Pintado**, the easternmost **great house** of **Chaco Canyon**.

A walk about the ruin reveals a three-story stone building with almost 140 rooms. An enclosed plaza is pocked with the depressions of several round **kivas**. Nearby, another of these shallow pits is almost fifty feet in diameter, the remains of a ceremonial **great kiva.** The ground is littered with thousands of broken potsherds, the black-on-white **ceramics** that were the hallmark of the prehistoric **Puebloan** peoples.

Surrounding the great house are a number of small mounds, the ruins of small pueblos that formed part of the Pueblo Pintado community. Cutting through these small houses is a shallow depression about thirty feet wide that runs in a surprisingly straight line. It marks the path of an ancient Chacoan **road** that connected Pueblo Pintado to the heartland of the **Chacoan World**, twenty miles to the west.

As impressive as Pueblo Pintado is, it is modest compared to the wonders found in Chaco Canyon. Here, by the 1100s, stone great houses stood up to four stories high and contained as many as five hundred rooms and thirty ceremonial kivas. Even more remarkably, the Chacoans built twelve of these giant apartment houses along a ten-mile stretch of the canyon. Six were located within the one-square-mile area known as **Downtown Chaco.** Most of the great houses were nestled against the sheer sandstone cliffs on the north side of the canyon, although a few stand like sentinels on the mesas above. Almost all have south-facing, terraced rows of rooms that took advantage of solar heating during the brutally cold winters. Each contains hundreds of pine, fir, or spruce beams that were cut in the distant mountains and carried as far as a hundred miles to the canyon.

On the south side of Chaco Canyon, dozens of **small house sites** top the hillocks at the base of the cliffs. In distinct contrast to the great houses, these stone pueblos have only ten to twenty rooms and an informal quality of architecture, but their pottery and kivas suggest ties to the residents of the great houses who lived across the canyon at the same time.

At several places in the canyon are sets of wide stairs carved into the sandstone cliffs. These are part of the network of formal roads that linked the canyon great houses to many **outlier communities** similar to Pueblo Pintado. Each has a great house surrounded by dozens of small house sites. The connecting roads are a standard thirty feet wide, were leveled and cleared, and were often lined with stone curbs. They run for miles in nearly straight lines and were built with earthen ramps, raised roadbeds, and cuts through hillsides.

At its height, between A.D. 1050 and 1120, Chaco Canyon was undoubtedly the most complex and technologically advanced culture in the Southwest. But it is also the most perplexing. Modern visitors and archaeologists marvel at the architecture and road systems and ask themselves, "How did such a sophisticated level of technology and social organization arise so quickly among the pre-historic Puebloans? And why here in Chaco Canyon, a place where it is so difficult to make a living?" Archaeologist Alfred V. Kidder may have said it best: "It is hard to see how life in the Chaco could have been anything but a continual struggle for bare existence."

After more than a century of systematic investigations, many of the questions that strike a first-time visitor still puzzle archaeolo-gists. While the fallen walls and broken pottery have yielded many clues to the nature of Chacoan society, definitive answers to the big-gest questions are still elusive. For example, how did people make a living in a region of poor soils, frigid winter temperatures, and only about 8.5 inches of rainfall a year? Archaeologists have discovered **water control** devices and **gridded fields** that suggest the skillful Chacoan farmers were harvesting the torrents of water that rushed from side canyons to irrigate their fields of **corn**, beans, and squash.

But could this canyon possibly feed as many as six thousand people living there? Some archaeologists think so. They see the great houses as large residential centers for a people who had mas-tered the art of desert farming and had developed a complex social system that could accommodate large groups. As the population grew, they built more apartments and farms along the canyon floor. Other researchers believe that the population of the canyon was much lower, perhaps never more than two thousand people. They tend to view Chaco as a ceremonial complex, with huge buildings that served as a combination ritual center and lodging place for hundreds of pilgrims who came to Chaco from settlements scat-tered throughout the **San Juan Basin**. In this case, the only perma-nent residents of the great houses are thought to have been the religious leaders and their helpers who carried out the rituals and maintained the facilities.

Archaeologists are also baffled by the construction of so many great houses in such a small area, especially by the presence of four major great houses within the immediate vicinity of **Pueblo Bo-nito**. Because the great houses were built along the length of the canyon in three distinct periods of construction that spanned almost three centuries, Downtown Chaco may have simply resulted from a natural process of population growth. Others believe the locations of Pueblo Bonito and its neighbors had special spiritual significance or were based on celestial alignments. Whether an urban residential hub or a ceremonial center, the concentration of architecture is remarkable.

The sophistication of Chacoan architecture is also remarkable. Constructed at the same time as the Romanesque cathedrals in France and Italy (the Leaning Tower of Pisa is a late example of this style), these buildings were the finest expression of Puebloan stone architecture in the prehistoric Southwest. Not only did Chacoans build the tallest and most complex buildings in the region, they did so when most of their neighbors were erecting simple ten- or twelve-room pueblos using less-sophisticated masonry techniques. And why did Chacoans display such an extravagant passion for architecture? Builders spent thousands of hours finishing details that would never be seen; they used scarce **timbers** in pairs and triplets when one would have sufficed.

The same question can be asked about the extensive network of roads that connected Chacoan communities over an area of at least ten thousand square miles. With no wheeled vehicles or domestic draft animals, it is unclear why Chacoans built such an elaborate system of roadways. In this terrain, a simple dirt path could have easily served to link these settlements, but at Chaco, road builders even cut deep steps into sandstone slopes that any toddler could have walked up. Some archaeologists have advanced theories about practical needs for these broad avenues: moving military troops to quell uprisings in the hinterlands; providing crews carrying timber with an efficient route; or allowing passage for large groups of pilgrims on their way to the ceremonial center. Others argue that the overbuilt roadways may have helped to integrate local communities, or may have served as symbolic links to outlier communities as visible reminders of their cultural, social, and economic ties to Chaco Canyon.

What was the nature of these outlier settlements? Again, there are several ideas, but no definitive answers. In the final stages of Chaco Canyon's development in the late 1000s and early 1100s, relatively small great houses were built at existing small house communities, primarily south, west, and north of the canyon. Eventually, most were linked to Downtown Chaco by one of at least five major roadways. But who lived in the great houses? They may have been community leaders who emulated the Chacoan political/religious/ economic system, or Chacoans may have been extending their domain far beyond the confines of the canyon. Some think this may have been an effort to expand their political and economic influence, but others believe that hard times in the canyon forced the Chacoans to splinter and find new homes while maintaining ties to the cultural center of their world.

For many people the most intriguing question is why the last generation of Chacoans left the canyon and the monumental great houses their ancestors had worked so hard to build. **Tree-ring dating** shows that in the mid-1100s the Chaco region was plagued by several decades of drought. Many archaeologists believe that people moved to areas where water was more plentiful: first to the Animas and San Juan Rivers, and later to the Rio Grande Valley, Acoma, and **Zuni**. The oral histories of modern Puebloan peoples contain repeated stories of ancient ancestors who left settlements throughout the Southwest before migrating to their present homes.

We will never know the full story of Chaco, but we can continue to ask new questions and search for answers. For all of those interested in Chaco—park visitors, archaeologists, and American Indians—the canyon is a special place that instills wonder and an appreciation of the accomplishments of these ancient peoples.

THE RISE OF CHACO: A BRIEF HISTORY

The silent walls and broken potsherds of Chaco Canyon will never reveal the answers to all of our questions. They can tell us much of the story, but every answer raises new questions, and some secrets will never be told. Nevertheless, the results of more than a hundred years of archaeology have answered many of the most basic questions about the growth and development of Chacoan culture: How old are the buildings? How many sites are there within the canyon? How did the people who lived there farm in such a dry and unforgiving climate? But archaeologists still struggle with seemingly simple questions such as "How many people lived in **Pueblo Bonito**? How many people lived in the canyon? What role did the **great houses** play in Chacoan culture?"

Let's start with some of the things that we do know about life at Chaco. We know that Chaco Canyon, and the larger **San Juan Basin** that surrounds it, is one of the most difficult places to make a living in the entire southwestern United States. It is extremely dry, averaging less than nine inches of rain per year, with temperatures that range from 106° (41°C) in the summer to –24° (–31°C) in the winter. The frost-free growing season can be as short as 120 days, making agriculture very difficult. Firewood is scarce, and trees large enough to serve as building **timbers** for the great houses had to be carried from mountains forty to a hundred miles away. You could hardly find a place less suited for a large number of people to support themselves and build a civilization.

We also know that most of the Chacoan great houses that we see today were built over many decades, even centuries. Their final form evolved as the local population grew in number and complexity, new construction techniques were developed, and new design concepts were introduced. The great houses, although "cast in stone," were actually vital entities that changed to meet the needs of their builders and residents.

Chacoan culture was part of a **Puebloan** cultural tradition that had deep roots in the Four Corners region. While the explosion of sophisticated architecture progressed very rapidly at Chaco, all indications are that the builders were the direct descendants of people who had lived in the region for centuries. When people left Chaco, they moved on to settle at new pueblos in central New Mexico, southwestern Colorado, and Arizona. This pattern of settlement, growth, and then migration to new homes was not uncommon among prehistoric peoples of the Southwest, especially Puebloans.

Although there is evidence that ancient peoples lived in this area for more than ten thousand years, the story of the people related to Chaco Canyon as we know it began about three thousand years ago. At that time, **Archaic** hunters and gatherers were living throughout the Chaco area, including a site known today as **Atlatl Cave**. Here they sought shelter from storms in a small overhang at the base of a sheer cliff. They built their fires in stone hearths; cooked rabbits, pack rats, and other small game; and kept grass seeds and pinyon nuts in nearby storage pits. They may also have experimented with gardening, producing small quantities of **corn**, beans, and squash, but agriculture was not a mainstay of their life. Instead they moved from place to place to gather the fruits of the desert, erecting simple brush structures for shelter from the wind and rain. They lived lightly on the land, and no more than a handful of people stayed in the canyon at a given time.

By A.D. 500, Chaco Canyon had a larger, more settled population scattered throughout the canyon, with many groups living in villages on the mesas above. At one settlement, **Shabik'eshchee Village**, nearly fifty **pithouses** were clustered near a **great kiva** that served as a community center for social and religious activities.

These **Basketmaker** people, as they are called by archaeologists, built permanent houses excavated slightly into the ground, erecting a log framework to support a covering of sticks and brush that was plastered with mud. The great kiva, about forty feet in diameter, was also partially underground.

The Basketmaker people had mastered the art of farming in the arid desert, and they kept their surplus of corn and beans in small storerooms behind their pithouses. They were skillful weavers and made beautiful baskets and bags as well as durable yucca sandals, sleeping mats, and clothing. At about this time, potters were perfecting their craft, making ceramic jars and bowls as well as storage vessels to keep mice and rabbits away from next winter's corn and beans.

About A.D. 700, a change appeared at Chaco Canyon that occurred throughout the **Puebloan** region: the slow transition to Puebloan architecture. At that time people began to enlarge their stone-lined storerooms and link four or five together in a row behind their pithouses. Later, open shade **ramadas** were built to cover the work areas in front of the room-sized storage areas. Eventually, the sides of the ramadas were filled in with stone masonry, forming a large living room with two smaller storerooms attached at the rear. This three-room suite—home for a nuclear family group—became the basic building block of Puebloan architecture and persisted for centuries. By A.D. 800, the typical community consisted of a crescent-shaped room block of four or five linked suites fronting on one or more **kivas**, a vestige of the earlier pithouse. Along with stone architecture, people began to make a much higher quality **pottery**. Both are signs of a sedentary society that relies heavily on agriculture.

Throughout the Four Corners area, Puebloan peoples were building similar structures, with some regional differences. However, at Chaco Canyon things took a very sudden and radical turn about A.D. 850. At a few sites on the north side of the canyon, daring builders raised the walls of their small rectangular room blocks two, and even three, stories. Suites were added until the buildings had grown to compact clusters of up to fifty rooms. Masons laid up the walls using wider sandstone slabs in a sophisticated **core-and-veneer** technique that provided the strength necessary to support multistory walls. In another important innovation, builders terraced the rows of rooms from north to south so that all would be warmed by the winter sun.

Although these early architectural experiments were on a modest scale, development of the great houses of Pueblo Bonito, **Peñasco Blanco,** and **Una Vida** had begun. At the same time, the tradition of "small house" pueblos continued on the south side of Chaco Canyon. Obviously aware of the radical new building styles developing in the canyon, these people chose to continue with the older building type that was common throughout much of the San Juan Basin.

Why did builders on the north side of the canyon develop such a different building style? We may never know, but some archaeologists point to the distinct similarities between the floor plan of Pueblo Bonito and contemporary sites such as the one-story McPhee Pueblo in the Dolores Valley of southwestern Colorado. Were the builders of the Chacoan great houses northern immigrants who left their homes during a drought in southern Colorado and moved to Chaco Canyon in the mid-800s?

By A.D. 900, the population of the canyon had grown since the earlier Basketmaker days. But how were so many people able to survive? Game was becoming scarce, and in such an arid climate, farming was difficult at best. Only improved agricultural techniques could have provided enough food to carry the people through long cold winters and times of drought.

All three of the earliest great houses were located near large tributaries of the **Chaco Wash**. It is likely the Chacoans had already begun to harvest the runoff that poured over the canyon cliffs following summer rainstorms, diverting the water into their fields using a system of brush dikes and ditches. If so, this move toward intensive agriculture may have been what spurred the growth of the Chacoan great house communities that created such magnificent architecture, abundant wealth, extensive trading systems, and a complex social system.

Building on the innovations of the previous century, the Chacoans on the north side of the canyon enlarged their three great houses during the early 900s. At Pueblo Bonito, two arcing wings were added at either side of the central room block, increasing the total number of rooms to about 150. Several round kivas were built within the plaza area created by the two wings. Peñasco Blanco grew into a gently curving arc of about 65 rooms, all much larger than those found in small house sites. Una Vida had more modest beginnings than its sister sites, but similarities in architecture and the addition of an arced wing clearly define it as part of the great house tradition.

There are also signs that in the 900s Chaco Canyon was already becoming a social center of the larger San Juan Basin, with resources flowing into the canyon. Faced with the problem of spanning the roofs of larger rooms, builders imported **timbers** from distant forests, including those of the **Chuska Mountains**. Households relied increasingly on imported ceramics, with as much as 85 percent of the pottery found in the canyon during the Early Pueblo period coming from outside sources.

In the 1020s, rapid growth at the great houses changed the face of the Chaco community as well as the nature of its social life. Chacoan leaders began a preplanned building campaign that defined a new aesthetic, and in the 1050s, the arced wings of Pueblo Bonito were remodeled to follow rectangular lines, while three new great houses with angular floor plans were planned along a six-mile stretch of the canyon and on the mesa to the north.

Crews of masons, laborers, and foremen put in long hours as the initial room blocks of **Chetro Ketl**, **Pueblo Alto**, and **Hungo Pavi** were erected during a twenty-year period. Millions of building stones were quarried from the cliffs above the canyon and carried to the scaffolds surrounding the rising walls. Masons developed new patterns in their core-and-veneer walls, and resident engineers developed new techniques to haul the massive beams to the roofs of third-story rooms. Tree-ring dates suggest that the builders of the great houses cooperated throughout the canyon, with work carried out first at one great house, then another, and then another.

And perhaps somewhere, a select group of elders sat discussing the vision that they hoped to accomplish through this massive outlay of time, energy, and resources. These buildings were obviously carefully planned in advance, with labor managed on a community-wide basis. The leaders of each of the great house communities may even have met to chart a course of growth spanning the canyon. Of course, throughout these building phases, farmers still had to produce food, and local trade and religious activities had to continue uninterrupted. Fitting these huge construction projects into ongoing life at Chaco Canyon implies a complex society with some sort of authority system to manage and integrate a growing population.

A key element in the success of the building program was an effective agricultural system that could produce abundant food surpluses. There is evidence that by the mid-1000s a full-blown **water control** system was developed on the north side of the canyon to serve the great houses. Diversion **dams, canals,** and water gates directed floodwaters to gridded fields to make the most efficient use of scarce rainfall. However, on the south side of the canyon, farmers living in small house settlements continued their *akchin* gardening.

The second half of the 1000s saw an explosion of building activity, during which several of the great houses were completed in the final D-shaped plan, with a plaza enclosed by an arc of rooms. New kivas were built in many existing great houses, bringing the total at Pueblo Bonito to more than thirty. Although the design of each great house was unique, it also appears that each one attained a final form that met established criteria.

The vision of the Chacoans did not end with the completion of the canyon great houses. In the late 1000s, great house construction and Chacoan influence extended into the farthest reaches of the San Juan Basin. In every direction, as far as 120 miles from Chaco Canyon, small to medium-sized great houses sprang up in small **outlier communities.** In almost every case, the great house was surrounded by a cluster of **small house sites** and often had a great kiva nearby. Even more remarkably, these outlier communities often were linked to the canyon by a system of engineered **roads** that ran in straight lines across mesas, through washes, and even up sheer cliffs. In some places, four parallel sections of road were built no more than sixty yards apart. Some of the outliers had four-story **tower kivas** dominating the horizon that may have served as **sig-**

nal stations along these roadways. Whether the roads were built as practical routes for foot traffic or as symbolic links to tie the outliers to Chaco, at its zenith just after 1100, the Chacoan sphere of influence linked a network of communities covering more than ten thousand square miles.

At the time the outlier system was growing, significant changes were taking place in Chacoan architecture. A new style of architecture emerged in the canyon as a new generation of great houses was built in the early 1100s. Known as **McElmo style**, these new great houses were built as compact squares or rectangles and lacked the open plazas of the earlier classic Bonito-style buildings. Also different were the masonry techniques and even the type of stone used for construction. **New Alto**, **Kin Kletso**, **Casa Chiquita**, and virtually all of the northern outlier great houses were built in this style. Most of these McElmo-style buildings were smaller than their earlier counterparts. However, two contemporary Bonito-style great houses built during this period on the San Juan and Animas Rivers—**Salmon Ruin** and **Aztec Ruins,** respectively—rivaled some of the canyon great houses in size.

Ironically, this expansion of the Chacoan system marked the beginning of the end of one of the most remarkable civilizations known in North America. By 1150, the great houses in the canyon stood empty, and two decades later the same was true of the outliers. Although it is difficult to make specific links, there are indications that segments of the canyon population may have first moved northward to settle at the San Juan River outliers. A few may have joined the Puebloan peoples living in the cliff dwellings at **Mesa Verde**. Indeed, when Mesa Verde was abandoned two centuries later, some stayed briefly in the abandoned great houses at Chaco Canyon. Others moved to the east, the south, and the west. Descendants of the Chacoans are among the modern Puebloans living in the many settlements along the Rio Grande and farther west at Acoma, **Zuni,** and **Hopi**.

Why did the Chacoans leave the canyon? Most archaeologists agree that it was due to an extended period of drought, but this is one of the many questions that lead them to continue their quest for new information. While every new archaeological survey or excavation produces some small answers, the big questions remain largely unanswered. How did Chacoans maintain a successful agricultural economy in such a severe environment? What was the relationship of the small house communities to the great house communities on the opposite side of the canyon? Were the residents of the outlier communities Chacoans who left the canyon, or "country folk" imitating their sophisticated neighbors?

While these questions address complex social issues, many of the practical questions remain unanswered. How did work crews transport the vast quantities of timbers and stones used in the great houses? Why are so few burials found in and around the great houses? And did people actually live in them, or were they religious centers for a small priestly class?

To an extent, unanswered questions are an unavoidable part of archaeology. The remains of the past can never reveal all of the details of the lives of people long gone. But Chaco Canyon presents some of the most enduring and intriguing questions of any prehistoric site in the world. Its sophisticated architecture and dense population are remarkable, but even more so when viewed in the context of the arid climate and lack of available resources. Visitors and archaeologists alike ask themselves, "How did people at Chaco build such a sophisticated civilization? And how did they do it here, of all places?" Perhaps this is the biggest mystery of Chaco Canyon.

EXPLORATION AND INVESTIGATION OF THE CHACO RUINS

For several centuries after the last Chacoans left their canyon home, the **great houses** and **kivas** stood silent. The massive walls slowly crumbled, greasewood bushes took root in the plazas, and desert sands drifted into the vacant rooms. What had once been the monuments of a great civilization slowly became haunting ruins strewn with building stones and fragments of broken pottery.

Of course, the **Puebloan** descendants of the Chacoan people did not forget this important place, and memories of what had happened there were passed down for many generations. But as newcomers came to this isolated land, each in turn "discovered" the canyon and the greatness that once dwelled within it. In the 1400s, the **Navajo** arrived from their distant homeland in northwestern Canada and settled the arid plateaus within sight of the great houses and **outliers**. Three centuries later, Spanish explorers and settlers arriving from the south may have heard stories of this remarkable place, but expeditions led by soldiers and priests skirted the **San Juan Basin**. There is no evidence that any of them stumbled upon the ruins of the ancient civilization.

It was not until 1823, two years after Mexico gained independence from Spain, that the governor of New Mexico, José Antonio **Vizcarra**, entered the canyon with a company of troops on a campaign against Navajo raiders. Vizcarra made the first historical reference to the great houses, "which were of such antiquity that their inhabitants were not known to Europeans." With more pressing matters at hand, he did not dwell long on his discovery.

The earliest U.S. visitors to Chaco were largely members of military expeditions, geological survey parties, and mapmakers. When the United States took possession of New Mexico Territory after the Mexican War in 1848, a series of expeditions was launched to inventory this vast acquisition and chart the course for a new overland route to California. In 1849, the governor of New Mexico led his own military campaign against the Navajo through Chaco Canyon, camping for the night at **Pueblo Pintado** at the eastern end of the canyon. A member of the expedition, Lt. James **Simpson**, a surveyor with the Army Corps of Topographical Engineers, was captivated by the ruins. Led by Francisco **Hosta**, the governor of Jemez Pueblo, Simpson and artist Richard **Kern** spent two days exploring the canyon's major ruins. Simpson marveled at the Chacoans' engineering skills, describing their masonry as "a combination of science and art which can only be referred to a higher stage of civilization and refinement than is discoverable in the works of Mexicans or Pueblos of the present day."

During their brief stay, Simpson and Kern made extensive notes, took measurements, and sketched the ruins, noting such important features as the basic floor plans and dimensions of several great houses, the presence of "circular apartments sunk in the ground" (kivas), the unique style of masonry, and the fact that the great houses lay on the north side of **Chaco Wash** against the canyon walls. The archaeology of Chaco Canyon had begun.

With the publication of Lieutenant Simpson's report in 1850 and the completion of Kern's dramatic lithographs of the ruins, word of Chaco Canyon slowly spread among the staunch group of soldiers and surveyors charged with exploring the new territory. In the two decades following the Civil War, several topographic survey parties visited the canyon. On one of these expeditions photographer William **Jackson** and a crew of five mapped several ruins and discovered **Pueblo Alto** and the **Jackson Staircase** cut into the cliff behind **Chetro Ketl**. He took dozens of photos, but on his return to Washington, he was heartbroken to find that a new experimental film was faulty, and none of the images developed.

The actual archaeological investigation of Chaco Canyon began in 1895 when Richard **Wetherill**, a Colorado rancher, turned his attention to the San Juan Basin. Wetherill had created a reputation for himself in archaeological circles when a roundup of stray cattle in 1888 led to his discovery of several of the largest and most impressive cliff dwellings at **Mesa Verde**. He mined these sites for pottery and other treasures and sold them to museums, a legal enterprise in those days. For similar collecting expeditions to the Grand Gulch, Utah, area in the early 1890s, he arranged financial backing from brothers Talbot **Hyde** and Fred Hyde Jr., heirs to a New York soap fortune.

In 1895, Wetherill received a visitor at his ranch, Sidney Palmer, an amateur archaeologist from back east who had set out to see for himself the wonders of Mesa Verde and the mysterious Chaco Canyon. Although he had never visited Chaco, Wetherill was easily convinced to leave his ranching duties to his brothers and guide Palmer on a month-long journey to the canyon.

Wetherill's survey of the canyon ruins and exploratory digs at several sites convinced him of Chaco's rich potential. Upon his return to Colorado, he contacted the Hyde brothers and urged them to finance long-term excavations under the auspices of the **Hyde Exploring Expedition**. They agreed to fund a full season of fieldwork in 1896, but asked Frederic Ward Putnam, curator of the Peabody Museum at Harvard, to direct the work to ensure the scientific value of the investigations. Putnam declined but offered to send a student, George H. **Pepper**, in his stead.

In May of 1896, digging began at **Pueblo Bonito** led by Wetherill and Pepper, codirectors and sometimes rivals. With the assistance of Navajo laborers, they set to clearing rooms in the oldest part of the great house, removing tons of collapsed roof timbers, fallen building stones, and windblown sand. By the standards of their time, the archaeological work was of high quality, and the two took detailed notes, made sketches, and photographed the progress of the excavations. At the end of the season, a freight car filled with pottery, **turquoise** jewelry, and stone tools headed off to the American Museum in New York City, which would announce the wonders of Chaco Canyon and the success of the undertaking.

Excitement ran high as the Hyde Exploring Expedition prepared for a second season of fieldwork. They continued their explorations of Pueblo Bonito, which yielded even richer treasures, including high-status **burials**, caches of **pottery** and turquoise, and a carved and inlaid jet frog. By the end of the fourth season in 1899, the pair had excavated 190 rooms at Pueblo Bonito, had dug in **trash mounds** at numerous **small house sites,** and had located several prehistoric **irrigation** systems and roadways. Unfortunately, the **roads** and irrigation **canals** would be ignored by later archaeologists for several decades.

Wetherill and the Hydes undoubtedly considered their crowning achievement to be the thousands of impressive artifacts that were rapidly filling the storerooms of eastern museums. Ironically, this would lead to the end of their operations in 1900. In the late 1800s, most anthropological research in the Southwest was conducted by scholars from the eastern establishment. Some of the most active—such as Jesse Walter Fewkes, Frank Hamilton Cushing, and Matilda Coxe Stevenson—collected extensively for their institutions. Before long, anthropologists at fledgling universities in New Mexico and Arizona raised concerns over the wholesale removal of the region's cultural heritage by the "carpetbaggers."

In 1900, Edgar L. **Hewett**, an antiquarian and president of New Mexico Normal University, lodged complaints with the U.S. Land Office that the Hyde expedition was vandalizing sites at Chaco Canyon and selling artifacts on the open market. Although two investigations failed to uphold his claims, the Hyde expedition stopped work after the 1900 season. Hewett continued to press his case, however, and his efforts resulted in passage of the federal **Antiquities Act of 1906**, which protected cultural and historic sites on government land. Under the act, Chaco Canyon became a national monument in 1907.

Although the work done by Wetherill and Pepper yielded tremendous new information, its full potential was not realized. Pepper produced only four short articles by 1909, and his volume of field notes on Pueblo Bonito was not published until 1920. With the population explosion of the western states and the growth of scholarship in archaeology during the first two decades of the 1900s, Chaco Canyon cried out for further investigations.

Hewett responded with a five-year plan for excavations at Chetro Ketl to begin in 1919, while New Mexican archaeologist Earl **Morris** was embarking on a six-year investigation of the Aztec West Ruin, a Chacoan outlier. But again, it was an eastern institution that took the lead at Chaco. In 1920 the research committee of the **National Geographic Society** recommended that the society conduct a study of the canyon to determine the most effective plan for a long-term research project at one of the ruins. Neil **Judd**, a young southwestern archaeologist at the **Smithsonian Institution**, was chosen to direct the project.

When Neil Judd met Edgar Hewett in Chaco Canyon during the summer of 1920 to begin his study, he was accompanied by Earl Morris and Harvard archaeology students Alfred Kidder and Sylvanus Morley. This meeting hinted at Chaco's future role as a training ground where the deans of southwestern archaeology worked side by side with the best and the brightest of the upcoming generation of scholars. By summer's end, Judd had outlined a plan to conduct further excavations at Pueblo Bonito and begin new explorations at nearby **Pueblo del Arroyo.** Combined with ongoing work at Chetro Ketl, Judd's study would result in the thorough investigation of the three major sites that Hewett believed comprised a Chacoan town.

Beginning in May 1921, Pueblo Bonito buzzed with activity as Judd's Navajo and **Zuni** work crews erected a tent city, cleared rooms in the southeast room block, dug test trenches in the west trash mound, and excavated the **great kiva** in the courtyard. Aided by Pepper's field notes, Judd was able to build on previous knowledge and avoid duplication of effort. Unwilling to share the professional spotlight, Hewett suspended work at Chetro Ketl.

In eight field seasons, Judd's work revealed not only the extent and grandeur of the four-story Pueblo Bonito, but also much of the history of the "Bonitians," as he called the people of Chaco Canyon. He excavated most of the rooms and kivas to ground level and stabilized many of the stone walls. Through subsequent studies, Judd was able to establish a chronology of the four Chacoan **masonry types**, which allowed him to chart the growth of the pueblo as well as the sophisticated engineering knowledge of its builders. He also directed the work of a graduate student, Frank **Roberts** Jr., who sorted the confusing array of pottery types found in disturbed trash mounds into a firm chronological sequence. And, of course, he amassed an inspiring collection of artifacts that spoke to the wealth, skill, and aesthetics of the ancient Chacoan people.

With help from Andrew **Douglass**, inventor of the science of **tree-ring dating**, Judd was also finally able to answer Chaco Canyon's most puzzling question: How old were these pueblos? Beams that only two decades earlier were cursed as worthless, heavy debris, and even burned as firewood, now proved to be one of an archaeologist's most valuable resources. But in other cases, the National Geographic excavations led only to further questions: Why were there so few burials? Were these sheer walls and enclosed courtyards defensive?

In 1929, Hewett resumed his work at Chetro Ketl under the auspices of the **School of American Research** and the newly founded Department of Archaeology at the University of New Mexico. As department head, he looked to Chaco Canyon as a fertile training ground for his students and established a summer field school. Assisted by staff and students, he conducted extensive excavations of Chetro Ketl, revealing, in his words, "a community-residence (an ancient apartment house) which, if set down in a modern American city, would pretty fully occupy two average blocks. As a dwelling house, built by people for their own domestic purposes, I know of nothing to compare with it in the world—ancient or modern." He also excavated a sixty-foot-diameter great kiva in the plaza and was startled to discover an earlier great kiva hidden twelve feet below.

Hewett's work did not stop at Chetro Ketl, however, and he soon turned his attention to the intriguing issue of the small house sites on the south side of the canyon. Hewett assigned student **Gordon Vivian** to excavate **Casa Rinconada**, a great kiva associated with a cluster of small house pueblos, to provide further comparisons. Another student, Florence **Hawley**, made an extensive collection of tree-ring samples at Chetro Ketl that provided detailed, specific dates for the pueblo and the four different **veneer styles** used by Chacoan masons.

Other archaeologists turned their attention to Chaco in the 1930s. Among them was Harold **Gladwin**, who had recently made his mark in southwestern archaeology with excavations that had defined the **Hohokam** culture of southern Arizona. Convinced that great houses evolved from an earlier small house tradition, he set out to prove Hewett and his students wrong in their belief that they coexisted, and he conducted his own surveys, excavations, and tree-ring sampling to arrive at a chronology for Chaco Canyon. While some of his terminology for phases of development is still used today, there is no doubt that great houses and small houses were occupied at the same time.

Although the University of New Mexico's Chaco field school continued until the mid-1940s, activity declined somewhat after 1936. The following year, Gordon Vivian assumed the post of National Park Service archaeologist at Chaco and began an active program of research and the critically important stabilization of the excavated ruins at Pueblo Bonito and other great houses. His interests were varied, and over the next three decades he investigated the relationship of small houses and great houses, **water control** systems, ceramic styles, and the nature of the later **McElmo-style** great houses. He also reexcavated the **tri-wall structure** at Pueblo del Arroyo and dug the **Kin Kletso** great house and numerous other sites throughout the **Chaco Core.**

By 1970, more than 390 sites had been located within the Chaco Canyon National Monument, and it seemed that each excavation produced more questions than answers about the nature of what Cynthia **Irwin-Williams** called "the **Chaco Phenomenon.**" That year, the Park Service announced plans to launch a ten-year research initiative at Chaco in cooperation with the University of New Mexico. Directed first by Robert **Lister** and then by James **Judge**, the **Chaco Project** proposed to look at "big picture" questions such as the reasons for the rapid development of Chaco Canyon, the nature of Chacoan agriculture, the role of great houses, the use and distribution of scarce resources, and the reasons for the decline and abandonment of the canyon.

Fueled by federal dollars, intense academic curiosity, the expertise of its staff, and a ready supply of the field's brightest graduate students, in 1971 the Chaco Project began far-reaching surveys, extensive mapping projects, and excavations in a number of untouched sites. By the end of fieldwork in 1982, they had located 2,528 sites, had dug or tested 27 sites (including Pueblo Alto), and had collected more than 300,000 artifacts. Intermittent fieldwork continued after 1983, including research carried out by Thomas **Windes,** an archaeologist from the Chaco Project hired by the National Park Service. Windes also was involved in writing final reports on the excavations at Pueblo Alto and several small house sites. These reports were part of the more than twenty volumes produced by the Chaco Center under the direction of Joan **Mathien** and Robert Powers (Powers took over direction of Chaco Project activities from Judge).

Chaco Project staff members made significant progress toward answering the "big picture" questions posed in 1970. The relationship of great and small houses was addressed in a variety of ways, including comparative skeletal analyses carried out by Nancy Akins and John Schelberg, and research on site variability in ceramic and lithic collections conducted by Catherine **Cameron,** Thomas Windes, and Wolcott **Toll.** Detailed architectural comparisons of small and great houses sites were reported by Marcia Truell and Peter McKenna. Stephen **Lekson**'s milestone publication on great house architecture and his work with Jeffrey Dean on the architecture and dendrochronology of Chetro Ketl shed new light on the role of great houses in Chacoan prehistory.

As the Chaco Project started, other researchers began to focus on the relationship of sites throughout the San Juan Basin to the Chaco Core. In 1971 **Gwinn Vivian**, interested in the nature and extent of the water control systems discovered by his father, tested a **canal** running from Pueblo Alto to Pueblo Bonito. He was surprised to find that the supposed waterway was actually a thirty-foot-wide paved roadway with stone curbs. Although Wetherill and others had noted these roads earlier, they had been forgotten for decades. This "discovery" set off a wave of excitement and interest in roads that led quickly to analysis of aerial photography through the

Chaco Project's Division of Remote Sensing. Gretchen Obenauf continued this work, using aerial photographs and ground surveys to document hundreds of miles of roadways extending throughout the San Juan Basin.

These roadways invariably led to outlier communities, and in the 1970s and 1980s, many archaeologists broadened their perspectives on Chaco and their field of study. Robert Powers, who had joined the Chaco Project in 1976, conducted an extensive survey of outlier sites and, with Chaco Project colleagues William Gillespie and Stephen Lekson, reported on 36 of an estimated 180 outliers. While Powers's project focused on the northern San Juan Basin, a similar project in the southern basin was carried out by Richard Loose, John **Stein**, and Michael Marshall for the Public Service Company of New Mexico, the state's largest energy company. Meanwhile, digs at several outliers, such as Cynthia Irwin-Williams's landmark work at the **Salmon Ruin,** helped piece together the relationship of peoples and communities within a Chacoan sphere that is now known to extend more than fifty miles from the canyon in every direction.

Following the close of Chaco Project fieldwork in the Park in the late 1980s the National Park Service initiated a detailed survey of new lands that had been added to the Park near Kin Klizhin and Kin Bineola as well as a zone to the south of the Park and to the east on the Chacra Mesa. Both environmental and archaeological data were recorded and the Chaco Additions final report is now available online at the Chaco Research Archive (www.chacoarchive.org). Thomas Windes continued to collect tree ring samples from many Chacoan sites and environmental data from a number of field stations. And the National Park Service, recognizing the need for a synthesis of information generated by the Chaco Project, contracted with Stephen Lekson to plan and produce this volume.

Two decades of intense interest in Chacoan prehistory stimulated scheduling the 1997 Pecos Conference in Chaco fifty years after the conference was last held there. Almost five hundred people attended and discussed the state of Chacoan archaeology. Among other topics, Mesoamerican links to Chaco was again a focus of interest. Christy Turner, an archaeologist at Arizona State University, proposed that the Toltec had used cannibalism as a means of social control in Chaco and elsewhere in the Southwest, and Stephen Lekson presented his **Chaco Meridian** theory.

The first decade of the twenty-first century brought notable changes to research activities in Chaco. With one exception, the period of intense fieldwork in the Park ceased. This was in part a response to the concerns of several Native American groups who viewed excavation and even testing as culturally intrusive. The single instance was the reopening in the early 2000s of Neil Judd's three trenches through and between the two Pueblo Bonito trash mounds. The work in this case was approved because it involved removing only "back dirt" that Judd's crew had replaced in his trenches. University of New Mexico archaeologists Wirt "Chip" **Wills** and Patricia **Crown** with a number of students conducted this work. Initial results included the discovery of **cacao** residue on recovered fragments of cylinder jars.

Though excavation was curtailed in the Park, several Chacoan-related sites outside the Park were investigated during this period including the Salmon Ruin near Farmington, New Mexico, the **Bluff Great House** in the village of Bluff, Utah, and the smaller but important Chacoan community, Blue J, in the Red Mesa Valley, New Mexico.

As fieldwork ended the literature on Chacoan history and prehistory increased significantly. The long-planned synthesis of Chaco Project research in the Park resulted in two landmark publications: Stephen Lekson's edited *The Archaeology of Chaco Canyon: An Eleventh-Century Pueblo Regional Center* and Joan Mathien's *Culture and Ecology of Chaco Canyon and the San Juan Basin* (see Selected Annotated References). Many journal articles also were published, one of the most important being Barbara J. Mills's "Recent Research on Chaco: Changing Views on Economy, Ritual and Society" in a 2002 issue of the *Journal of Archaeological Research*.

Notably, new books on Chaco have been published almost every year since 2000. Popular accounts include Brian Fagan's *Chaco Canyon: Archaeologists Explore the Lives of an Ancient Society*, David Noble's edited volume *In Search of Chaco: New Approaches to an*

Archaeological Enigma, and Florence **Lister**'s *Chaco's Vanished Past: Hogans, Tents and Ruins*. Though it was not necessarily written as a popular account, Stephen Lekson's *A History of the Ancient Southwest* will no doubt attract a wide public and professional audience with an interest in Chaco. Archaeologists' and the public's fascination with Chacoan great house architecture is reflected by Jill Neitzel's edited volume, *Pueblo Bonito: Center of the Chacoan World*, Stephen Lekson's *The Architecture of Chaco Canyon, New Mexico*, and Anna Sofaer's *Chaco Astronomy: An Ancient American Cosmology*. Ruth **Van Dyke**'s *The Chaco Experience: Landscape and Ideology at the Center Place* employs great house architecture as a medium for better understanding Chacoan belief systems. Two detailed reports on important Chacoan structures outside Chaco Canyon were published: Paul Reed's edited three-volume *Thirty-five Years of Archaeological Research at Salmon Ruins, New Mexico*, and Catherine Cameron's *Chaco and After in the Northern San Juan: Excavations at the Bluff Great House*. (See Selected Annotated References for summaries of these and other sources on Chaco.)

Complementing publications on new research are archival data now made available through the **Chaco Research Archive**. This critically important source provides access for the first time to unpublished archaeological information including photographs and maps. Given the limitations on collecting new data from Chaco, these materials will become increasingly important for archaeologists and the interested public. Scholars at the University of Virginia where the Archive was initiated intend to add to this source when needed.

As trends in Chacoan research activities have changed in the past decade, so too have interpretive scenarios shifted. In a sense, within a decade we have moved from Puebloan farmers to Chacoan kings. One wonders what we might expect in the next decade. What we can expect is many decades of limited fieldwork, particularly in the Park. This could have a positive effect on research as Chacoan scholars, particularly new young archaeologists, turn to large existing bodies of information for framing and testing interpretive models concerning Chacoan culture. These include but are not limited to the Chaco Research Archive, the Salmon Ruin archives, and new data from investigations by Wills and Crown, Cameron, and Reed. And as Joan Mathien noted in her synthesis volume, perhaps the most underutilized wealth of information is the Chaco Project database and published technical volumes. Opportunities for significantly furthering our understanding and appreciation of those hardy folk, the Chacoans, are almost limitless. We can hope that scholars and interpreters of the Chaco story will meet this challenge.

In 1823 José Antonio **Vizcarra**, Governor of New Mexico and the first known European to travel through **Chaco Canyon**, recorded seeing several **great houses**. However, other than commenting on their great antiquity and their unknown occupants, Vizcarra had no time for or possibly little interest in speculating on these sites.

Twenty-six years later it was a different story when Lieutenant **Simpson** first encountered the ruins of **Pueblo Pintado**. His journal makes it clear that his mind was filled with questions about these ancient inhabitants of the northern plateau. He queried one of his guides, Francisco **Hosta**, the governor of Jemez pueblo, about the nature of the pueblo but Hosta revealed little information. As Simpson inspected the large site, he found clues that gave some information about the prehistoric inhabitants. Like a modern archaeologist, he interpreted the archaeological record—artifacts and architecture—to arrive at conclusions about the lifestyles of the residents of Pueblo Pintado: the multistoried, masonry great house bore a resemblance to the living peoples in nearby pueblos; the vast quantity of **ceramics** suggested a sedentary people, most likely farmers; the sophistication of the **pottery** and architecture suggested a people who had a relatively advanced technology.

As Simpson continued down-canyon and discovered a series of massive ruins, he found these simple answers lacking. One pueblo could fit within his preconceptions of the present occupants of northeastern New Mexico. However, a community of so many large villages within the short length of arid Chaco Canyon was another matter. As he came to realize the extent of what came to be called the "**Chaco Phenomenon**," he groped for an explanation that could account for such a remarkable concentration of people and monumental architecture. Who were these people who had built such an incredible array of massive pueblos? What was the nature of the political and social organization that allowed leaders to marshal labor and resources on such a large scale? How did they solve the engineering challenges of raising five-story walls? How did the large population, suggested by the number of great houses, feed itself in such an arid environment? As he grappled with these questions, he came to the conclusion that the level of sophistication was far beyond the cultural traditions of the local **Puebloan** peoples; he decided that these prehistoric ruins could only be explained as the remains of the Aztecs, the sophisticated residents of the central valley of Mexico, whose monumental temples and cities were already known to explorers.

Like generations of archaeologists who followed Lieutenant Simpson into Chaco Canyon, he found that the Chacoan ruins demanded an explanation far greater than simply interpreting the pottery, stone tools, and masonry to determine how people lived their daily lives. Whatever had gone on in this canyon was incredibly complex and required equally complex explanations to give an adequate understanding.

Although Simpson did not grasp the full sophistication of the Chaco Phenomenon, his explanation of **Chaco** as an Aztecan civilization foreshadowed the questions for which future archaeologists would continue to seek answers nearly two centuries later. Over the course of decades of research projects, archaeologists developed numerous theories to answer the same basic questions:

1. Who were the Chacoans? Where did they come from? What was their relationship to other prehistoric Puebloan peoples? Where did the Chacoans go when they abandoned the canyon? Are their descendants still living in the Southwest today?
2. Why did the Chacoan people seem to follow a different

"cultural trajectory" from other prehistoric Puebloan peoples in the region? Why did they develop such a sophisticated architecture so early and so rapidly?

3. What was the nature of the ethnic and social differences between residences of **small house** communities and the great houses?

4. What was the social and political nature of the **outlier communities**? Were these colonies founded by Chacoans or settlements founded by people adopting aspects of Chacoan culture?

5. How did Chacoans feed and support seemingly large populations in such an arid environment?

6. What was the nature of the social and political organization in Chaco that allowed them to plan and implement such large-scale community structures, including the procurement of resources from throughout the region?

7. What was the function of Chacoan great houses, **roads**, and other structures?

As archaeologists searched for answers to these questions, they used a variety of resources. Of course, their primary document was the archaeological record of Chaco itself—the artifacts, architecture, and environment of the canyon. Because early archaeologists focused their attention on the great houses, their answers and even their questions themselves were shaped by the importance they accorded these architectural monuments. Their understanding of Chaco was shaped by other factors as well. As archaeologists developed theories to explain Chaco, other archaeologists reacted by developing new theories that refined previous ideas or opposed them. Archaeologists also reacted to popular trends in American archaeology and their research applied new ideas to interpretation of Chacoan culture. In addition, new technologies such as **dendrochronology** and aerial photography shaped theory as well as practice. Together, these influences along with the creative ideas of several generations of archaeologists have produced an ever-changing and increasingly diverse array of theories to attempt to explain the Chaco Phenomenon.

As with archaeologists who followed him, Lt. Simpson's theory that the Chacoans had ties to the Aztecs of central Mexico drew on then current trends in archaeological knowledge. Frederick Catherwood's *Incidents of Travel in Yucatan*, published in 1843, shocked and enlightened antiquarians of the day with the sophistication of New World civilizations. Simpson logically assumed that such a highly developed culture had ties to **Mesoamerica**.

Richard **Wetherill** had a copy of Simpson's report in his library but when he and George **Pepper** began their investigations of **Pueblo Bonito** in the 1890s they quickly rejected Simpson's theory. Wetherill's experience in the **Mesa Verde** cliff dwellings and his familiarity with sites throughout the Four Corners region gave him a distinct advantage in interpreting the evidence he found at Chaco. At the time, American archaeology, centered in the eastern universities, was largely a descriptive discipline—practitioners uncovered artifacts, identified them, and deduced their function. As a trained archaeologist, Pepper did a thorough job of clearing rooms in Pueblo Bonito and meticulously recording his finds. Wetherill was able to determine that the pottery, tools, stone implements, and building techniques were consistent with those of other prehistoric Puebloan peoples. Together, they concluded that the builders of the Chacoan great houses were not Aztec immigrants, but local agricultural people who achieved a remarkable degree of technological sophistication.

By the second decade of the twentieth century, archaeology had entered a new era. As eastern scholars gained a broader knowledge of the extent and variety of prehistoric ruins in the Southwest, they began to piece together a loose chronology of the region. Archaeologists focused on the creation of a culture history for the region and specific sites. Wetherill, recognizing the basic principles of **stratigraphy**, had learned at Mesa Verde that **pithouses** preceded stone pueblos and that pottery designs varied from early to late periods. Yet, they were unable to assign calendar dates to changes in architecture and ceramics.

Neil **Judd**'s excavations at Pueblo Bonito were at least partly directed toward the development of a culture history of Chacoan great houses. To do so, he incorporated the science of dendrochronology—tree-ring dating—that was being developed at the University of Arizona by Andrew **Douglass**. In 1923 Judd provided Douglass with samples of beams from Pueblo Bonito for dating. Based on the breakthrough in prehistoric dating provided by the third **Beam Expedition** in 1929, Judd eventually was able to determine dates for specific rooms in Pueblo Bonito and provide a chronology for the growth of the great house.

With this information, Judd was also able to precisely place the Chacoan great houses within the context of general Puebloan developments. Surprisingly, and significantly, he found that the majestic great houses were earlier than many of the other known Puebloan ruins. The great houses were not the final chapter in a sequence of architectural evolution; rather, the Chacoans were exceptional innovators and pioneers.

Shortly after Judd's excavations at Pueblo Bonito provided exciting new understanding of the culture history of Chaco, Edgar **Hewett** initiated major excavations at **Chetro Ketl** in 1929. Despite his stature in Southwestern archaeology, Hewett was not known for his theoretical contributions to the field. His strength was in attracting a dynamic cadre of brilliant young students who feasted on the intellectual challenge that Chaco offered. Students flocked to Hewett's field school, anxious to both learn and develop new archaeological techniques. With Hewett's annual University of New Mexico (UNM) field school, the driving force of Chacoan archaeology began to shift from eastern institutions to those in the West.

While working at Chetro Ketl with Hewett, students including Bertha Dutton, Anna Shepard, and Florence **Hawley** pushed to investigate small house sites on the south side of the canyon across the **Chaco Wash** from most great houses. Hawley had correlated the dendrochronology of room beams and associated pottery styles of Chetro Ketl to arrive at a ceramic typology that could be used to provide general dates for ruins throughout the canyon. She applied these techniques to excavations at small house sites across from Pueblo Bonito and came to a surprising discovery: the small house sites were occupied at the same time as the great houses. This required a major overhaul of the culture history developed by Harold

Gladwin that proposed that small houses were the forerunners of great houses.

In response to this theoretical vacuum, Clyde Kluckhohn, a director of the field school in 1936, postulated that small house and great house residents were actually of different ethnic backgrounds, a little-noted idea that would gain importance in later years. Following closure of the UNM field school during World War II, most archaeological research in the canyon shifted to archaeologists working for the National Park Service. **Gordon Vivian**, one of Hewett's former students, reexamined Kluckhohn's theory as he puzzled over the meaning of the different types of architecture and ceramics in the Canyon. Following his excavations at **Kin Kletso** in the early 1950s, he drew on Kluckhohn's initial theory to propose an even further-reaching explanation of the complex structure of Chacoan society. Vivian believed the canyon was home to three migrant groups: residents of small house sites had moved in by at least A.D. 500 from the south; occupants of early great houses had migrated from the north several hundred years later; and builders of the **McElmo-style** great houses arrived in Chaco in the late A.D. 1000s from their homeland near present-day Cortez, Colorado.

By the 1960s, new trends in American archaeology again influenced the approach to explaining the Chaco Phenomenon as scholars focused on the significant role that environmental conditions played in shaping a people's culture. A new generation of dendrochronologists, led by Jeffrey Dean at the University of Arizona, attempted to investigate the prehistoric environment through the detailed analysis of the patterns of rainfall and drought reflected in the annual growth rings of trees. Drawing on new techniques of capturing prehistoric pollen in the soil and identifying bone remains, archaeologists were able to "recreate" the prehistoric landscape and even the diets of ancient Chacoans. Using knowledge about nearby contemporary and historic Puebloan peoples, scholars hoped to better understand the cultural choices made by the prehistoric residents of the canyon.

One devotee of this environmental approach, as well as the scientific approach of the New Archaeology, was **R. Gwinn Vivian**, who grew up spending his summers at what was then Chaco Canyon National Monument assisting his father, Gordon, with his investigations. The younger Vivian grappled with the question of how the large canyon population that lived in the large great houses was able to feed itself in such a severe, arid environment. He and his father combed the canyon for evidence of farming, assured that such evidence would unlock some of the secrets of the nature of Chacoan society. Their tireless efforts revealed significant answers. On the north side of the canyon near Chetro Ketl, they discovered evidence of large **gridded fields** fed by a system of **dams** and **canals** that would have allowed the residents to harvest summer rains to water their **corn**, beans, and squash. Such intensive agricultural techniques would have provided for the large populations that many archaeologists assumed lived in the canyon great houses. On the south side of the canyon among the small house communities, the Vivians found only limited evidence of this high-tech farming, a fact that furthered their belief that the canyon's inhabitants were distinctly different peoples.

The Vivians' research into Chacoan canals led to a puzzling "discovery"—irrigation canals that flowed uphill! Upon further investigation in 1971, Gwinn Vivian determined that these "canals" were actually roads, a fact that was nearly as astonishing as the gravity-defying canals. Within a few years, researchers and surveyors had discovered a series of roads radiating in several directions from the canyon, with many of the longest converging on **Pueblo Alto**. Chacoan society took on a whole new aura of sophistication as archaeologists came to recognize that many of the outlying pueblos of the **San Juan Basin** were linked by roads in a very large, and undoubtedly complex, social system. Now, totally new theories were required to explain a much larger Chacoan society.

In the 1970s, the **Chaco Project** would generate a huge body of new information and, eventually, new theoretical explanations of the growing Chaco Phenomenon. For the first time in almost thirty years, Chaco Canyon was again a major focus of research by archaeologists outside of the National Park Service. The large funding base and the opportunity to work in Chaco Canyon attracted a whole new generation of young students and recent graduates of archaeology programs, including Stephen **Lekson**, Joan **Mathien**,

Wirt "Chip" **Wills**, and Wolcott **Toll**. Initially, the project focused on creating an inventory of archaeological resources by conducting field surveys, sampling of sites, and some limited excavations. Then intensive excavation was carried out in sites representative of the long Chacoan culture history.

The extensive discoveries of the 1970s eventually led to radically different interpretations of the nature of Chacoan lifestyle and radically different theoretical explanations. James **Judge**, the Project's director in its later years, also looked for explanations of how the Chacoans responded to their arid environment. But, where Vivian had seen agricultural technology as the primary response, Judge looked for answers in the social realm. He theorized that the great houses were not residential structures, but rather huge warehouses. To deal with the arid climate and periods of drought, Chacoan rulers directed the flow of surplus corn and other resources produced throughout the San Juan Basin. Judge theorized that an elite class of rulers used the surplus to consolidate power and wealth, organizing the massive labor projects required to build the impressive monuments. A linchpin of his theory was a series of test excavations at Pueblo Alto that revealed rooms with few hearths and other features that archaeologists use to identify residential room suites in a typical pueblo.

However, later Chaco Project excavations yielded no evidence of storage and redistribution. Goods flowed into Chaco, but what was sent out in return? Judge revised his theory, proposing that the great houses were neither storehouses nor apartments, but rather large ceremonial centers tended by a relatively small population of elite resident priests. Judge proposed that seasonally people from outlier communities traveled the roads leading to the canyon, bringing pottery, food and other luxury goods, and in return, participated in ceremonies that maintained the well-being of the universe. This "pilgrimage fair" model of Chaco, with the assumption of a hierarchical society ruled by an elite corps of residential priests, became the dominant explanation of the Chacoan Phenomenon in the 1980s.

Gwinn Vivian never accepted the conclusion that only a few priestly leaders occupied great houses. His work on **water control** systems, agricultural techniques, and other aspects of Chacoan culture left him convinced that the residents of the canyon were able to produce enough food to support a relatively large population. Vivian maintains that no explanation of the Chaco Phenomenon is complete unless it includes the residents of the small house communities on the south side of the canyon. He proposes that their social and political organization may have been similar to historic and contemporary Puebloan peoples. He sees great house peoples organized like the contemporary Tewa, a community of **Tanoan**-speakers of the Rio Grande Valley. They practice a system of "dual division," with two segments of the pueblo alternating political and religious responsibility every six months. He believes small house residents may have been organized like the **Hopi**, with several clans sharing community ceremonial and social duties. These two sociopolitical systems may have operated symbiotically at Chaco for several hundred years, much like the Tewa pueblo of Hano which was founded on First Mesa at the Hopi pueblos around 1700. Vivian theorizes that outlier sites were home to affiliated peoples or perhaps seasonal residences that provided additional agricultural potential during sporadic droughts.

While some archaeologists such as Vivian still looked to surrounding modern Puebloan communities for an explanation of Chacoan society, a process called "ethnographic analogy," many others pursued Judge's theory that the Chaco system was a hierarchical society—what might be called a chiefdom, a kingdom, or even a city-state. In the 1990s, David Wilcox proposed that Chacoan lords ruled the surrounding region through force, using the roads to move their armies to collect food as tribute and to quell any potential rebellions. Christy Turner, a physical anthropologist, supported a theory of violence and warfare, citing isolated evidence of mass murder and even **cannibalism** in the San Juan Basin. Others had less violent explanations. Nancy Akins analyzed the burials in the oldest part of Pueblo Bonito and cited the large quantities of **turquoise** and other luxury goods found with them as evidence of hereditary ruling families. Lynne **Sebastian** theorized that great house leaders' political power was based on competitive control of agricultural production that enabled them to harness the local labor force for massive construction projects. As the number and diversity of

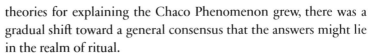

theories for explaining the Chaco Phenomenon grew, there was a gradual shift toward a general consensus that the answers might lie in the realm of ritual.

This trend was strengthened in the later stages of the Chaco Project by investigations at Pueblo Alto and a survey of the "outlier" great house communities. Excavations of trash mounds at Pueblo Alto revealed vast amounts of broken pottery. Wolcott Toll believed the amount of pottery was far in excess of that which would have been used by its residents and he interpreted this as evidence of ceremonial feasting, with the colorful serving bowls smashed in tribute. Through his mapping of outliers, John **Stein** noted the existence of numerous road segments that extended only a short distance from the remote great houses. He later theorized that these road segments were "bridges through time," connecting outliers to great kivas or other older structures—a connection to a cultural memory.

Beginning in the 1980s, other archaeologists began to pursue the idea that Chaco Canyon had a much deeper religious meaning than simply a ceremonial center. They came to view the "built environment" of the canyon as a ritual center that portrayed astronomical knowledge and cosmological principles. Exploring this concept, Norman Yoffee would later label Chaco a "rituality"—a concentration of purely ceremonial architecture rather than a city-state with economic and political functions. One of the most well known of these rituality theories explains Chaco as an astronomical facility designed to denote the timing of celestial events that were important to an agricultural people. In 1977, artist Anna **Sofaer** discovered the "**Sun Dagger**" petroglyph on **Fajada Butte** that marked the day of the summer solstice. Further research led to the discovery of numerous shrines and great house building features that appear to mark astronomical events. Enlisting a team of scholars that included astronomers and American Indian elders, she documented that many of the great houses are aligned to solstices, equinoxes, and even the lunar standstills that occur only once every 18.6 years. Her work seemed to establish Chaco Canyon as a monumental astronomical device that celebrated and preserved the collective knowledge of generations of prehistoric scholars. Such calendrical information is typical of knowledge that is preserved by Puebloan priests today and celebrated in their religious ceremonies.

In the 1990s, others pursued the rituality model in a different direction, explaining elements of the landscape and great houses as a symbolic representation of Chacoan cosmography. Using an approach termed "phenomenology," Ruth **Van Dyke** applied principles of contemporary Puebloan views of the cosmology to interpret the great houses, roads, and their alignments. Noting the significance of the six Puebloan directions—east, west, north, south, zenith, and nadir—and the prevalence of the balance of opposites, she interpreted numerous applications of these concepts in the Chacoan world. For example, the **Great North Road** represented the spiritual direction of the sacred underworld hidden below the rim of Kutz Canyon, where its last visible trace seemed to abruptly end; the **South Road**, which led to the base of the looming **Dutton Plateau**, represented the visible zenith of our physical world and the celestial realm. Van Dyke also saw roads as ceremonial links back to various great houses whose religious leaders competed for allegiance and control over the outlying populations. Such symbolism would have been readily apparent to those who experienced this living model of the universe from a Chacoan perspective—another aspect of a shared "cultural memory."

John Stein, an archaeologist for the Navajo Nation, concurred in this interpretation of Chaco as a symbolic rituality but introduced new interpretations as well. Stein theorized that roads represented spiritual pathways and also served as processional approaches to great houses. Architectural elements of the canyon were viewed as a spiritual and religious "theater" that served as a stage for the performance of a variety of ceremonies. At **Kin Bineola**, where Gwinn Vivian—the pragmatist—saw a canal, John Stein—the ritualist—saw a processional pathway. Consistent with trends of the 1990s, Stein also listened closely to American Indians who were willing to share their oral histories. Drawing on information held by several Navajo clans, Stein believes that the history of Chaco can be traced to a despotic figure known as the **Gambler**, *Nihwiilbiih* or *Noqoîlpi* in **Navajo**, who came to the Four Corners region from the south sometime between A.D. 400 and 800. According to some contemporary Navajo, the Gambler was not only skilled at games of chance, but was also a sorcerer who used his considerable power for evil, enslaving the people and forcing them to build the great stone buildings as he expanded his empire. Eventually, the people rebelled, beheaded the Gambler, and shot him like an arrow back toward the south. Based on this oral history, Stein views Chaco Canyon as the center of an occult system with powerful, tyrannical rulers.

For generations, archaeologists had largely dismissed American Indian perspectives and information on Chaco. With the emphasis on ethnographic analogy in the 1960s and an increasingly inclusive view of history that developed in the 1970s and 1980s, scholars sought out and gave greater credence to the information that native Southwesterners were willing to provide. Many Puebloan peoples have extensive knowledge of their clan's history, but often this knowledge is not to be shared with outsiders. We know from Hopi historians, for example, that Chaco was a stopping point for clans who journeyed through the prehistoric Southwest as they discovered and perfected *Hopivötskwani*, the Hopi Path of Life. Some clans actually lived at the great houses of *Yupköyvi*, while others came from different places in the region to perform their powerful ceremonies. Eventually, these clans abandoned Chaco and some migrated to Hopi, where they were accepted if they could prove their knowledge of *Hopivötskwani* and fulfill their destiny.

The concept and practice of migration is common to the oral histories of many Puebloan peoples today. Some pueblos have their own names for Chaco and consider themselves descendants of people who once lived there. Although the information they provide is often less detailed than archaeologists might like and sometimes is framed in symbolic terms, what scholars have previously described as "myths" can provide a valid and important perspective on the Chacoan past. Indeed, there may be quite detailed histories that are still repeated in pueblo kivas today, but only for those who are intended to receive such privileged information. In many cases, these stories point in the same direction as archaeological research as scholars search for increasingly fine-grained explanations of the nature of Chacoan society.

In the first decade of the twenty-first century, one scholar gained a growing reputation for his far-reaching and detailed theory of what drove Chaco's brief, but dynamic, cultural trajectory. During his tenure with the Chaco Project, Stephen **Lekson** was known primarily for his work on Chacoan architecture, especially great houses. In 1999, he introduced a new theory that caused considerable discussion within the archaeological community. Noting the precise north-south alignment of **Casa Rinconada**, Pueblo Alto, and the Great North Road, Lekson maintained that Chaco was the physical manifestation of a people driven by their obsession with the ceremonial significance of the "**Chaco Meridian**," longitude 107° 57' 25". Lekson believes that the great houses of "**Downtown Chaco**" constitute a ritual center aligned along this axis. When environmental conditions in the canyon became unlivable in the mid-1100s, he theorizes Chacoans followed the Great North Road and repeated the layout of the major components of Downtown Chaco at the **Aztec Ruin** site on the San Juan River. A few generations later, the Chacoans' descendants moved approximately five hundred miles due south to establish **Paquimé**, also known as **Casas Grandes**, in Chihuahua, Mexico. His theory combined elements of hierarchical political power, ritual symbolism, astronomical alignments, and **Mesoamerican** influences to explain those who would be Chacoan kings. As evidence, he cited architectural features such as **T-shaped doorways**, pottery, **macaws**, and the huge stone **discs** found in kivas. He drew his inspiration from archaeological evidence, anthropological theory, and American Indian oral history and symbology.

Lekson spent nearly a decade defending his thesis in the face of considerable criticism from some of his colleagues before presenting an even grander vision in his 2009 treatise, *A History of the Ancient Southwest*. Never one to shy away from controversy, he expanded on his previous ideas, presenting a detailed, three-thousand-year history of the prehistoric people of the American Southwest that integrated the **Anasazi** of the north, the **Hohokam** of the Arizona deserts, the Mimbres people of southwestern New Mexico, and the urban center of Paquimé. Here, he set forth the theory that "urbanism" was a concept that spread northward from Teotihuacán and other cities in the central valley of Mexico to the Hohokam communities of southern Arizona. Eventually, leaders in the Four Corners area adopted the concept of hierarchical political power that was expressed through the monumental symbols of great houses, establishing both a community and a power base at Chaco Canyon. Lekson states that these kings transformed ancestral Puebloan society as they asserted their political, economic, religious, and military power among a lower class of commoners, extending their power through the system of outlier communities. They imposed a peace among the diverse peoples of the San Juan Basin, but demanded tribute in return. Eventually, a rift formed as the newer faction of the Chacoan Meridian competed with the older adherents to the solstitial worldview that held that cultural values were linked to astronomical events and not a north-south meridian. After the Chacoan leaders and their subjects moved northward to Aztec about A.D. 1150, the system began to fall apart. The kings sent their armies to subdue surrounding communities, but instead, their residents fled eastward to settle along the Rio Grande and to the south and west at the modern pueblos of Acoma and Hopi. As people abandoned the northern plateau, Chacoan rulers moved south, with some establishing themselves as kings among Classic-period Hohokam communities. By A.D. 1400, the residents of southern Arizona overthrew these rulers and the descendants and heirs of the Chacoan kings moved farther south to the rising urban center of Paquimé. Having rejected the last vestiges of elite political power, the Puebloan people of the north and the O'odham people of southern Arizona returned to egalitarian sociopolitical systems that the earliest Spanish explorers encountered in the late 1500s.

Lekson's latest theory has created as much controversy as his earlier ideas about the Chaco Meridian. As detailed as his history is, it is just as tenuous. But, it serves as a far-reaching explanation of Chaco and its role within the greater history of the Southwest that deserves further investigation and testing through further archaeological research. As Linda Cordell and James Judge wrote in 2001, "we are weary and wary of grand stories and scenarios that go unevaluated." In a way, though, Lekson's history symbolizes and manifests the limitations of archaeology, oral history, and the investigation of prehistory. Every question is broader than the answers that can be discerned from crumbling stone walls, scattered potsherds, and the histories passed down through generations in kivas.

For generations, the ruins of Chaco Canyon have intrigued explorers and archaeologists. Yet, as they try to refine their explanations through better technology, additional data, native perspectives, and creative theories, definitive answers often slip through their fingers. In the end, there have been few definitive answers to the most intriguing questions. For the present, the mystery of Chaco Canyon remains just that—a mystery.

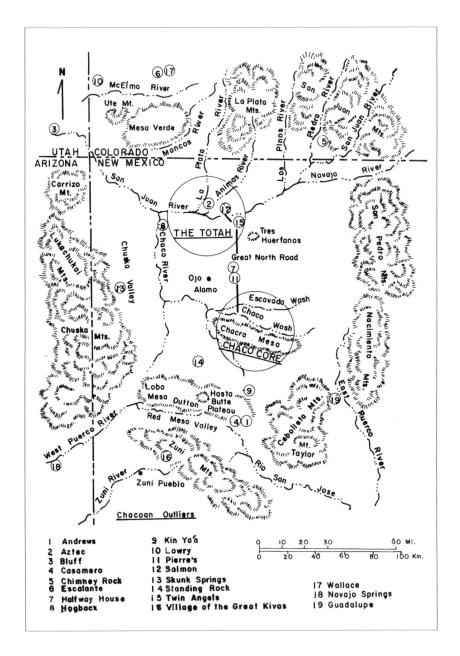

MAP 1. The San Juan Basin's major topographic and hydrologic features, and locations of the Chaco Core, the Totah, and cited Chacoan outliers. (After Vivian 1990: Figure 2.1.)

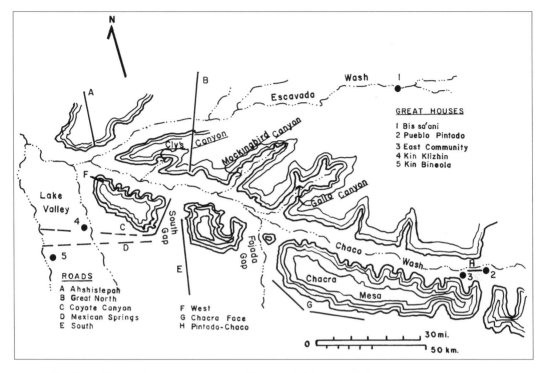

MAP 2. The Chaco Core's primary topographic and hydrologic features, and the locations of five great houses and eight roads.

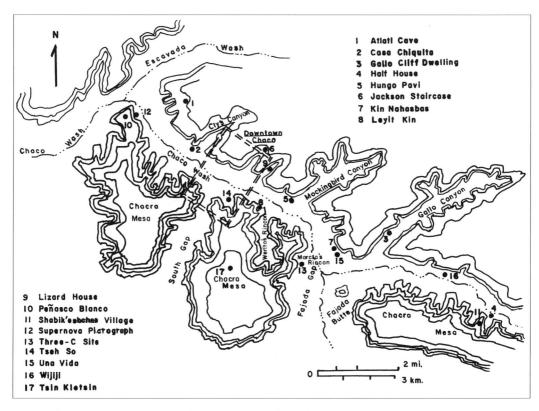

MAP 3. Chaco Canyon's major sites and primary topographic and hydrologic features. (See Map 4 for sites in Downtown Chaco.)

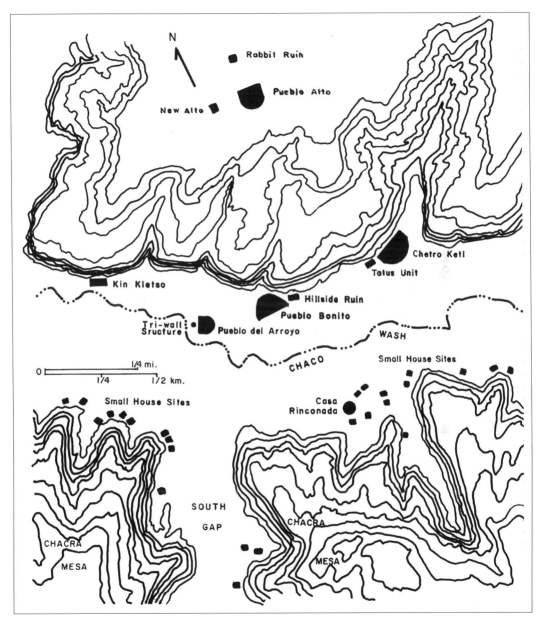

MAP 4. Locations of the great houses within the central canyon zone identified by Lekson as Downtown Chaco. Also shown are the Casa Rinconada great kiva, some small house sites, and the tri-wall structure.

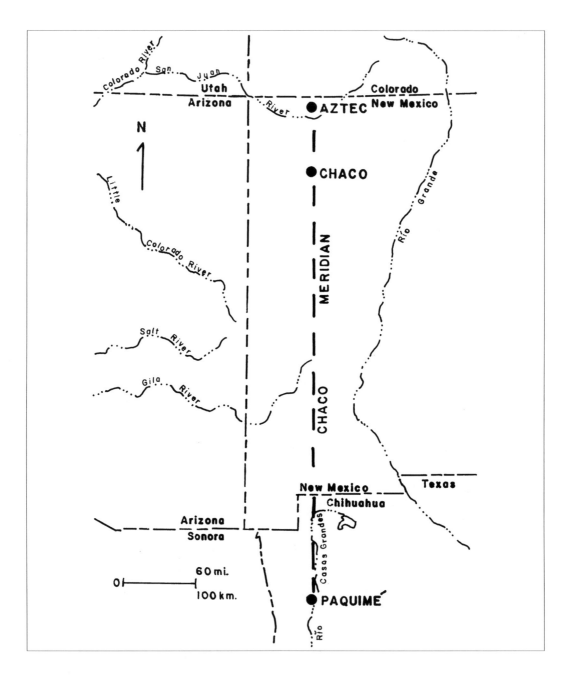

MAP 5. Lekson's postulated "Chaco Meridian" linking Chaco, Aztec, and Paquimé. (After Lekson 1999: Figure 1.1.)

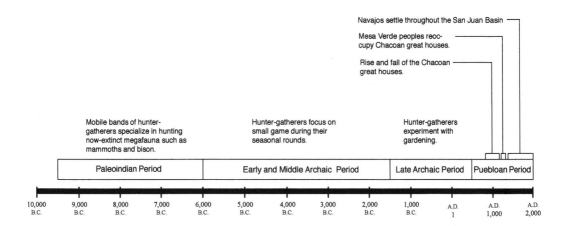

Navajos settle throughout the San Juan Basin

Mesa Verde peoples reoc-
cupy Chacoan great houses.

Rise and fall of the Chacoan
great houses.

Mobile bands of hunter-
gatherers specialize in hunting
now-extinct megafauna such as
mammoths and bison.

Hunter-gatherers focus on
small game during their
seasonal rounds.

Hunter-gatherers
experiment with
gardening.

| Paleoindian Period | Early and Middle Archaic Period | Late Archaic Period | Puebloan Period |

| 10,000 B.C. | 9,000 B.C. | 8,000 B.C. | 7,000 B.C. | 6,000 B.C. | 5,000 B.C. | 4,000 B.C. | 3,000 B.C. | 2,000 B.C. | 1,000 B.C. | A.D. 1 | A.D. 1,000 | A.D. 2,000 |

TIME LINE 1. American Indian occupation of the San Juan Basin.

TIME LINE 2. Initial construction dates in the San Juan Basin.

Time scale: A.D. 850 — A.D. 900 — A.D. 950 — A.D. 1000 — A.D. 1050 — A.D. 1100 — A.D. 1150 — A.D. 1200

Phases: Early Bonito Phase 900–1040 | Classic Bonito Phase 1040–1100 | Late Bonito Phase 1100–1140 | Abandonment 1140–1180

Water Control Systems

Chacoan Roads

Outliers in Northern San Juan Basin
- Wallace 1060?
- Lowry 1086
- Salmon 1088
- West Ruin 1110
- Aztec
- Pierre's 1120
- Escalante 1130

Outliers in Southern San Juan Basin
- Andrews Outlier early 900s
- Guadalupe Outlier early 900s
- Village of the Great Kivas 1060
- Kin Ya'a 1087

Small Houses in Chaco Canyon
- 3C Site 870
- BC 50 early 900s
- BC 59
- Leyit Kin

Great Houses in Chaco Core
- East Community early 900s
- Pueblo Pintado 1065
- Kin Klizhin 1086
- Kin Bineola 1110
- Bis sa'ani 1130

Great Houses in Chaco Canyon
- Pueblo Bonito 860
- Una Vida 860
- Peñasco Blanco 900
- Hungo Pavi 990
- Chetro Ketl 1010
- Pueblo Alto 1020
- Pueblo del Arroyo 1065
- Casa Rinconada 1075
- Casa Chiquita
- Wijiji
- New Alto
- Tsin Kletsin 1110
- Hillside 1130

TIME LINE 3. Periods of intense building activity at Chacoan great houses.

TIME LINE 4. Occupation dates of sites in the Chaco Core.

TIME LINE 5. Occupation dates of selected Chacoan outliers in the San Juan Basin. (After Powers et al. 1983: Figure 140.)

A

Abandonment
A process common throughout the prehistoric Southwest in which people moved away from habitation sites and even entire regions. In most cases, these departures appear to have been planned, because portable items such as **pottery**, tools, and clothing were removed from the rooms. In some sites, however, many of these items have been found by archaeologists, and it is assumed that the departure was hurried and unplanned. Archaeologists can often trace these movements of people from one locale to another based on the presence of similar artifacts—usually distinctive pottery types—in the two areas at different dates.

Many theories have been proposed for the abandonment of prehistoric sites, but archaeological, climatological, and hydrological evidence strongly suggests that inadequate rainfall was often one cause. Warfare and raiding may have contributed to some population movements, but they probably did not account for most of the changes documented in the Southwest.

The oral histories of **Puebloan** peoples contain many references to migrations of clans and other kin groups in past times. The Puebloans do not consider any ancestral site "abandoned"; rather, they believe that their ancestors' spirits still reside in the buildings they constructed.

Chacoans left their **great houses** and **small house sites** in Chaco Canyon by at least the late 1100s. Archaeological evidence from the Chaco area and the greater **San Juan Basin** indicates that movement out of the canyon probably started in the early 1100s and continued into the mid- to late 1100s. This movement likely was stimulated by a twenty-five-year period of below-average rainfall that began about A.D. 1130. The climatic change affected residents of both small house sites and great houses. Post-1150 Chacoan sites have not been positively identified in the archaeological record, and documenting the late evolution of Chacoan culture remains a problem. Some archaeologists believe that Chacoan culture persisted in canyon great houses into the 1200s, but supportive data are inconclusive.

Portions of some canyon great houses were remodeled and occupied in the mid- to late 1200s by people making **Mesa Verde Black-on-white** pottery, presumably residents of **Mesa Verde** who began moving out of southwestern Colorado in the mid-1200s. The **Aztec** and **Salmon** outliers provide some of the best evidence for reoccupation of Chacoan great houses by people moving south and east from Mesa Verde in the mid-1200s. This reoccupation was short-lived, and Chaco Canyon and most outliers probably were completely abandoned by A.D. 1300.

Ahshislepah Road

(Map 2)

A Chacoan **road** connecting Ahshislepah Canyon to the western end of Chaco Canyon. The road enters Chaco Canyon from the west at the cliff overlooking the confluence of the Chaco and **Escavada** washes. A series of seven sets of masonry and rock-cut steps descend into the bottom of the canyon. From this point the road may have continued east up the canyon to the **great houses** of **Downtown Chaco**, or it may have proceeded up the cliff on the south side of **Chaco Wash** and across the mesa to **Peñasco Blanco**.

From the top of the seven sets of stairs, the road leads west for slightly more than three miles to the edge of Ahshislepah Canyon, and a rubble mound in the canyon below is probably the remains of a ramp. The road has never been traced beyond Ahshislepah

Canyon. If it crossed the canyon, its bearing would have taken it toward the **Hogback outlier**, but it may have been routed down Ahshislepah Canyon to the south and west.

Akchin Farming

A type of **floodwater farming**. The name comes from a Tohono O'odham word meaning "at the mouth of the wash." Where water fans out over the desert at the mouth of usually dry desert riverbeds, runoff deposits water, soil, and nutrients, creating natural garden plots that were watered several times during the growing season by violent summer thunderstorms.

Akchin agriculture was often practiced in arid regions where river irrigation was not possible. Washes could channel runoff from miles away, an advantage in the desert when summer rains were scarce. Chacoan farmers almost certainly used the *akchin* technique, especially on the south side of **Chaco Canyon**, where many small washes entered the floodplain. Chacoan peoples living outside the canyon also probably relied on this effective technique of harvesting desert rainfall.

Anasazi

A term used by archaeologists since the 1930s to describe the prehistoric **Puebloan** peoples of the Four Corners region and to distinguish their culture from other ancient southwestern cultures such as the **Mogollon** and **Hohokam**. The Anasazi are believed to be the ancestors of modern Puebloan people.

Anasazi culture varied by region, and there were distinct differences between the Anasazi living east and west of the modern-day Arizona/New Mexico state line. Chacoan culture is usually considered to be Eastern Anasazi, whereas the Kayenta culture of northeastern Arizona is considered Western Anasazi.

The word "Anasazi" is an English corruption of a **Navajo** (Diné) term meaning "enemy ancestors." Today, Puebloan peoples prefer to use the term "**Ancestral Puebloans**" rather than the Navajo word, which they find disrespectful.

Ancestral Puebloan (see *Anasazi*)

Andrews Outlier

(Map 1; Figure 1)

A Chacoan outlier community located about fifty miles due south of Chaco Canyon, notable for having three **great kivas**. One lies near the great house, while the other two are located among approximately thirty small house sites that make up the community.

Andrews is one of several outlier communities in the **Red Mesa Valley** in the southern sector of the **San Juan Basin**. No Chacoan **roads** have been conclusively located at Andrews, but they are present at neighboring outliers. Analysis of ceramic styles found at the site indicate that it was occupied from about A.D. 900 to 1100. No excavations have been conducted at this outlier, but Ruth **Van Dyke's** careful analysis of visible architecture suggests that the local population constructed the buildings for community ritual.

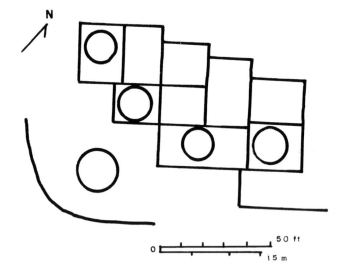

FIGURE 1. Andrews Outlier great house ground plan. The site has not been excavated, but the locations of kivas and rooms have been estimated from present surface evidence. The curved plaza wall may have enclosed a larger area at one time. A nearby associated great kiva is not shown.

The great house is owned by the Archaeological Conservancy, and the outlier community is protected by the Bureau of Land Management.

Antiquities Act of 1906

Federal legislation passed during the presidency of Theodore Roosevelt to protect prehistoric and historic ruins and objects of antiquity on U.S. public lands. The act also provided for the establishment of national monuments by presidential proclamation and national parks by act of Congress.

Chaco Canyon was pivotal in the passage of the bill. Edgar L. **Hewett**, a prominent archaeologist in New Mexico at the time, lobbied heavily for the act because of his concern about large-scale excavations at Chaco conducted by Richard **Wetherill** and the **Hyde Exploring Expedition**.

Chaco Canyon was among the first eighteen national monuments named by Theodore Roosevelt in 1907. The monument achieved park status in 1980 and became Chaco Culture National Historical Park.

Archaeoastronomy

A branch of archaeology that investigates possible relationships between the placement of buildings, features in buildings, stone pillars, **rock art,** and other man-made objects and the celestial movements of the sun, moon, planets, stars, and constellations. Natural features may also be a part of such observations. Some of these celestial markers are thought to chart major astronomical events that may have been used in prehistoric ritual and planting calendars, such as the solstice and equinox.

The best-known example of archaeoastronomical features at Chaco Canyon is the **Sun Dagger** on **Fajada Butte,** where fallen rock slabs direct sunlight onto a cliff face **petroglyph** on the same day each year. Several features in Chaco Canyon, such as **corner doorways** and **shrines,** are believed to have had astronomical significance. Anna **Sofaer,** Jonathan Reyman, Michael Zeilik, and Ray

Williamson, among others, have conducted archaeoastronomical investigations at Chaco.

Archaeomagnetic Dating

A dating technique based on the movement through time of magnetic north, a location that differs slightly from the Earth's geographic pole, known as true north or the North Pole. The Earth's magnetic field is constantly changing, and the movement of magnetic north can be traced back into time.

When clay in soil is baked at high temperatures, iron particles in the clay will permanently align with the earth's magnetic direction. As long as the clay is not reheated and realigned, the particles can be pegged to a certain point in time when magnetic north matched the alignment of the particles. Archaeologists carefully record the location of a soil sample and then measure the alignment of the clay particles in a laboratory to obtain a date.

In the southwestern United States this movement has been plotted for a period of about 2,000 years using particle magnetic alignment in fired clay features such as fire pits and hearths in rooms that have been dated by other means.

Archaeomagnetic dating is especially useful in prehistoric sites that cannot be dated by tree-rings or other means, and it has been used in some early Chacoan sites.

Archaic

A term used by archaeologists to describe a prehistoric time period and a way of life that was known throughout most of North America. Within the Southwest it is usually dated from about 6000 B.C. to A.D. 100. The Archaic period is seen as a long transition between the earlier **Paleoindian** big game hunters and the later agricultural peoples of the Southwest (**Anasazi**, **Mogollon**, and **Hohokam**).

Throughout most of the Archaic period, people lived by hunting small game and gathering wild plant foods. Extended family groups moved within their territories on a seasonal basis, often coming together in larger winter camps. Late in the Archaic period, people began to experiment with growing corn and making primitive ceramics.

A number of Archaic sites, including **Atlatl Cave,** have been identified in Chaco Canyon and also throughout the **San Juan Basin.**

Astronomical Alignments (see *Archaeoastronomy, Sofaer, Anna*)

Atencio, Agapito and Charlie

Two brothers of a local **Chaco Navajo** family who assisted early archaeologists in the excavation and stabilization of ruins at Chaco Canyon. The Atencio family has lived in the lower reaches of Chaco Canyon and along the **Escavada Wash** since at least the 1890s, and probably much longer.

Agapito Atencio was probably the first workman hired by Richard **Wetherill** in 1896 for excavations in **Pueblo Bonito.** He may have continued to work for Wetherill, and was later employed by Neil **Judd** for excavations at Pueblo Bonito, at least during the 1923 season. He served as an informant for Francis H. Elmore, a student at Edgar **Hewett**'s 1935 field school, who was beginning to collect data for a book on Navajo ethnobotany. Agapito's brother Charlie was employed by the National Park Service in 1925, and both men worked for **Gordon Vivian** in the Ruins **Stabilization** Unit in the late 1930s and 1940s. Charlie Atencio's son, who was known as Charlie Atencio Sr., also worked for the National Park Service in Chaco.

Judd recorded information on the Atencio family, and they are cited frequently in David **Brugge**'s *A History of the Chaco Navajos.*

Atlatl Cave

(Map 3; Figure 2)
A rock shelter near the western end of Chaco Canyon with traces of a Late **Archaic** occupation dating to the early 900s B.C. **Chaco Center** excavations in the cave in the 1970s did not reveal any man-made structures, but archaeologists found plant food remains, including

FIGURE 2. Atlatl Cave,
Chaco Canyon. A rock shelter that was occupied during
the Archaic period, probably
seasonally.

Indian rice grass, pinyon nuts, yucca, and hackberry seeds. They also
recovered a yucca fiber sandal, small seed beads, coiled basketry, and
rabbit fur fabric. **Carbon-14** dates in the 900s B.C. were derived from
these **organic materials** as well as from a partial atlatl—a small, flat
wooden stick with an end notch used for increasing arm length
when throwing a short spear. This site yielded very important information because most Archaic sites in Chaco Canyon are "open" sites
(not rock shelters) with little or no preservation of plants and other
organic materials.

Aztec Ruins

(Map 1; Figures 3, 4)
The largest northern Chacoan **outlier community,** located near the
junction of the Animas and San Juan rivers in the vicinity of Aztec,
New Mexico, fifty miles north of Chaco Canyon. This national
monument is best known for the excavated and stabilized Aztec
West Ruin, but the community encompasses three tri-wall structures
(including the **Hubbard** Site), the unexcavated East Ruin and Earl
Morris Ruin, and the recently rediscovered Aztec North Ruin, a col-

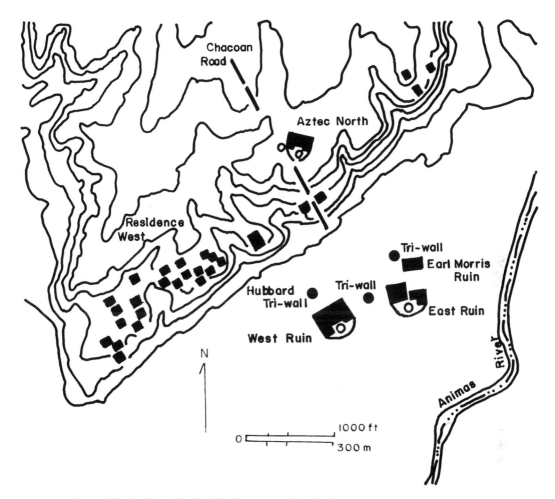

FIGURE 3. Aztec Ruins site plan. The site includes remains of multiple great houses, three tri-wall structures, small house communities, and a road.

lection of **great houses** and associated features on a gravel terrace north of the East and West Ruins.

Completed about A.D. 1115, the 400-room West Ruin pueblo with its D-shaped floor plan and twelve **kivas** has all of the classic features of a Chacoan great house. It is the third largest of all Chacoan great houses, and its reconstructed **great kiva** is among the biggest in the northern region. A segment of Chacoan **road** has

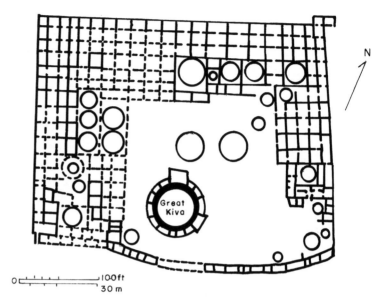

FIGURE 4. Aztec West Ruin great house ground plan. Dashed lines represent unexcavated portions of the site. Open doorways are shown.

been documented for the Aztec complex, and there are numerous **small house sites** in the area. The Aztec complex played an important role during the last stages of the **Chaco Phenomenon**. Some archaeologists believe the community may have become the center of the Chacoan system as Chaco Canyon was abandoned in the mid-1100s. It flourished for more than a century but was abandoned about 1275.

Excavations in the West Ruin were initiated by Earl **Morris** in 1916, and he continued to work at the site on a seasonal basis for several more years. During this time he cleared much of the building and the great kiva in the courtyard. Morris returned in 1934 to restore and roof the great kiva. He also avidly collected wood samples at Aztec for the new science of **dendrochronology**. Analysis of this wood showed that most of the building had been constructed between A.D. 1110 and 1120.

The ruins were named in the 1870s by Anglo farmers and ranchers settling along the Animas River who believed the buildings were constructed by the Aztecs of Mexico. The community of Aztec, New Mexico, took its name from the ruins.

B

Backfilling

The process of replacing soil removed from rooms and other structures following the archaeological excavation of a site. Backfilling is a preservation measure that protects the features and walls of excavated buildings so that they will not deteriorate further. It also preserves information in the building that might be extracted in the future with more-refined archaeological techniques.

Richard **Wetherill** backfilled at **Pueblo Bonito** in the 1890s, but largely as a means of dealing with vast quantities of backdirt produced during his investigation. Previously excavated rooms served as convenient places for dumping the rock and dirt removed from adjacent rooms undergoing excavation. During the later work in **great houses** carried out by **Judd** and **Hewett,** rooms and **kivas** were left open so that the public might better appreciate the architectural complexity of the sites.

Open rooms collect large quantities of water, and moisture moves up the room walls by capillary action. This process damages the mortar and eventually causes the walls to collapse. To curtail this process, the National Park Service has initiated a program of partial backfilling in great houses and **small house sites** within the park.

Badlands

A landform commonly found in southwestern deserts, created when water erodes dense clay or soft rock deposits that have little or no covering vegetation. Badlands formations are usually composed of narrow ridges whose sides are cut with many deeply eroded channels. The ridges are often separated by large, open flat areas. The Painted Desert in northern Arizona is a good example of badlands.

Badlands frequently occur to the north and northwest of Chaco Canyon, especially in the Bisti and De Na Zin Wash region around **Ojo Alamo.** These formations contain a variety of colored clay deposits and outcrops of petrified wood. Because badlands soils are not productive for farming and water is scarce, these areas were not heavily utilized by prehistoric peoples. However, **Pierre's Outlier** is located at the eastern edge of the De Na Zin Wash area, and **Bis sa'ani** is on a badlands ridge bordering the **Escavada Wash**.

Basketmaker

A term used by archaeologists in the Southwest to identify early time periods and lifeways in the development of Ancestral **Puebloan** (**Anasazi**) culture. Richard **Wetherill** first used the term "Basket Maker" in the 1890s to describe cultural materials, including many finely woven baskets, that he found beneath levels with pottery in southern Utah rock shelters. At the first **Pecos Conference** in 1927, Alfred Kidder recommended that the long Anasazi cultural sequence be divided into Basketmaker and Pueblo periods. The resulting **Pecos Classification** defined three Basketmaker periods and five Pueblo periods (I through V), each with distinguishing characteristics. Archaeologists have since recognized that time periods and cultural attributes vary somewhat by region.

The Basketmaker I period, which dates before A.D. 200, is not used by southwestern archaeologists, who prefer to call this period Late **Archaic**. In general, the Basketmaker II period dates from about A.D. 200 to A.D. 500, and Basketmaker III from A.D. 500 to A.D. 700. The earlier Archaic hunting and gathering lifestyle grew more complex in Basketmaker II. People relied more on farming, spending much of the year in small villages of **pithouses** near their garden plots along streams and rivers. Late in the period they began making ceramic cooking pots and storage vessels.

During Basketmaker III times, villages grew in size, and early **great kivas** were built to serve social and religious needs. **Pottery** grew more sophisticated, and regional styles developed. The invention of the bow and arrow greatly increased a hunter's efficiency.

Many Basketmaker sites have been located in Chaco Canyon and the **San Juan Basin**, including **Shabik'eshchee Village**, an early reference site that defined Basketmaker III culture for the Eastern Anasazi.

Bc Sites

A numbering code for archaeological sites in Chaco Canyon according to a site designation system developed by the University of New Mexico and used from the 1930s to the early 1960s. In this system, states were identified by a capital letter, archaeological regions within the state were assigned a lowercase letter, and sites were numerically listed as they were found and recorded. Thus, all sites in Arizona were identified first with an "A." Sites in New Mexico were identified with a "B," and the Chaco region with a "c." Site Bc50 in the **Casa Rinconada** group was the fiftieth site recorded in Chaco Canyon. There were numerous problems with this code—for example, defining the limits of each region—and it was replaced with Smithsonian Institution site designation numbers in the 1970s. The use of "Bc" should not be confused with the dating term B.C. ("before Christ").

Beam Expeditions

An organized search for **timbers** with tree rings that would link **dendrochronology** samples from the prehistoric and historic periods in the Southwest. Dr. Andrew **Douglass**, an astronomer at the University of Arizona, initiated the study of dendrochronology in 1904. By 1923 he had amassed a large collection of timbers from prehistoric sites. However, he could not establish actual dates for these ancient timbers until he could connect them to tree-ring samples with known dates from the historic period.

To assist in this effort, and to tie beams collected from **Pueblo Bonito** into the master chronology, Chacoan archaeologist Neil **Judd** persuaded the **National Geographic Society** to sponsor Douglass's project. Throughout the summer of 1923, wood was collected from **Mesa Verde**, Chaco Canyon, Canyon de Chelly, and other areas with intensive prehistoric occupation, but samples with the needed range of dates were not found. During a second expedition in 1928, wood was collected from the **Hopi** pueblos, but again without success. The following year Emil Haury and Lyndon Hargrave, leaders of the third beam expedition, discovered a log at the Show Low Ruin in central Arizona that had rings spanning the missing period.

Berm

A linear earthen ridge or mound bordering a Chacoan **road**, usually occurring where roads approach outlier **great houses**, as at the **Navajo Springs Outlier.** Fred Nials, an archaeologist with the Bureau of Land Management's Chaco Roads Project, originally defined berms as "broad, low, linear ridges of earthen or rubble materials paralleling the roads at the margins." Later, John **Stein,** Stephen **Lekson,** and others identified berms as a major component of what they termed "Anasazi ritual landscapes," which included architectural elements consciously designed to enhance and be enhanced by their natural location.

These ritual landscapes were most obvious at certain **outlier communities** where the great house was encircled by a below-grade road surrounded by an above-grade berm, usually one to two feet high. This pattern characterized the **Bluff Great House** outlier in southern Utah which was investigated by Catherine **Cameron.** She summarized Chacoan earthen architecture in her book on this important site. Often there were breaks in the berm where radiating roads intersected. Stein noted that the berms fronting the building were often identified as **trash mounds.** He also referred to the joint road and berm composition as the site "aureola," and the crescent berm as the site *nazha*, a Navajo term for this form.

Beyal, Hosteen

A **Navajo** elder who provided Neil **Judd** with some of the earliest known recollections of Chaco Canyon. When Beyal was interviewed by Judd in 1927, he was about ninety-five and considered to be the oldest Navajo in the Chaco area. He reported that he came to the region as a young boy, which would have placed him in the vicinity of the canyon at the time of Lieutenant **Simpson**'s expedition. He remembered Chaco Canyon during his boyhood as being much less arid and having several permanent springs. There was no entrenched wash in the canyon bottom, which was flat with shallow pools and cottonwoods in several places. He also recalled small stands of ponderosa pine in **Mockingbird Canyon** and in several **rincons** on the south side of Chaco Canyon. When asked about

canals and **roads**, he described a number of each within and outside the canyon.

Beyal and his extended family lived in the Kin Bineola–**Lake Valley** region to the southwest of Chaco Canyon, and his descendants still live there today. His great-grandson George worked for the National Park Service Ruins Stabilization Unit for many years and retired in 1997.

Bis sa'ani [Navajo for "clay in place"]

(Map 2; Figure 5)

A small **great house** of about thirty-five rooms with an associated **small house** community located on the south side of the **Escavada Wash** about eight miles northeast of **Pueblo Bonito.** The site lies within the **Chaco Core** and is not considered a true **outlier**, though it is outside Chaco Canyon itself. Two components (East and West) of the great house are situated on portions of a long, narrow ridge of **badlands** formation; **small house sites** are scattered to the south of the great house. No **great kivas** are present, and no **roads** have been located within the community boundaries. Occupation of the site was limited to the early 1100s.

The great house and other community structures were excavated by archaeologists from the Navajo Nation Cultural Resource Management Program in the 1980s. Portions of the great house were **backfilled** to preserve them. The site is also known as Bisgháá' kini, Navajo for "house on top of clay."

Bluff Great House

(Map 1; Figure 6)

A three-, possibly four-story **great house** located above the north bank of the San Juan River in southeastern Utah approximately 130 miles northwest of **Chaco Canyon.** Containing between fifty and sixty rooms and four **kivas**, it was built between A.D. 1075–1150 in at least two construction episodes, remodeled between A.D. 1150–1200, and abandoned by A.D. 1250. Significant earthen landscaping features were also located at the site, including two **road** segments

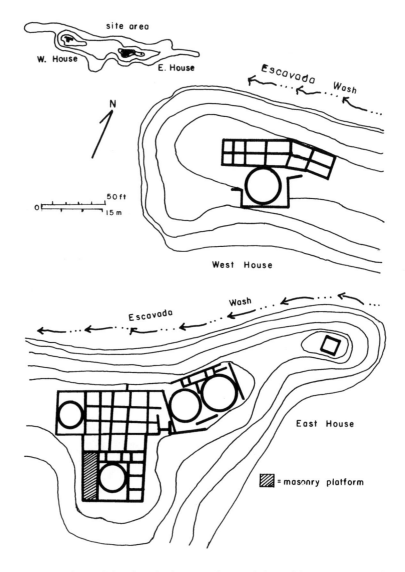

FIGURE 5. Bis sa'ani site plan. Site layout and ground plans of the East House and West House are shown. The site is located on a badlands remnant bordering the Escavada Wash.

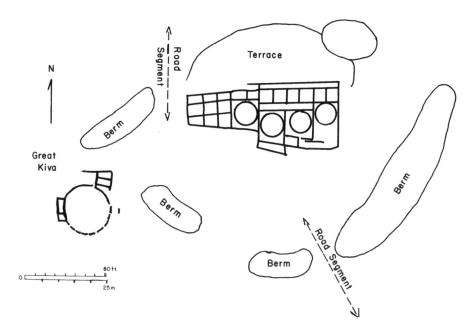

FIGURE 6. Bluff great house ground plan. The terrace on the north side of the structure is shown as are berms surrounding the front portion of the building and two road segments. The great kiva lies outside the berms to the west of the great house.

and several discrete **berms** to the south of the great house. Similar berms apparently were leveled on the north side of the great house to create a terrace, a rare feature in Chacoan architecture. Several berms separated the great house from a **great kiva** to the west of the great house. There is little evidence for an associated **small house site** community.

The Bluff Great House site was partially excavated by Catherine **Cameron** and Stephen **Lekson** from 1996 to 2004 through a partnership of archaeologists, students, and cultural preservationists including the Southwest Heritage Foundation, Abajo Archaeology, the University of Colorado, and citizens of the community of Bluff, Utah. Cameron's publication on this work, *Chaco and After in the Northern San Juan: Excavations at the Bluff Great House*, proposes that the great house was established by people from Chaco Canyon who then interacted with both **Mesa Verde** and Kayenta groups until at least A.D. 1150. After this time, Cameron believes the late Chacoan complex centered at **Aztec** may have dominated the northern San Juan region and restricted local power at places such as the Bluff Great House.

Bonito Phase

A term used by some archaeologists working in the Chaco area to identify the time period associated with the development of **great house** architecture. The Bonito phase is divided into three subphases:

Early Bonito phase	A.D. 900–1040
Classic Bonito phase	A.D. 1040–1100
Late Bonito phase	A.D. 1100–1140

When this system was first devised in the 1980s, it was believed that great house architecture started about A.D. 920. It is now known that construction at **Pueblo Bonito, Una Vida,** and **Peñasco Blanco** began almost a hundred years earlier. Thus, the Early Bonito phase may have started even earlier than A.D. 900. The Classic Bonito phase spans the period of most great house construction, which ended in the Late Bonito phase.

Brugge, David M.

An archaeologist and ethnohistorian who recorded historic sites for the **Chaco Project** and supervised the excavation of the Doll House Site, the only **Navajo** site excavated by the Chaco Project. Brugge's thorough archaeological and historical documentation of Spanish, Mexican, and Anglo-American settlement of the Chaco area greatly expanded knowledge of these little-known periods. His major works on the **Chaco Navajo,** *A History of the Chaco Navajos* and *Tsegai: An Archaeological Ethnohistory of the Chaco Region*, prove the importance of integrating archaeological evidence, historical documents, and oral history in creating a more complete history of a local native people. Brugge is held in high regard by the local Chaco Navajo for his work in documenting their past.

Brushy Basin Chert (see *Chert*)

Bryan, Kirk

A geologist with the U.S. Geological Survey who worked with Neil **Judd**'s survey and excavation program in Chaco Canyon in 1924 and 1925. Bryan accumulated critical data on the geology, erosional processes, and water resources of Chaco Canyon. In a work of special significance, *The Geology of Chaco Canyon, New Mexico, in Relation to the Life and Remains of the Prehistoric Peoples of Pueblo Bonito*, he traced the prehistoric channel of the **Chaco Wash.**

Bryan's early life in New Mexico probably prompted his interest in both the archaeology and water resources of this semi-arid region. His studies of groundwater and surface water in New Mexico and Arizona (published in the U.S.G.S. Water Supply Papers) are considered classics. In his archaeological work, he focused primarily on the **Paleoindian** period and made major contributions to the analysis of early sites, including Lindenmeier, Sandia Cave, and Ventana Cave.

Burials

A common method of attending the dead practiced by the **Ancestral Puebloans** throughout the **Anasazi** region. Some other peoples of the Southwest, such as the **Hohokam,** practiced cremation.

One of the enduring mysteries of Chaco is why so few burials have been found at the **great houses.** Several of those unearthed by **Wetherill** at **Pueblo Bonito** appear to have been people of high status who were buried with a wealth of ceremonial objects, jewelry, and **pottery.** The scarcity of burials at great houses has led to speculation that they were not residential buildings but ceremonial centers with a small priestly staff who were given special treatment at burial. Other explanations may account for the lack of burials at great houses, including the presence of undiscovered cemeteries within or outside Chaco Canyon. Burials at **small house sites** are more numerous and appear to reflect a residential occupation.

Nancy Akins, a **Chaco Project** staff member, published a detailed analysis of burials from Chaco Canyon in 1986 that included a discussion of mortuary practices. This work also identified physical differences in the human remains in Pueblo Bonito, suggesting to Akins that two different groups of people inhabited this great house. Based on later analyses, other archaeologists believed that populations at Pueblo Bonito may have been linked to Rio Grande and **Zuni** Puebloan groups.

C

Cacao

A neotropical **Mesoamerican** tree, *Theobroma cacao*, whose pulp and seeds are the source of chocolate or cocoa. The seeds were highly valued among prehistoric Mesoamerican peoples and were used as a type of currency by the Aztecs. The Maya used cacao for a beverage prepared and served in cylindrical jars.

In 2009, archaeologist Patricia **Crown** submitted pieces of Chacoan **cylinder jars** for chemical analysis to W. Jeffrey Hurst at the Hershey Center for Health and Nutrition in Hershey, Pennsylvania. His tests revealed the residue of a chocolate beverage, producing the first evidence of prehistoric use of cacao north of the U.S.-Mexican border. Crown believes that the consumption of the beverage was limited to ritual specialists or an elite group, reflected by the fact that cylinder jars were found almost exclusively in the oldest section of **Pueblo Bonito**. The presence of cacao, along with **parrots** and **macaws**, provides strong evidence that aspects of Mesoamerican ritual were part of religious ceremonies at **Chaco Canyon** by the A.D. 1000s.

Cameron, Catherine

A prominent Southwestern archaeologist and scholar who has made major contributions to Chacoan studies in the areas of **lithics**, craft specialization, architecture, and trade. Cameron began her Chacoan research analyzing stone tools discovered at the **Salmon Ruin Outlier** for Cynthia **Irwin-Williams**. She pursued this interest in lithics and trade as an archaeologist with the **Chaco Project,** investigating the importation of **Narbona Pass Chert** and other high-quality stone into **Chaco Canyon**. Her work at Chaco stimulated a broad interest in **outliers**, regional architecture, site abandonment, and migration. Her diverse studies are reflected in her many books, such as *Hopi Dwellings: Architecture at Orayvi,* a classic investigation of architectural continuity and change. *Chaco and After in the Northern San Juan: Excavations at the Bluff Great House* provides in-depth analysis of multiple topics including the Chaco regional system, its expression in southeastern Utah, and earthen architecture. Cameron and husband Stephen **Lekson** have coauthored many Chaco-related publications including *Chaco Panache: Feathers and 11th Century Political Power*; and *The Abandonment of Chaco Canyon, the Mesa Verde Migrations and the Reorganization of the Pueblo World.*

Canals

Large ditches found in Chaco Canyon used to carry runoff from summer rains to fields. Prehistoric farmers in the canyon built an elaborate **water control** system of **dams**, canals, and gates to collect this runoff and distribute it to large **gridded fields.** Canals were used to carry the water to fields from diversion dams at the mouths of nearly all the short side canyons on the north side of Chaco Canyon. Canals varied in width and depth, but the largest were up to sixteen feet wide and six feet deep. Some were walled on one side or faced with sandstone slabs. Large canals with similar features also were constructed at **Kin Bineola** and **Kin Klizhin**. In these cases runoff came from major drainage basins carrying great volumes of floodwater.

Cannibalism

The practice of eating the flesh of other humans. Several archaeologists have proposed that Ancestral Puebloans (**Anasazi**) practiced cannibalism. As evidence, they point to sites with jumbled piles of human bones that have cut marks and "pot polishing" (smoothed edges that could result from stirring while cooking) similar to those found on animal bones in trash piles. Human bones from Chaco Canyon have been listed as part of this evidence.

The leading proponents of this theory, Christy and Jacqueline Turner, also argue that cultists and warriors from Mexico used the threat of cannibalism to force Chacoan populations into constructing **great houses**, **roads**, and other major architectural features during the 1000s and early 1100s. Although there is evidence for isolated acts of cannibalism in the Southwest, the archaeological record does not support the Turners' "cannibalism as terrorism" theory.

Carbon-14 Dating

A **dating technique** based on the absorption by plants and animals of carbon 14, an unstable isotope of carbon that has eight neutrons rather than the six in carbon 12. Carbon 14, or radiocarbon, is constantly produced in small amounts in the atmosphere and is found in all living organisms. Plants absorb radiocarbon through carbon dioxide; animals absorb radiocarbon by eating plants or animals. The ratio of carbon 14 to carbon 12 is constant in all living beings.

When a plant or animal dies, the absorption ceases and radiocarbon begins to decay, converting back into the more stable carbon 12. It is known that carbon 14 decays at a set rate (50 percent after 5,730 years). Methods have been developed to measure the minute amounts of carbon 14 left in a sample, thereby providing a date of the death of the plant or animal. However, because the annual quantity of carbon 14 in the atmosphere changes from year to year, radiocarbon years can differ from calendar years by as much as 15 percent. Therefore, archaeologists use calibration programs to convert radiocarbon years to calendar years before the present, usually shown as "cal BP." Calendar years may also be shown as a date with a margin of error (for example, A.D. 275 ± 50).

Radiocarbon dating can be used on any carbon-bearing **organic material:** yucca fibers, wood, cotton cloth, and even bones. Carbon-14 dating is most useful at sites that do not have wood suitable for tree-ring dating, or ceramics produced during known time periods.

Carravahal

A guide for Colonel Washington's 1849 military expedition that passed through Chaco Canyon. Lieutenant **Simpson** stated in his journal on August 23, 1849, that "a Mexican, by name Carravahal, whose residence is at San Ysidro," accompanied the troops as a guide. Simpson reported that upon arrival at the first Chacoan **great house**, various names were given to it but that Carravahal, "who probably knows more about it than anyone else," called it **Pueblo Pintado**. This suggests that Carravahal also may have accompanied José Antonio **Vizcarra**'s 1823 campaign against the **Navajos**, the first known European expedition through Chaco Canyon.

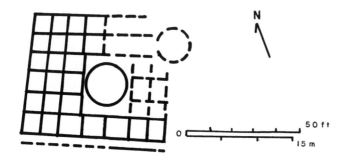

FIGURE 7. Casa Chiquita great house ground plan. The site has not been excavated. Solid lines represent the portion of the building with standing wall; rooms and kivas shown as dashed lines are estimated from surface evidence. Doorways are not shown.

Casa Chiquita [Spanish for "little house"]

(Map 3; Figure 7)

A late McElmo-style **great house** near the mouth of **Cly's Canyon** in the western half of Chaco Canyon. This small, essentially square building has a central **kiva** surrounded by approximately thirty-four ground-floor rooms. A second kiva may be present in the badly collapsed northeast corner of the building. The building is terraced, rising from one to three stories from the front (south) to the rear (north).

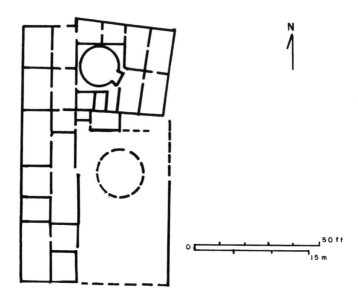

FIGURE 8. Casamero Outlier great house ground plan. The structure has been largely excavated, and doorways are shown. Dashed lines represent structures estimated from surface evidence.

Veneer on the **core-and-veneer** masonry is **McElmo style:** large blocks of soft yellowish sandstone are finished with a dimpled or pecked surface. Three tree-ring dates in the 1060s probably represent wood recycled from an earlier building because Casa Chiquita's plan and **veneer style** are typical of McElmo great houses dating from A.D. 1100–1130. The site has not been excavated.

Casamero Outlier

(Map 1; Figure 8)

A Chacoan **outlier community** approximately forty miles south of Chaco Canyon. The community includes a small **great house**, an associated **great kiva**, and more than thirty **small house sites.** The L-shaped great house has about twenty ground-floor rooms and was probably two stories high on the west side. A partially enclosed plaza at the front of the rooms created a rectangular building plan. A great kiva is located approximately 200 feet south of the great house. No Chacoan **roads** have been identified at this outlier.

The great house and community have been dated to approximately A.D. 1000–1125 on the basis of associated ceramics. The great house was partially excavated by the Cottonwood Gulch Foundation in the late 1960s. The site is on Bureau of Land Management land and is protected by that federal agency. Robert and Florence **Lister** believe this site may be **Casa Morena**.

Casa Morena [Spanish for "dark brown house"]

A "lost" Chacoan site that has intrigued generations of archaeologists. Casa Morena was first reported by Stephen **Holsinger,** who was sent to Chaco Canyon in 1901 to investigate charges that Richard **Wetherill** and the **Hyde Exploring Expedition** were vandalizing Chacoan **great houses.** Holsinger spent four weeks in the area visiting sites and making notes for a thorough report. He was told about Casa Morena and included a location for the site without actually visiting it. When Chaco Canyon National Monument was established in 1907, the location he gave for Casa Morena was included, yet there was no Chacoan site at the place he described.

Some archaeologists, including the **Listers,** believe that Holsinger was told about **Casamero,** but that he miscalculated its location. However, Edgar **Hewett** believed Casa Morena was actually Mesa Pueblo, a late Chacoan site perched on a low mesa about ten miles northeast of Hospah, New Mexico.

Casa Rinconada [Spanish for "cornered house" or "house within a corner"]

(Map 4; Figures 9 and 10)

A **great kiva** on the south side of Chaco Canyon whose unique floor features may have been used by ritual specialists to perform "kiva magic" for the residents of a cluster of nearby **small house sites.** An "isolated" great kiva not associated with a **great house,** Casa Rinconada (also known as just "Rinconada") was partially dug into the top of a long sandstone and shale ridge bordering a small house site community opposite the great houses of **Pueblo Bonito** and **Chetro Ketl.** With an interior diameter of slightly more than sixty-three feet, it is the largest of the excavated great kivas in Chaco Canyon.

FIGURE 9. Casa Rinconada great kiva during excavation. (Courtesy of National Park Service.)

Casa Rinconada displays all of the standard great kiva features: an encircling inner bench; a raised firebox; four pits to hold support beams for the roof frame; raised masonry vaults, or **foot drums**; and small niches built into the inner wall, presumably for holding ritual objects. Masonry steps provided entry on both the north and south, though a single northern entry is common in most other canyon great kivas. Small antechambers are present at both entrances. A masonry fire screen that protected the firebox from drafts through the south entry is no longer visible.

Rinconada also has two features not found in any other excavated great kiva. The first is a thirty-nine-foot-long underground passage extending from the floor of a room in the northern antechamber to near the northwestern support beam pit, passing under the bench and below the floor of the kiva. The passage ends just within the second unique feature, a shallow and narrow masonry trench that was sunk into the kiva floor and encircled the northwestern support pit. If the passageway were covered and a wooden-slat screen, small poles,

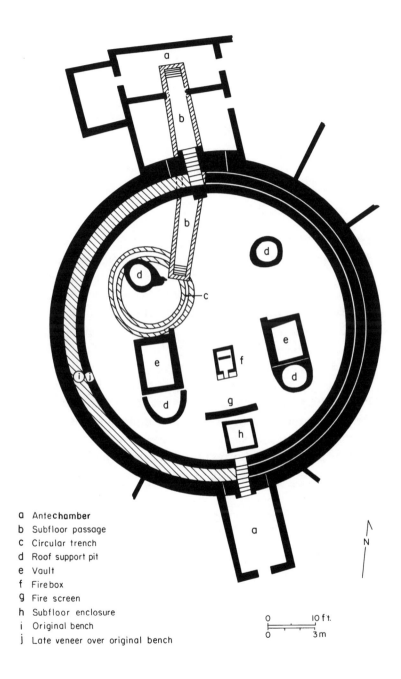

a Antechamber
b Subfloor passage
c Circular trench
d Roof support pit
e Vault
f Firebox
g Fire screen
h Subfloor enclosure
i Original bench
j Late veneer over original bench

0   10 ft.
0   3 m

FIGURE 10. Casa Rinconada great kiva ground plan showing interior features.

or branches placed in the trench, it would have been possible to enter this enclosure unseen and then appear to emerge from the "underworld." The passageway was intentionally filled before the last use of the kiva.

This great kiva was excavated during the summer of 1931 by **Gordon Vivian** as part of the University of New Mexico's archaeological field program. It was partially restored in the summer of 1933, when Vivian repaired the walls and floor, and placed the large pine beams in the two entryways.

Casas Grandes [Spanish for "big houses"]

A large prehistoric site in northern Chihuahua, Mexico. Stephen **Lekson**, a southwestern archaeologist, believes that Casas Grandes was the third and final "capital" of a **Puebloan** group that originated in Chaco Canyon in the early tenth century. In Lekson's scenario, the elite rulers of this long dynasty moved the capital from Chaco to the **Aztec Ruins** on the Animas River north of Chaco in the early 1100s, and some one hundred years later to the largest complex of buildings at Casas Grandes, known also as **Paquimé**. The major occupation at Paquimé was from approximately A.D. 1275 to 1450. Lekson uses similarities in architecture (**colonnades**, **room-wide platforms**, and carved stone **discs**) to support his theory and also cites the close alignment of all three capitals on a single north-south line of longitude, which he calls the **Chaco Meridian**.

Ceramics (see *Pottery*)

Cerrillos Turquoise Mines

Ancient mines in the Cerrillos Hills, about twenty miles southwest of Santa Fe, New Mexico. Chacoan jewelry makers collected or traded for **turquoise** from several mines in the Southwest, but much of the turquoise found at Chacoan sites probably came from the Cerrillos mines. It is not known if Chacoan peoples traded for the blue-green stones from these mines or had "mining rights." Several contemporary **Puebloan** groups in the Rio Grande Valley claim to have had ownership of these mines in the prehistoric past.

Chaco

A term with several meanings, often used as a shorthand name for Chaco Canyon, but now commonly used to refer to the larger Chacoan culture area of the **San Juan Basin.** The term also describes the cultural system or prehistoric lifeway associated with the canyon's distinctive architecture.

The meaning of the word itself is not certain but may stem from the **Navajo** word for the **Chacra Mesa**, "Tzak aih," meaning "white string of rocks." According to David **Brugge**, an archaeologist and ethnohistorian, a variation of the word, "Tsegai," is a contraction of Navajo words for "rock" and "white." Alternatively, Richard Van Valkenburgh, who wrote a geographic dictionary of Navajo country, has suggested that the Navajo word for "box canyon," *tsekooh*, (also spelled *tsekho* [*tse* "rock" + *kho* "opening"]) was applied to the entire Chaco Canyon.

Almost certainly, "Tzak aih" or "Tsegai" was Hispanicized as "Chaca." As a place name, this word appeared on a map drawn in 1777 by a Spanish surveying engineer, Don Bernardo Miera y Pacheco. The word was inscribed on the map near the southern edge of a large area marked as the "Provincia de Nabajoo" and at the base of a flat-topped mesa capped by two small rounded dwellings, presumed to be Navajo hogans. It is also the same place as "Mesa de Chaca," referenced in a Spanish land grant document of the same period.

Neither "Chaca" nor "Chaco" was used by José Antonio **Vizcarra**, Mexican governor of New Mexico, when he passed through the canyon in 1823 on a mission to enforce a treaty with the Navajos. The term "Rio Chaco" does appear in the 1849 journal of U.S. Army Lt. James H. **Simpson**, recorded during an American campaign against the Navajos. "Chaco" appears regularly in the literature thereafter.

Chacoan Communities

Social units in the **San Juan Basin** usually centered on a Chacoan **great house** and associated **small house sites.** This type of community is fairly easy to distinguish outside Chaco Canyon where open space around the settlement helps to define its outer limits. Within the canyon, however, drawing lines between communities is difficult because dense occupation leaves little space between clusters of small house sites.

Dozens of small house sites are present on the south side of Chaco Canyon opposite the great houses of **Pueblo del Arroyo, Pueblo Bonito,** and **Chetro Ketl,** but "site packing" makes it almost impossible to associate a "set" of these small houses with individual great houses. Communities outside Chaco Canyon, often called **outlier communities,** may also have one or more Chacoan **roads** and one or more **great kivas** near the great house.

Chacoan World

A space in the **San Juan Basin** that may have represented the sacred geography of the ancient Chacoans. This concept is based on the fact that **Puebloan** and other Native American peoples often construct sacred landscapes based on the location of physical landmarks and the movement of mythological beings within that landscape. For example, Alfonso Ortiz has defined the Tewa world within a framework of four expanding zones around each Tewa pueblo and the four cardinal directions. Moving from the center—the pueblo plaza and its four sides—the Tewa world is then marked by four shrines surrounding the pueblo. The third zone is marked by encircling flat-topped hills, again in the four directions. The fourth zone is defined by four sacred mountains on the horizon as seen from the pueblo.

We cannot know what landmarks may have been important to the Chacoans, but based on the knowledge we have of Puebloan sacred worlds, we can guess that major horizon features probably helped to define the outer limits of the Chacoan World. If so, a Chacoan standing at **Pueblo Alto** facing north would have seen the La Plata and San Juan mountains on the horizon, and **Tres Huerfanos** mesa in the foreground. To the west, the primary landmark is the long mountain chain beginning in the north with Carrizo Mountain and extending south through the Lukachukai and **Chuska** ranges. The southern horizon is dominated by the much nearer **Dutton Plateau** and **Hosta Butte**. Beyond the eastern corner of the plateau, Mount Taylor is a striking landmark. Far on the eastern horizon the Jemez and Nacimiento ranges form a thin blue ridge carrying the eye back to the north. Landmarks within these boundaries undoubtedly also had special significance.

Chaco Black-on-white

(Figure 11)

A **Cibola White Ware** that has come to epitomize the height of ceramic development in Chacoan culture. Produced from about A.D. 1075 to 1150 in the central San Juan Basin, Chaco Black-on-white was made in limited quantities but is well-known because of its high quality and precision in painting. Chaco Black-on-white was named and described by Florence **Hawley** based on her work in Chaco Canyon.

As with other Cibola White Wares in Chaco, this type was decorated with black designs executed in mineral paints derived from hematite or other iron oxides found throughout the San Juan Basin. However, unlike other contemporary and earlier Cibola wares, closed forms such as square-shouldered pitchers were far more common than bowls. This pottery type is especially known for the spectacular **cylinder jars**, found primarily at **Pueblo Bonito**.

FIGURE 11. Chaco Black-on-white pitcher and bowl forms with decorative motifs and design layout common to this ceramic type.

Chaco Black-on-white designs consist only of hatched elements, many similar to those used on **Gallup Black-on-white** but without opposing (or "counterchanged") solid motifs. Triangular pennants, stepped triangles, interlocking rectangular scrolls, and wide framing bands filled with hatching are most common. As in Gallup Black-on-white, the design field on all shapes was increasingly filled with decoration.

Though Chuska Black-on-white from the **Chuska Valley** and Mancos Black-on-white from the **Mesa Verde** area have been compared to Chaco Black-on-white, both contain solid elements in design construction and can easily be differentiated from true Chaco Black-on-white. Cooking ware associated with Chaco Black-on-white was indented **corrugated.**

Chaco Canyon

(Maps 2, 3, 4)

The home of Chacoan peoples from the Late **Archaic** period to the mid-1100s, a span of more than 2,000 years. Chaco Canyon runs largely east-west for just over twenty miles, with most Chacoan **great houses** located in the lower (western) twelve miles of the canyon.

A unique topographic feature in the **San Juan Basin**, Chaco Canyon was formed when water flowing west from the Continental Divide cut through a *cuesta*, a large uplifted and tilted landform with a higher, sheer face toward the south and a downward slope toward the north. Thousands of years of erosion from water flowing westward carved the canyon.

When the **Chaco Wash** cut through the *cuesta*, it created the **Chacra Mesa**, a long, fairly narrow uplifted and tilted strip of land along the south side of Chaco Canyon. Visitors entering Chaco Canyon from the southern approach first see the uplifted face of the *cuesta*. Those entering or leaving the canyon from the north see the gradual lowering of the *cuesta* as side canyons such as **Gallo Canyon** and **Mockingbird Canyon** become more shallow to the north.

The slope of the *cuesta* is also displayed in the cliff walls of Chaco Canyon, which are composed of two major geologic deposits laid down during the Late Cretaceous period about eighty million to sixty-five million years ago. The lower Menefee deposit is mostly visible on the south side of the canyon where it is the brownish layer at the base of the more vertical, yellowish sandstone cliffs. The Menefee—a mixture of sandstone, mudstone, shale, and very poor grades of coal—formed at the swampy edge of a marine sea. This formation is much softer than the overlying Cliffhouse Sandstone and tends to erode under the upper sandstone, causing the cliffs to break off, fall, and create talus slopes of broken rubble. Exposures of the Menefee and the talus erosion process can be seen on the trail through the **small house sites** near **Casa Rinconada**.

The higher Cliffhouse Sandstone layer forms most of the cliffs on the north side of the canyon, though some exposures of Menefee are present, as behind the **Hungo Pavi** great house. There is less undercutting on the north and fewer talus slopes, though some large slabs of cliff face may break off, as in the case of **Threatening Rock**.

The geology on the north and south sides of Chaco Canyon created different patterns of runoff following summer rains, a fact that probably had important implications for farming methods and **water control** systems in the canyon.

Chaco Center

An administrative facility created in 1971 by the National Park Service and the University of New Mexico to carry out new surveys, excavations, and related multidisciplinary research in Chaco Canyon and surrounding areas to better interpret Chacoan prehistory for the public. Alden **Hayes**, James **Judge**, and Robert **Lister** were responsible for directing Center activities at different times. Hayes supervised much of the initial survey, Judge oversaw most of the excavations, and Lister provided general scientific support.

Chaco Core

(Maps 1, 2)
The heartland of Chacoan culture and the most densely settled part of the **San Juan Basin** in the eleventh century. This small zone

extends from the headwaters of the **Chaco Wash** at the Continental Divide on the east to the confluence of the Chaco and Kin Bineola washes at **Lake Valley** on the west. It encompasses Chaco Canyon and the **Chacra Mesa** on the south side of Chaco Canyon, and extends to the **Escavada Wash** drainage on the north.

Chaco-McElmo Black-on-white

(Figure 12)

A late type of **Cibola White Ware** produced from approximately A.D. 1100 to 1150 and associated with **McElmo-style** great houses. It is the only Cibola White Ware decorated with "carbon paint," which was derived from plants (such as Rocky Mountain beeweed) rather than mineral pigments. The Chaco-McElmo type was named and fully described by Thomas **Windes,** who identified it as a ware produced in Chaco Canyon and the **Chuska Valley.** Earlier, **Gordon Vivian** had classified much of this pottery as McElmo Black-on-white, equating it with a contemporary type of the same name produced in the **Mesa Verde** area.

Bowl forms are most common for this pottery type, but as with **Chaco Black-on-white** there is a high frequency of square-shouldered pitchers. Mugs, a hallmark of Mesa Verde Black-on-white from the **Mesa Verde** area, appeared for the first time in the Chaco area in the Chaco-McElmo wares. A few examples of **cylinder jars** using Chaco-McElmo designs are also known. Windes

FIGURE 12. Chaco-McElmo Black-on-white pitcher and bowl forms with decorative motifs and design layout common to this ceramic type.

described the design elements of Chaco-McElmo as a mixture of Cibola, Mesa Verde, Chuska, and Little Colorado motifs. The use of hatching declined, however, and the most common elements consist of parallelograms, checkerboards, dots in open squares, and interlocking frets. The design fields of jars and pitchers covered most of the vessel walls; the interior top half or more of bowls was decorated, but the bottom was often left open.

Chaco Black-on-white and **Gallup Black-on-white** were produced during most of the time Chaco-McElmo was popular. All three of these were the last Chaco Series types produced in Chaco Canyon. Cooking ware commonly used with Chaco-McElmo Black-on-white was indented **corrugated.**

Chaco Meridian

(Map 5)

A hypothetical north-south alignment connecting the prehistoric sites of Chaco, the **Aztec Ruins**, and **Paquimé**, a large residential and ceremonial center in the **Casas Grandes** Ruins in northern Chihuahua, Mexico. Stephen **Lekson**, an archaeologist specializing in Chacoan research, maintains that the location of these sites on the same approximate line of longitude (107°57'25") is not mere coincidence, but rather a "constructed feature" which may have had ceremonial significance. The Chacoan **Great North Road** generally follows this line, and Lekson believes that other roads followed the meridian to link these important sites.

Lekson has proposed that the abandonment of Chaco Canyon was guided in part by the Chaco Meridian. He believes Chacoans moved first to the Aztec Ruins in the mid-1100s and from Aztec to Paquimé in the mid-1200s. In support of this theory, he cites certain "Chacoan" architectural features at Paquimé such as stone **discs**, **colonnades**, and **room-wide platforms.**

Chaco Navajo

A term used to refer to Navajos living in the vicinity of Chaco Canyon. The history of Chaco and the surrounding **San Juan Basin** is as much about the Navajo people as about the ancient Chacoans. Chaco is at the southern boundary of the "Dinetah," the sacred Navajo homeland, and much of **Navajo** mythology is centered on landmarks in the **Chacoan World**.

Navajos have resided in the Chaco area since at least the late 1600s, and their early occupation of the **Chacra Mesa** and Chaco Canyon is marked by numerous stone pueblitos and forked-stick **hogans**. A Navajo clan, the Tall House People, is believed to have originated at the Chacoan outlier **Kin Ya'a**.

Most of the Navajos residing near Chaco Canyon today are descendants of early migrants into the area from the Dinetah. The present Navajo occupation of the Chaco area is centered on the **Escavada Wash** to the north, **Pueblo Pintado** to the east, and in the **Lake Valley** region to the west near the Chacoan outlier **Kin Bineola**.

Places in Chaco Canyon such as **Werito's Rincon** and **Cly's Canyon** take their names from early Navajo families living there. Others, including the **Atencios**, Padillas, **Weros**, Trujillos, **Mescalitos**, and **Newtons**, have deep cultural roots in the area. *A History of the Chaco Navajos*, written by David **Brugge**, an archaeologist and one of the foremost scholars on the Navajo, is an excellent source of information. Neil **Judd** collected histories of the Chaco area from several older Navajos, such as Hosteen **Beyal, Wello**, and Tomas **Padilla**, during his work in the canyon in the 1920s. These are summarized as "Navaho Notes from Chaco Canyon" in Judd's 1954 publication, *The Material Culture of Pueblo Bonito*.

In 1948, a few Navajo families living within the boundaries of the park (then a national monument) were moved by the National Park Service to areas outside the park.

Chaco Phenomenon (or Chacoan Phenomenon)

A term coined by Cynthia **Irwin-Williams**, a prominent southwestern archaeologist who directed the excavation of the **Salmon Ruin**, to describe the distinguishing features of Chacoan culture in the 1000s and early 1100s in the **San Juan Basin**. These included the location of Chacoan sites in an environment marginal for agriculture, the occurrence of a few **great houses** in the **Chaco Core**, the presence of many contemporaneous **small house sites**, and the late establishment of Chacoan **outliers** on the basin's peripheries.

Chaco Project

An extensive program of fieldwork conducted by the **Chaco Center** as a joint effort of the National Park Service and the University of New Mexico. The Chaco Project began with an archaeological survey in the summer of 1971 and continued for more than a decade with additional surveys, testing, excavation, and analysis of Chacoan sites throughout the **San Juan Basin.** Robert **Lister**, Alden **Hayes**, and James **Judge** directed various aspects of the project and were assisted by a staff composed primarily of archaeology graduate students, most of whom continued professional careers in the discipline. The project achieved significant results, including the recording of more than 2,500 archaeological sites, the testing or excavation of 27 sites, and recovery of more than 300,000 artifacts.

Chaco Project personnel also made significant advances in interpreting Chacoan prehistory, including excellent summaries of survey data by Hayes, Judge, and David Brugge. Analyses of Chacoan **great house** architecture were prepared by Stephen **Lekson** and Peter McKenna, and similar studies of **small house** architecture and settlements were completed by McKenna and Marcia Truell Newren. A major investigation of Chacoan **outlier communities** by Robert Powers, Lekson, and William Gillespie added critical information to a growing new field in Chacoan studies.

The importance of documenting ancient environmental data (**paleoclimate**) and past use of natural resources for interpreting the archaeological record was established in botanical and hydrological analyses carried out by Mollie Toll, Nancy Akins, Gillespie, Anne and Jack Cully, Marcia Donaldson and others. Characteristics of human populations such as sex, age at death, and disease were investigated through osteological and **burial** analyses by Akins and John Schelberg. Numerous material culture studies, including investigations of **pottery** and **lithics,** were conducted by Catherine **Cameron**, Joan **Mathien**, Wolcott **Toll**, Wirt **Wills**, Lekson, and others.

Perhaps the most inventive, thorough, and all-encompassing

project work was carried out by Thomas **Windes,** who has spent more than thirty years immersed in Chacoan archaeology. There is scarcely an aspect of Chacoan research that has not been furthered by his contributions. Several people not on the project staff also contributed to various studies, including important **dendrochronological** and climatic reconstruction analyses by Jeffrey Dean.

The Chaco Center produced more than twenty volumes on project work, most of them edited by Mathien. The National Park Service contracted in the late 1990s with Lekson to convene scholars to produce a complete synthesis of all Chaco Project studies.

A synthesis, *Culture and Ecology of Chaco Canyon and the San Juan Basin*, was written by Joan Mathien and published in 2005 as part of the Chaco Canyon Studies series. Lekson took a different and broader approach by enlisting both Chaco Project and non-Project scholars not only to review what the Chaco Project had accomplished but to evaluate the significance of Project work in the context of Southwestern and even Mesoamerican archaeology. The results of this undertaking were edited by Lekson and published in 2006 as *The Archaeology of Chaco Canyon: An Eleventh-Century Pueblo Regional Center.*

Chaco Research Archive (CRA)

An online resource (www.chacoarchive.org) that provides access to extensive archaeological research data on **Chaco Canyon.** The Archive was conceived in 2002 by Stephen Plog with students and staff at the University of Virginia and developed with a group of Southwestern archaeologists. The goal of the project is to increase the availability of archival photographs, field notes, inventory lists, and unpublished manuscripts.

The Archive includes extensive research and materials collected during explorations and excavations in the late nineteenth and early twentieth centuries. The website organizes the information into the following sections:

- *Explore the Canyon* features an interactive map of the Chaco Park region for users to zoom in and view many sites and to overlay historical aerial photographs taken fifty years ago.
- *Image Gallery* allows users to search and examine over ten thousand photographs including the first images of Chaco taken by the **Mindeleff** brothers in 1877.
- *Sites* provides descriptions, photographs, **tree-ring dates**, and artifact information from more than thirty settlements. Users can download unpublished documents from the excavations.
- *Query the Database* allows users access to a large relational database on rooms and kivas at many sites.
- *Architectural Stabilization Images* includes over nine thousand photographs of Chacoan **stabilization** projects over the past seventy years.
- *Bibliography* lists all known publications on Chaco including theses and dissertations as well as unpublished papers. The bibliography was compiled by prominent Chacoan scholar, Joan **Mathien** and is regularly updated by CRA staff.
- *Tree-Ring Dates* features a downloadable spreadsheet of all available samples, dates, and locations.
- *Digital Monographs* provides access to Neil **Judd**'s publications on **Pueblo Bonito** and **Pueblo del Arroyo**, as well as the only published monographs on **Small House Sites** Bc 50 and Bc 51 near **Casa Rinconada**.

Funding for the CRA was provided by the Andrew W. Mellon Foundation, the National Science Foundation, the Institute for Advanced Technology in the Humanities, and the Dean of Arts and Sciences at the University of Virginia. Cooperating archives included the National Anthropological Archives, the American Museum of Natural History, and the Chaco Culture Museum Collections.

FIGURE 13. Chaco Wash below Peñasco Blanco near its confluence with the Escavada Wash.

Chaco Wash (and Chaco River)

(Maps 1, 2, 3, 4; Figure 13)
The primary watercourse draining the interior of the **San Juan Basin**. Originating as the Chaco Wash on the western slopes of the Continental Divide twenty miles east of Chaco Canyon, the drainage runs through Chaco Canyon and joins the **Escavada Wash** at the canyon's western end. Many maps show the Chaco River beginning below this confluence, though the name has significance only after major summer rains since the riverbed is dry most of the year.

Continuing its westward course, the Chaco River makes an abrupt turn to the north about forty miles west of Chaco Canyon at a point known as "the Great Bend of the Chaco." From this point the wide, dry riverbed continues its final sixty miles to join the San Juan River near Shiprock, New Mexico.

Chacra Face Road

(Map 2)
One of at least eight Chacoan **roads** that entered Chaco Canyon. The Chacra Face Road, identified through analysis of aerial photographs,

enters the canyon through the **Fajada Gap**, a break in the **Chacra Mesa** at **Fajada Butte**. The road leads toward the **great house** of **Una Vida,** its probable end point. Outside the canyon, the road curves around the base of Chacra Mesa and can be traced to the east for several miles. It may have connected Una Vida to the **Guadalupe Outlier**, one of the easternmost Chacoan **outlier communities**.

Chacra Mesa

(Maps 1, 2, 3, 4)

A flat-topped mesa, or plateau, averaging a mile in width and rising some 500 feet above the canyon floor on the south side of Chaco Canyon. Without the Chacra Mesa, life for the prehistoric Chacoan people would have been difficult because the mesa's higher elevations provided more water and several zones of resources, including pinyon nuts, mule deer, firewood, and yucca.

Chacra Mesa is the dominant landform in the central **San Juan Basin** and passes across the Continental Divide to the east. It forms the southern edge of Chaco Canyon and is broken in the canyon at two places, the **Fajada Gap** and **South Gap**.

The word "Chaca" appears on a Spanish map made in 1777. It may be the Hispanicized version of the Navajo name for Chacra Mesa, "Tzak aih," meaning "white string of rocks." The uppermost sandstone formations on Chacra Mesa occur as light-colored knobs, rock fins, and small buttes and may possibly be the "white string of rocks." The word **"Chaco"** is almost certainly derived from "Chaca."

Chert

A cryptocrystalline quartz, often occurring as pebbles or nodules, that was well suited for making stone tools such as arrowheads, drills, knives, and scrapers. Because of its almost pure silica content, it produces very sharp edges when broken.

Studies by Catherine **Cameron**, an "alumna" of the **Chaco Project**, have shown that several kinds of chert were used by Chacoan toolmakers, including three exotic cherts imported from the edges of the **San Juan Basin**. Morrison Chert came from the northwestern basin, and one of its most common pale green forms, Brushy Basin Chert, was traded into Chaco Canyon from the 800s through the 1000s.

During this same period, Washington Pass Chert, now known as Narbona Pass Chert, was also imported in greater quantities than any other exotic stone. This orange to light orange rock is found in deposits in the **Chuska Mountains**. Cameron's studies have shown that despite its wide appeal in Chaco, relatively small quantities were imported. Based on samples taken during excavations at the **Pueblo Alto** great house, Cameron estimated that one man could supply ten canyon **great houses** with this chert by making only 1.2 trips to the Chuska Mountain source per year.

The third exotic, Zuni Spotted Chert, was brought into the canyon in the 1100s after trade in the other two cherts declined. This material was collected to the south of Chaco in the Zuni Mountains and is easily identified by its butterscotch color with small, dark brown spots.

Obsidian was the only other important lithic imported into Chaco Canyon.

Chetro Ketl

(Map 4; Figure 14)

A Chacoan **great house** located less than a half mile east of **Pueblo Bonito**. The ground plan is the classic D-shape characteristic of the 1000s. Chetro Ketl has the largest surface area of any Chacoan great house (more than 250,000 square feet) although it has only about 400 rooms, approximately one hundred fewer than Pueblo Bonito. The building may have risen to four stories in some places on the north side, but only three stories remain. A balcony running along most of the back wall is marked today by a horizontal slit in the masonry at the second story. Hundreds of tree-ring dates place the major construction period in the mid-1000s.

Two **great kivas** were situated in the large open plaza, and a **tower kiva** was constructed near the middle of the central room block. Excellent examples of stone **discs** found in great kiva seating pits can be seen in the excavated great kiva. The smaller great kiva

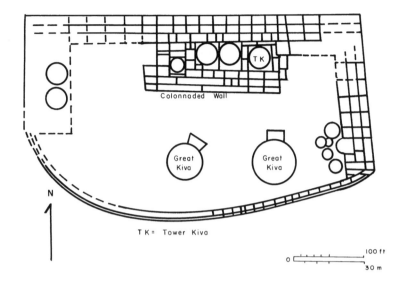

Colonnaded Wall

Great Kiva

Great Kiva

N

T K = Tower Kiva

0   100 ft
         30 m

FIGURE 14. Chetro Ketl great house ground plan. Dashed lines represent unexcavated portions of the site. Doorways are not shown.

was **backfilled** with soil following excavation, and its location is not readily apparent today.

A **colonnade** was built on the plaza-facing wall in the central room block; spaces between the columns were later filled with masonry. Several Chacoan **roads** are directed toward the site, and one ends at the **Talus Unit**, a detached room block a few yards west of the great house's northwestern corner.

Chetro Ketl was selected by Edgar **Hewett** in 1920 for excavations by the **School of American Research** and the Royal Ontario Museum. Hewett carried out work at the site through 1921 but stopped during the period Neil **Judd** was excavating Pueblo Bonito. Hewett returned in 1929 and used Chetro Ketl and other Chacoan sites for student field training in archaeology. Work at the site continued through 1934. Although Hewett did a poor job of documenting his work and published only generalized statements of the results, research here produced significant contributions to **dendrochronology**, architectural studies, and ceramic analysis.

An in-depth analysis of Chetro Ketl architecture and dendrochronology by Stephen **Lekson**, Peter McKenna, Jeffrey Dean, and Richard Warren was published by the **Chaco Center** in 1983. A delightful and perceptive foreword by Florence **Ellis** provides a strong historic link to Hewett's work in this great house.

The name "Pueblo Chettro Kettle" was reported to Lieutenant **Simpson** in 1849 by his "guide," probably **Carravahal**, who interpreted the name as Rain Pueblo. However, Washington Matthews, an early chronicler of Navajo culture, wrote in 1889 that he believed the great house was a structure in Navajo mythology known as Kintyél or Kintyéli meaning "Broad-house." This building figured significantly in Matthews's version of the Navajo legend of Noqoîlpi, the **Gambler**. In this story Pueblo people built the great house for the Gambler in exchange for part of the property they lost to him in various games. Other translated Navajo names for Chetro Ketl include "house in the corner" and "shining house."

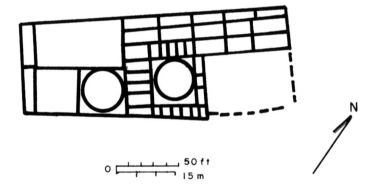

FIGURE 15. Chimney Rock Outlier great house ground plan. Dashed lines represent unexcavated portions of the site. Doorways are not shown.

Chimney Rock Outlier

(Map 1; Figure 15)

A Chacoan **outlier community** that may have served as a logging camp for workers cutting beams for **great houses** in Chaco Canyon. Archaeologist Allen Kane has suggested that large stands of ponderosa pine near this northern outlier may have been the reason for its establishment in southwestern Colorado. The nearby Piedras River may even have been used to float timbers to the San

Juan River and then downstream to a takeout point for overland transport to Chaco Canyon.

Chimney Rock is named for two prominent sandstone pinnacles that some archaeologists believe were used to chart certain celestial events, particularly lunar standstills, a phenomenon that occurs only once every 18.6 years.

The community includes a great house near the summit of the site area and seven clusters of **small house sites**. Two structures identified as **great kivas** share only some features with standard Chacoan great kivas. The great house and several small house sites were first excavated in the 1920s and then again in the 1970s. The site is located midway between Durango and Pagosa Springs, Colorado, and is protected and managed by the National Forest Service.

Chis-chilling-begay (or Chiisch'ilin Biye)

The man convicted of killing Chacoan archaeologist Richard **Wetherill** in an alleged livestock dispute on June 22, 1910, near **Cly's Canyon** in Chaco Canyon. Begay, a local **Navajo**, surrendered to authorities and stood trial for the murder. Conflicting accounts of the incident, created in part by Wetherill's bad relations with the Indian Service, may have contributed to Begay's reduced charges of voluntary manslaughter. He was sentenced to five to ten years in the state penitentiary in Santa Fe, New Mexico.

Begay's grandson, Andrew Charley, works for the National Park Service in Chaco Canyon.

Chuska Mountains

(Map 1)

The southern portion of a long range of mountains straddling the New Mexico/Arizona border from the Four Corners to Gallup, New Mexico. Looming on the western horizon as seen from **Pueblo Alto** or other high points around Chaco Canyon, they served as the western border of the **Chacoan World**. The mountains were also an important source of building **timbers** and stone (Narbona Pass **Chert**) used for arrow points and other chipped stone artifacts. "Chuska" is an English approximation of the **Navajo** word *chusgai*, meaning "white spruce."

Chuska Valley

(Map 1)

A valley about fifty miles west of Chaco Canyon that was the source of possibly thousands of **pottery** vessels, especially large cooking jars, transported to Chaco Canyon.

Archaeologists have confirmed this extensive trade in the A.D. 1000s through analysis of the **temper** in the ceramics. Much of the pottery produced in the Chuska Valley was tempered with a crushed, shiny greenish black rock called trachyte. Because this rock is limited to the western flanks of the **Chuska Mountains** near Narbona Pass, the source of the pottery was almost certainly the large **Anasazi** settlements in the Chuska Valley, including the **Skunk Springs Outlier.**

The people of Chaco probably imported pottery because of a lack of fuel wood in the canyon for firing the vessels. Perhaps, faced with the choice of importing firewood or pottery, they chose pottery. Although we can document this trade, we do not know what the Chacoans offered in exchange for the pottery.

Cibola White Ware

(Figure 16)

A **Puebloan** pottery tradition extending from Chaco south into the **Zuni** Pueblo area. Typical of **Anasazi** ceramics, most Chacoan decorated **pottery** featured black geometric designs painted on whitish backgrounds. Design motifs and layouts changed through time, and archaeologists classify each different design style as a ceramic "type." Similar types that share a common beginning are classified as a particular "ware." Many of the Chacoan ceramics are types of Cibola White Ware.

The Chaco Series of Cibola White Ware includes the following types:

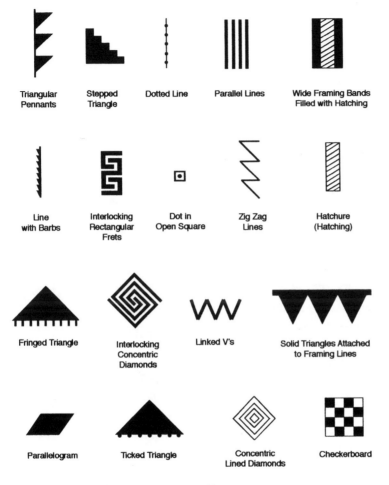

FIGURE 16. Cibola white ware pottery motifs.

La Plata Black-on-white	A.D. 600–850
Red Mesa Black-on-white	A.D. 875–1040
Escavada Black-on-white	A.D. 1000–1100
Gallup Black-on-white	A.D. 1030–1150
Chaco Black-on-white	A.D. 1075–1150
Chaco-McElmo Black-on-white	A.D. 1100–1150

Dates of production and use are approximate and may vary by area within the **San Juan Basin.** Production of some types overlapped temporally.

Cloisonné (see *Pseudo-cloisonné*)

Cly, Dan

A Navajo mason who worked on stabilization projects at Chaco. Cly and his family were well-known in the area, having lived for many years in **Cly's Canyon** and along the **Escavada Wash.**

Cly worked for Neil **Judd** at **Pueblo Bonito** from 1921 through 1925, when he may have acquired ruins **stabilization** skills. He began working with the National Park Service Ruins Stabilization Unit for **Gordon Vivian** in 1938 and continued into the 1940s. Ruins stabilization became a family tradition, and three of Dan's sons—Joe, John, and Pat—were employed on Vivian's crew for many years. Bessie Cly, Dan's granddaughter, also worked for the Park Service.

Dan Cly also served as a resource for information on **Navajo** culture and Chaco Canyon. In 1925, Judd's interest in local Navajo farming practices led him to map Cly's two floodwater corn fields in Cly's Canyon. He also shared his knowledge with two of **Hewett**'s students who were researching Navajo ethnobotany and place names in Chaco Canyon. The Cly family is frequently cited by David **Brugge** in his monograph, *A History of the Chaco Navajos.*

Cly's Canyon

(Maps 2, 3)
A major tributary side canyon, or **rincon**, on the north side of Chaco Canyon that has figured significantly in the prehistory and history of Chaco. The Chacoans built one of the largest prehistoric masonry **dams** in Chaco Canyon sometime in the A.D. 1000s near the mouth of Cly's Canyon to collect and divert floodwaters into **canals** that carried water to fields in the canyon proper. At a slightly later time,

the **McElmo-style** great house **Casa Chiquita** was built below the dam on the west side of Cly's Canyon.

Named for a Navajo family who lived there in the 1920s, Cly's Canyon was the site of a spring that probably served as a source of domestic water for the ancient peoples living in the **Pueblo Alto** great house on the mesa just to the east.

A road north out of Chaco Canyon was routed through Cly's Canyon in the early 1900s to replace the earlier **Wetherill** wagon route that ran to the western end of the Chaco Canyon before turning north and west to Farmington, New Mexico. Because of the new road, Cly's Canyon was known for a time as Rincon del Camino, or "Road Canyon."

Colonnades

(Figure 17)

A series of columns separated at regular intervals that often formed the base for a covered porch. Two examples of square masonry colonnades have been found in Chaco Canyon. The first is the well-known colonnaded gallery in a long room facing the main plaza at the **Chetro Ketl** great house. The room was later divided into smaller spaces and the openings between the columns were filled with masonry, but the original pillars are still visible. The second set, much less spectacular, is found at the **small house site** of Bc 51 in the **Casa Rinconada** small house community. Only the stubs of these square columns remain. Archaeologists are not certain what purpose the colonnades served in either of these two sites.

Colonnades are one of several architectural features in Chacoan sites that some archaeologists (for example, Charles **DiPeso**, Edwin **Ferdon**, J. Charles Kelley) believe are evidence for influence in Chaco from the high cultures of Mexico.

Colorado Plateau

A large, uplifted plateau covering approximately 150,000 square miles, bounded on the northwest by Cedar City, Utah, on the northeast by Aspen, Colorado, on the southwest by Flagstaff, Arizona, and

FIGURE 17. Colonnade at the Chetro Ketl great house. Spaces between the columns were filled with masonry at a later date.

on the southeast by Albuquerque, New Mexico. The Colorado Plateau is often associated with the Ancestral **Puebloan** culture, and the **San Juan Basin** and Chaco Canyon lie squarely within the southern portion of the plateau.

The second largest plateau in the world (second only to the Tibetan Plateau), this geologic province is actually a set of plateaus that have been generically lumped under one term. Its distinctive geology and topography are characterized by sedimentary rocks cut by canyons forming smaller plateaus, mesas, buttes, and similar landforms.

Communication System (see *Signal Stations*)

Community

A term used by archaeologists to define a cohesive group of people who have face-to-face contact in their daily work and living routines. Some archaeologists believe the term should be expanded geographically and socially to include the minimal number of groups necessary to ensure stability in subsistence and human reproduction.

These two levels of community have been identified as "the residential community" and "the sustainable community."

Michael Marshall, John **Stein**, and others first used the term "community" during early investigation of Chacoan outliers in the 1970s, and it has generally been used since to refer to the cluster of structures and features common to most Chacoan **outlier communities**. A collection of great house community studies, edited by John **Kantner** and Nancy Mahoney, and published in 2000, summarizes current interpretations of these settlements.

Copper Bells

(Figure 18)

Small ceremonial bells found at Chaco Canyon that demonstrate contact with the high cultures of Mexico. Copper bells produced in northwestern Mexico by the lost wax method were traded north into the **Hohokam, Mogollon,** and **Anasazi** areas. Although they are

FIGURE 18. Hohokam copper bells from the Point of Pines Ruin, Arizona. (Arizona State Museum, University of Arizona; Helga Teiwes, photographer.)

small (usually no more than one-half inch in diameter) and might not be easy to find in an excavation, the fact that only about twenty-five have been found in Chaco Canyon sites suggests that they were very rare. Even fewer (about five) are reported from the northern **San Juan Basin.** These bells almost certainly were used in ceremonies by priests and were not for personal adornment. For example, three bells from Chaco were recovered from the **Casa Rinconada** great kiva.

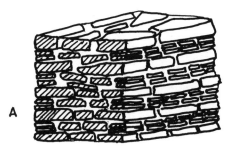
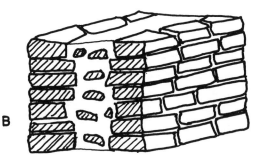

FIGURE 19. Cross sections of core-and-veneer walls: (A) solid core; (B) fill core.

Core-and-Veneer

(Figure 19)

One of three Chacoan **masonry types,** consisting of a core of rough "rubble" stone, often laid up with large amounts of mortar, faced on both sides with an outer layer of finished or "dressed" stones. The stones of the outer veneer layers interlock with the rubble core to form a more substantial block of solid masonry. The core stones were either laid up in courses or simply mixed with mud mortar to fill the cavity between the veneer walls. The weight of upper-story walls and roofing timbers rests on both the core and the facing layers so that the "veneer" is a major element of the load-bearing wall.

A true veneer is a thin layer of material applied to another surface. In actuality, the only true Chacoan core-and-veneer construction was the Type I **veneer style** used in the earliest great houses

(**Pueblo Bonito**, **Una Vida**, **Peñasco Blanco**). Walls in these buildings were built of wide, thin slabs of dark, tabular sandstone set in abundant mortar and then faced on both sides with a thick plaster. Thousands of small sandstone chips or **spalls** were then pressed horizontally into the plaster, creating a true veneer. In this case, the veneer was not load-bearing.

Wall construction in Chaco Type II masonry and all later veneer styles changed when the wall facings became load-bearing, and a rubble core was placed between them as the wall was built.

Almost all walls in Chacoan **great houses** were of core-and-veneer construction, though a few examples of other masonry types are occasionally present. Core-and-veneer masonry can be found in a few rooms at **small house sites**, but most small house construction was of simple or compound masonry.

Corn (see *Maize*)

Corner Doorways

(Figure 20)

Unusual doorways in the corners of some rooms in the **Chetro Ketl** and **Pueblo Bonito** great houses. Two good examples of Chacoan corner doorways can be found on the self-guided trail through Pueblo Bonito: look for them when passing through the series of deep rooms in the eastern portion of the **great house**.

Why build a corner doorway to provide access between diagonal rooms? They are seldom found in modern buildings, but Chacoan great house architects designed and built them. Jonathan Reyman, a southwestern archaeologist, has proposed that two corner doorways at the third-story level in Pueblo Bonito were used to record the winter solstice sunrise.

Another possibility is that the doorways made interaction between people living in parallel **suites** of rooms easier. Households in great houses consisted of several rooms running from the front to the back of the pueblo. Corner doors linked adjacent suites that may have been occupied by close relatives.

FIGURE 20. Corner doorway at Pueblo Bonito.

Corrugated Pottery
(Figure 21)

Ceramic containers in which the exposed coils of clay are pressed together to make three-dimensional bands. This process produces a rough but generally symmetrical surface. An "indented corrugated" pattern was produced when the moist clay in each band was slightly notched or indented with a stick or the tip of a finger. Fingerprints

FIGURE 21. Indented corrugated pottery jar.

can often be seen on these vessels. Corrugated vessels rarely had painted designs.

Heavy sooting on the exteriors of many of these vessels and their frequent location near hearths in **Puebloan** sites suggests that most were used for cooking. A corrugated surface may have aided in heat transfer, thereby reducing the time of cooking and the amount of fuel needed for the fire. Corrugating also reduced cracking in cooking pots exposed to frequent heating and cooling.

Many of the corrugated pottery vessels found in Chaco Canyon were imported from villages in the **Chuska Valley**. Archaeologists made this determination based on the identification of a distinctive **temper** material found only in deposits in that valley.

Coyote Canyon Road

(Map 2)

A Chacoan road reaching into the southwestern sector of the **San Juan Basin**. It is known from a number of documented segments extending from the **South Gap** in Chaco Canyon to the Gray Ridge community north of Gallup, New Mexico, but the entire roadway has not been traced.

The road has been defined from South Gap to a point outside the canyon where the **Kin Klizhin** great house is visible. A link between Kin Klizhin and **Kin Bineola** is assumed based on one short segment of road discovered between these two **great houses**. A connection between Kin Bineola and the **Standing Rock Outlier** is hypothetical; segments between Standing Rock and the Gray Ridge community are well documented. No traces of road have been found beyond the Gray Ridge community.

Crown, Patricia

A distinguished archaeologist with experience in both the **Hohokam** and **Chaco** regions who is highly regarded for her creative analysis of Southwestern ceramics. Crown and James **Judge** co-edited *Chaco and Hohokam: Prehistoric Regional Systems in the American Southwest*, a comparative examination of settlement pattern, subsistence, exchange, and sociopolitical complexity in the two areas. She is well known for *Ceramics & Ideology: Salado Polychrome Pottery*, a landmark study that argued that these fourteenth-century ceramics were emblematic of a widespread religious system, rather than a distinct cultural group. Crown later focused her interest in the symbolic aspects of ceramic decoration on an examination of motifs on sixteen Chacoan **cylinder jars**. She unexpectedly discovered surface modifications on some vessels including the obscuring of original designs or slipping and painting new designs. Crown concluded that these design changes did not reflect a design change during production or restoration of damaged motifs, but rather an intentional renewal of a vessel symbolizing participation in Chacoan ritual.

Crown's interest in cylinder jars continued following recovery of fragments of these vessels during the reopening of Neil **Judd**'s trenches through the **trash mounds** at **Pueblo Bonito** with Wirt "Chip" **Wills**. Analysis of residue on several fragments revealed traces of **cacao**, underscoring the potential ritual use of these vessels and Chacoan ties to **Mesoamerica**.

Cylinder Jars

(Figure 22)

Unusual cylindrical black-on-white **pottery** vessels found in caches at **Pueblo Bonito** and, rarely, at other Chacoan sites. One of the most exciting discoveries made by Richard **Wetherill** in his excavations at the Pueblo Bonito **great house** was a cache of 63 cylinder-shaped jars stacked in several layers in Room 28. Forty-eight similar vessels in the same room plus 8 more in an adjoining room brought the to-tal to 119 jars. Neighboring rooms also contained one or more ves-sels for a total of 192 cylinder jars. Only 18 others have been recovered from sites in Chaco Canyon and the northern **San Juan Basin**, including two **small house sites**.

All of these vessels are similar, being cylindrical but slightly flared at the bottom, averaging ten inches in height and four and one-half inches in diameter at the mouth. Many have small knobs or handles near the top. Most are painted white and decorated in black geometric designs typical of late Chacoan decorative styles. A few are decorated with only a red slip or wash of paint. The sheer dominance of numbers and clustering in Pueblo Bonito suggests some special purpose for these jars at that great house and perhaps elsewhere.

Patricia **Crown** and W. Jeffrey Hurst discovered that purpose in 2009 when analysis of residues on fragments of broken cylinder jars revealed evidence of **cacao**. It is believed that cylinder jars may have been used for mixing a cacao beverage for consumption during rit-ual activities.

FIGURE 22. Cylinder jar from Pueblo Bonito with de-sign motifs and layout typi-cal of the Chaco Black-on-white ceramic type.

D

Dams

Structures built to collect and hold surface water or to divert water to **canals**. Diversion dams channeled runoff to fields, and small check dams were probably constructed in minor drainages to collect water and keep soil from washing away. Large dams built to hold water in ponds for household use seem to be rare in Chaco Canyon.

Early reports of reservoirs that may have looked like modern stock ponds have not been confirmed but may lie undetected below the canyon floor.

Diversion dams used in farming systems are more common. Water was not held in ponds behind these dams. Rather, they channeled runoff into canals that carried it to nearby fields. One of the largest of this type of dam was built near the mouth of **Cly's Canyon**. The remaining part of the dam (evidence shows it was washed out, probably in prehistoric times) is 118 feet long, and the original length may have been almost twice that. A solid masonry section butting against the cliff wall on the west side was twenty-one feet wide and at least seven feet high. A four-foot-wide opening, or gate, separated this solid section from the part that extended toward the middle of Cly's Canyon. This portion was the same width and height, but consisted of a masonry wall built around a sand core. The use of this less solid construction technique may have been a fatal mistake, for the washout occurred in this area. Testing on the down-canyon side of the dam revealed canals and gates of a typical Chacoan **water control** system.

The one large masonry water impoundment dam known in Chaco Canyon was built near the head of a small canyon east of the mesa-top great house of **Tsin Kletsin**. This dam was at least 140 feet long, 7 feet high, and 9 feet wide. The area behind the dam was estimated to hold about one acre-foot of water (almost 326,000 gallons).

Dating Techniques

Methods used by archaeologists to determine the age of prehistoric materials and sites. Some methods, such as **dendrochronology**, **carbon-14** (radiocarbon), and **archaeomagnetic dating**, are "absolute" dating techniques that provide actual years or estimates of years (e.g., A.D. 950 ± 25 years). "Relative" dating techniques, such as **stratigraphy** and **pottery** sequences, tell us that one artifact or layer of artifacts is older or later than another.

In Chaco Canyon, tree-ring dating, or dendrochronology, has been the most important and successful dating method due to the large number of preserved roof timbers that can provide specific cutting dates when outside rings are present. Other techniques, such as carbon-14 and archaeomagnetic dating, are more useful for very ancient sites that do not contain wood suitable for tree-ring dating.

Dendrochronology

(Figure 23)

A **dating technique** used in several countries based on matching the pattern of annual growth rings in a tree to a master long-term growth-ring chart. Most trees add a ring of growth each year, and the width varies depending on climate. In the Southwest, dry years produce narrow rings, and wet years, wider rings. Trees of the same species in the same area generally produce the same pattern of ring growth. Beginning with modern trees, dendrochronologists can overlap ring patterns back into the past using older and older trees to establish a "master chronology" for an area.

To date a timber, a dendrochronologist uses a cylindrical boring tool to remove a sample of wood that cuts across all growth rings from the outer surface to the central core. This sample is moved along the master chronology until the patterns of wide and narrow rings match. The dendrochronologist then can tell when the tree began its growth (the core or center of the set of rings) and the year it was cut (the last ring in the section).

Unfortunately, interpreting building construction dates from tree-ring dates is not always simple. Archaeologists face problems such as recycled **timbers** (producing apparently early dates for later

FIGURE 23. Cross section and sample core of a tree cut in 1965. The varied widths of annual growth rings reflect increases (wider rings) and decreases (narrower rings) in annual precipitation.

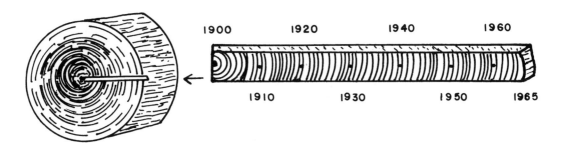

1900   1920   1940   1960

1910   1930   1950   1965

buildings) and timbers that were cut and stockpiled several years before construction. Nevertheless, dendrochronology provides some of the most accurate dates possible in archaeology.

With more than a thousand recorded tree-ring dates, Chaco Canyon is probably the most thoroughly dated prehistoric area in the Southwest. The first tree-ring specimens were collected during the 1920s in the early developmental stages of this dating science. The investigation continues today through the work of the Laboratory of Tree-Ring Research at the University of Arizona and such dendrochronologists as Bryant Bannister and Jeffrey Dean. The rich store of timbers in **great houses** not only helps to refine dating at Chaco Canyon, but also the dendrochronology dating process.

DiPeso, Charles

A southwestern archaeologist who served as director of the privately funded Amerind Foundation in Dragoon, Arizona, from 1952 to 1982. Much of DiPeso's work focused on the **Hohokam** culture area in southern Arizona and the **Casas Grandes** culture of northern Mexico. This research led to DiPeso's theory that many prehistoric southwestern cultures had been strongly influenced by the high cultures of **Mesoamerica**. He believed that trade was an important element of this influence, with a specialized group of traders, the *pochteca*, acting as agents of change.

DiPeso argued that Chacoan cultural development in the A.D. 1000s was the direct result of the *pochteca* establishing trading outposts in the **great houses** of Chaco Canyon. He also believed that southwestern peoples eventually turned against the *pochteca* and drove them from Chaco and other southwestern culture areas. Evidence supporting this theory is limited.

Discs, Stone

(Figure 24)

Large, round, flat stones, usually sandstone, often found beneath the massive vertical roof support posts in Chacoan **great kivas**. These posts were placed into round "seating pits" in the floor of the kivas. In many of the seating pits, archaeologists found one to four discs averaging four inches in thickness and up to three feet in diameter. Examples of these stone discs can be seen in the great kiva at **Chetro Ketl**.

FIGURE 24. Sandstone discs and roof-support pits in the great kiva at Chetro Ketl.

Some archaeologists believe the discs were placed at the bottom of seating pits as foundations to prevent the heavy posts from sinking into the earth. At **Casa Rinconada**, each of the four roof-support posts was at least two feet in diameter and twelve feet tall, weighing more than a metric ton even after a year of drying. In some cases, however, the discs sit directly on bedrock. It may be that they were used to compensate for unequal post length; if posts were recycled from abandoned great kivas, one or more discs could have increased the height of a short post. Some discs were also found below masonry support columns, as in the great kiva at the **Aztec** West Ruin, perhaps pointing to a ritual or symbolic use.

Stone discs are one of the features that Stephen **Lekson** cites as evidence supporting his **Chaco Meridian** theory.

Douglass, Andrew

The father of tree-ring dating, or **dendrochronology**. Douglass was an astronomer at the University of Arizona who believed that sunspot cycles had an effect on climate and that changes in climate might be reflected in the annual growth rings of trees. His analysis of tree rings from the Flagstaff and Prescott areas in Arizona confirmed his theory.

In 1918, Earl **Morris** sent Douglass sections of nine beams from the **Aztec Ruins** and **Pueblo Bonito** to help him investigate changes in rainfall. Neil **Judd** offered Douglass beam samples from Pueblo Bonito in 1921, again for climatic research.

In 1922, when Judd heard Douglass speak of cross-dating the Morris samples from Aztec and Pueblo Bonito, Judd realized the potential for establishing a tree-ring chronology for the Southwest. Support from the **National Geographic Society** led to the three **beam expeditions** of 1923, 1928, and 1929, and the establishment of a master dating chart for the Southwest that extended from A.D. 700 to 1930.

Douglass continued to participate in the developing science of dendrochronology but remained primarily interested in climate and cyclic phenomena.

Downtown Chaco

(Maps 3, 4)

A term coined by archaeologist Stephen **Lekson** to refer to the dense cluster of Chacoan buildings in the vicinity of **Pueblo Bonito**. He believes this architectural cluster to be a single settlement that achieved essentially urban status. The concept has important implications for the social and political organization of the Chacoan population. How other **great house** groups in Chaco Canyon related to this urban zone is an important question.

Over time, Lekson's "downtown" area has changed. In 1984, he first used the term to describe a three-square-mile zone extending from **Chetro Ketl** to **Kin Kletso** and from **Pueblo Alto** to **Casa Rinconada**. In 1999, the new "downtown" encompassed ten square miles, extending from **Hungo Pavi** on the east to **Cly's Canyon** on the west, and from **Pueblo Alto** on the north to **Tsin Kletsin** on the south. In 2009 "downtown" shrank to a two-kilometer-diameter zone surrounding Pueblo Bonito. All versions of "downtown" include **small house sites** and other man-made features.

Drought Cycles

Periods of decreased rainfall in the Southwest that threatened **Puebloan** farmers' agricultural way of life. Regional reconstructions of climate for the past 2,000 years show major dry periods lasting about 50 years that occurred about every 550 years. Lesser periods of drought every 275 years lasted about 20 years. Each of these major cycles was marked by much shorter but often vastly different moisture levels occurring in periods of a decade or shorter.

The effect of droughts on Chacoan farmers was that they always had to plan for the future. Like the historic **Hopi**, they very likely tried to reserve two to three years of stored **maize** (corn) for years when crops failed from lack of moisture. Some archaeologists believe an extended drought cycle may have led to the **abandonment** of Chaco Canyon.

The record of annual moisture in the **San Juan Basin** for periods before the use of rain gauges and other weather recording devices has been reconstructed mostly from tree rings. The pattern of wide and narrow tree rings not only shows the wet and dry years, respectively, but also longer cycles of wet and dry years.

Dry Farming

Dry farmed fields are watered only by rain falling directly on them. Where annual precipitation is low this is a risky form of agriculture. However, Chacoan farmers probably planted in sand dunes that conserved moisture in the loose sand. The Hopi have used **dune farming** successfully for centuries for a variety of crops, especially beans. The Hopi and almost certainly the Chacoans depended to a greater extent on various methods of **floodwater farming**.

Dune Dam

A long sand dune across the western end of **Chaco Canyon** at the confluence of the Chaco and **Escavada** washes. Southwesterly winds carrying sand upstream from the **Chaco River** created a dune barrier that at times dammed the **Chaco Wash** and created a shallow lake below the **Peñasco Blanco** great house.

Buried soil deposits and broken **ceramics** exposed in the banks of the Chaco Wash suggest that heavy floods in the wash around A.D. 900 breached the dune dam. At some time in the early A.D. 1000s, Chacoans plugged the breach with masonry. In 1901 Stephen **Holsinger** reported the remnants of a "rock **dam** and ditch" in this location as well as a large **reservoir** lined with stone slabs and clay. According to Neil **Judd**, the last vestige of the dam disappeared in 1920.

When the dam was in place the Chaco Wash did not erode into the canyon floor and the water table remained high—a critical factor for farming. The breach of the dam in the early A.D. 900s would have lowered the water table. Stephen **Lekson** has noted that a hiatus in **great house** construction started at about the same time but building resumed by A.D. 1020.

In 2010 Stephen A. Hall, a geologist with considerable experience in the alluvial stratigraphy of Chaco Canyon, questioned the presence of a saline lake behind the dam. This was based on the absence of lacustrine beds in the alluvial valley fill.

Dune Farming

(Figure 25)

An arid farming technique that uses the water that collects in sand dunes from rainfall or underground seeps. Because of its porosity, sand is capable of storing large amounts of water below the surface. Dunes conserve this stored water because the thin layer of dry surface sand works as a mulch to prevent evaporation.

Based on the farming practices of modern **Puebloans**, it is assumed that Chacoans also used dune farming. The **Hopi** grow many crops in dune fields, especially beans. They often build low brush windbreaks between rows of plants to stop blowing sand and to prevent evaporation. Several types of dunes are used, including large climbing dunes at the base of cliffs and two- to three-foot blankets of sand covering layers of bedrock.

In Chaco Canyon, dunes have formed in **Werito's Rincon** and at the junction of the **Chaco** and **Escavada washes**. These and other areas were probably farmed in the past. **Chaco Project** archaeologists

FIGURE 25. Hopi bean fields in dunes near Third Mesa, Arizona.

carried out experimental dune farming in Werito's Rincon in 1979 with moderate success.

Dutton Plateau
(Map 1)
A large land mass that dominates the skyline south of Chaco Canyon. The plateau and the prominent butte crowning it, **Hosta Butte**, likely had special significance in the Chacoan cosmography as they formed a major geographic feature in the **Chacoan World**. The western portion of Dutton Plateau is also known as Mesa de los Lobos, suggesting wolves may have once lived on its summit. The plateau is named for Captain Clarence Dutton, a member of the Hayden U.S. Geological and Geographical Surveys of the Territories undertaken from 1873 to 1876.

E

East Community
(Map 2; Figure 26)
A Chacoan great house community near the eastern end of Chaco Canyon, approximately twelve miles east of **Pueblo Bonito** and five miles west of **Pueblo Pintado**. East Community was known by archaeologists working in Chaco Canyon in the 1950s but was not studied until the late 1980s. This investigation showed that it was occupied by both Chacoans and Mesa Verdeans.

Eighty-two archaeological sites were inventoried in the community, including a **great house** and numerous **small house sites**. The great house is located on a knoll on the south side of the canyon, probably because the course of the **Chaco Wash** left few building locations and farmlands on the north side. Most small house sites are on the south side of the canyon in the vicinity of the great house.

The great house is D-shaped, single-storied, and contains about twenty-five rooms. The ground plan has a northern room block and short west wing with an arced row of rooms enclosing an open

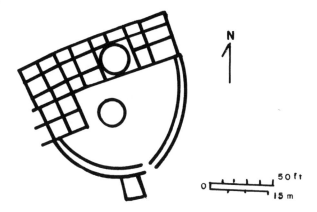

plaza. An opening may be present in this row of rooms. There is at least one **kiva** in the northern room block, and another in the plaza. No **great kiva** has been located at the site. The depression of a **road** arcs around the front of the building, but it is not known if it links to a road from Pueblo Pintado that enters the canyon about two miles east of the East Community great house.

Based on ceramics, it is believed that the building was constructed in the A.D. 900s, but the enclosing arc of rooms that created the plaza was erected in the 1000s. Small house sites in the community were built and occupied from A.D. 875 to 1300. Thirty-nine of these small house sites were occupied from A.D. 1175 to 1300 during the Mesa Verde period of canyon use. Thomas **Windes**, a National Park Service archaeologist and an authority on Chacoan prehistory, has intensively studied this community and believes that it was linked to other canyon great houses and Pueblo Pintado through a visual network of **signal stations** associated with mesatop **shrines.**

Effigy Vessels

(Figure 27)

Ceramic containers made in the shape of animals and people. Like many of the world's **pottery**-producing peoples, Chacoans made effigy vessels. They produced them in fairly limited numbers but in a

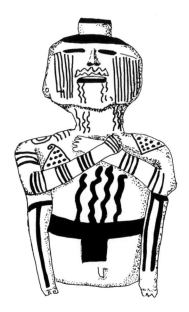

FIGURE 27. Chacoan effigy vessel. This human effigy jar was found during the Wetherill excavations at Pueblo Bonito.

wide range of bird, amphibian, and animal shapes, including ducks, frogs, bears, bighorn sheep, and badgers.

Human effigy vessels were rare in Chaco but almost always had the same general form. The figure usually is seated with the legs drawn up almost to the chest and the feet held flat. The head is generally wide, and the face flat with molded features. Genitalia are often shown, and most of the effigies are male. The body is hollow, and an opening on the top of the head encircled by a low rim of clay would have allowed the effigy to be filled with a liquid or a dry material such as cornmeal.

Human effigy vessels provide us with a valuable glimpse into Chacoan life. Potters created richly detailed "portraits" that included clothing and body decoration such as tattooing and pierced ears. Sandals and ornaments—including bracelets, anklets, and arm bands—are painted on many of the figures. Some of the effigies are hunchbacked, leading some archaeologists to speculate that there may be some connection with the legendary Kokopelli, or "Hunchback Flute Player," although only one instance of an effigy vessel with a flute is known.

The Chacoan human effigy vessels resemble similar containers from **Casas Grandes**, Chihuahua, although there are differences in manufacture and decoration, and the Casas Grandes examples were produced more than 200 years later.

El Faro

(Figure 28)

A prominent, cone-shaped hill at **Pierre's Outlier,** north of Chaco Canyon, that has been interpreted as a **signaling station.** The **Great North Road** passes just west of the site, and the presence of what may be a signaling station along the road implies communication links to Chaco Canyon.

Many of the major landmarks of the **Chacoan World** are visible from the top of El Faro, including Mount Taylor, **Hosta Butte, Fajada Butte,** and the Chuska-Lukachukai range. El Faro and other hilltop summits at Pierre's Outlier are, in turn, visible from several points on the south rim of the **Chacra Mesa.**

Although Chris Kincaid and others suggested during the Chaco roads project that the site may have been used as a signal station, Chaco Project archaeologist Robert Powers earlier described it as a

FIGURE 28. El Faro at Pierre's Outlier. The remains of the El Faro building unit are below the lower left slope of the cone. The Great North Road passes behind the cone.

three-room small house site with a hearth. Powers made a much stronger case for the presence of a signal station with burned rock and charcoal on the summit of a hilltop one half-mile west of El Faro.

The name "El Faro," Spanish for "lighthouse," is given to both the cone-shaped peak and a Chacoan building at the base of the cone that has about seventeen ground-floor rooms and three enclosures that may contain **kivas**. The masonry and ground plan suggest elements of both Classic Bonito and **McElmo-style** traditions.

Ellis, Florence Hawley (see *Hawley, Florence*)

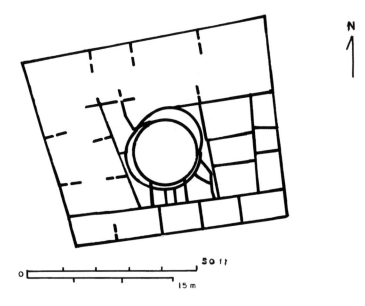

FIGURE 29. Escalante Outlier great house ground plan. Dashed lines represent unexcavated portion of the site. Several sealed doorways are not shown. Multiple remodeled kivas are shown in the center of the building.

Escalante Outlier

(Map 1; Figure 29)

A Chacoan outlier **great house** on the Dolores River north of **Mesa Verde**. Escalante Outlier was first discovered and reported on

August 13, 1776, by a Franciscan friar, Silvestre Vélez de Escalante, who was searching for an overland route from Santa Fe, New Mexico, to Spanish settlements on the California coast. It is partially excavated, stabilized, and open to the public at the Anasazi Heritage Center (managed by the Bureau of Land Management) just north of Cortez, Colorado.

This late **McElmo-style** great house with tree-ring dates in the A.D. 1120s contains about twenty-five rooms and a central **kiva**. Like many **outlier** great houses, Escalante was built on a point high above the surrounding countryside. About six **small house sites** are in the immediate vicinity, one of which, the Dominguez Ruin, was excavated and is interpreted by the Anasazi Heritage Center. There is no known association of the Escalante Outlier with a Chacoan **road.**

Escavada Black-on-white

(Figure 30)

A type of **Cibola White Ware** decorated pottery found at Chacoan sites dating to the A.D. 1000s. Manufactured throughout most of the San Juan Basin from roughly A.D. 1000 to 1100, Escavada Black-on-white featured black geometric designs on the white or gray body of the vessels. During most of this time another Cibola White Ware, **Gallup Black-on-white**, was also made. Escavada Black-on-white was first named and described by Florence **Hawley** based on her work in Chaco Canyon.

Like **Red Mesa Black-on-white**, most Escavada containers are bowls, though "closed" vessels such as jars, canteens, and pitchers were also produced. Archaeologists do not always agree on variation in design motifs for pottery types, and Escavada Black-on-white is an example of these differences of opinion. Usually, Escavada designs are identified as solid triangles often paired and attached to wide framing lines, heavy lines with multiple pennants, and heavy ticked triangles reminiscent of Red Mesa Black-on-white. The background wash or slip is often more gray than white, and the surface is rough. Most archaeologists agree that when hatched lines are incorporated into the design and the slip is whiter and polished, the pottery should be

FIGURE 30. Escavada Black-on-white pitcher and bowl forms with decorative motifs and design layout common to this ceramic type.

classified as Puerco Black-on-white, a contemporary of Escavada. Design layout usually consists of repetitive panels of similar elements encircling most of the interiors of bowls or the exteriors of jars and pitchers.

Pottery decorated with similar designs but in carbon paint (made from plants) was produced to the west of Chaco Canyon in the **Chuska Valley**, including Chuska Black-on-white. During the time Escavada was produced, the earlier neckbanded cooking ware was fully replaced by overall indented **corrugated** ware.

Escavada Wash

(Maps 1, 2, 3)

A major northern tributary of the **Chaco Wash** that begins near Lybrook, New Mexico, and flows south and west to join the Chaco Wash at the western end of Chaco Canyon. The **Bis sa'ani** community is located on the edge of this drainage north of **Gallo Canyon**, and numerous **small house sites** border the wash north of the **Pueblo Alto** great house. Farmers from Pueblo Alto may have farmed the floodplain of the Escavada much like the **Navajos** did during the late historic period.

The **Great North Road** crosses the wash north of Pueblo Alto. The **Ahshislepah Road** crosses the Escavada at its confluence with the Chaco Wash.

F

Fajada Butte

(Map 3)

One of the most prominent landmarks in Chaco Canyon, located in the **Fajada Gap**, a break in the Chacra Mesa south of the National Park Service Visitor Center. This remnant piece of the Chacra Mesa remained standing as other portions eroded away to form the gap. "Fajada," which means "belted" or "banded" in Spanish, refers to the wide band of low-grade coal and dark carbonaceous shale that encircles the butte about midway up from its base.

The butte can be seen from many points in the **Chacoan World** and must have been a major landmark in the ancient Chacoan cosmography. This is supported by the presence near its summit of the **Sun Dagger**, a celestial rock art marker that records the summer and winter solstices, the equinox, and phases of the moon.

The butte was first mentioned in José Antonio **Vizcarra**'s journal as "Cerrito Fajado," a place he camped near in Chaco Canyon on August 25, 1823, while returning from a Mexican campaign against the **Navajos**. Lieutenant **Simpson**, who chronicled Colonel Washington's march through the Chaco area in 1849, also records a Chaco Canyon campsite near "Mesa Fachada."

Fajada Gap

(Maps 2, 3)

A wide break in the **Chacra Mesa** south of the National Park Service Visitor Center and the **Una Vida** great house. The location of the gap is marked by **Fajada Butte**, a remnant of the Chacra Mesa. Drainage into Chaco Canyon through the gap may have created an especially fertile zone, accounting for the presence nearby of many **small house sites** and the Una Vida **great house**, one of the three earliest great houses in Chaco Canyon.

The gap also offered easy access into Chaco Canyon. The Chacoan **South Road** may enter the canyon through Fajada Gap and could have been routed toward Una Vida. The **Chacra Face**

Road also enters here, running along the base of the mesa to the east of Fajada Butte. This road may have gone to Una Vida.

Ferdon, Edwin

A student of Edgar **Hewett**'s who worked in several Chaco Canyon sites, including **Chetro Ketl** and **Kin Kletso**. Ferdon's major contribution to Chacoan prehistory came a number of years later when he published his monograph, *A Trial Survey of Mexican-Southwestern Architectural Parallels*. In this report he proposed that a number of architectural features found in **Anasazi** and **Hohokam** sites were derived from the high cultures of **Mesoamerica**.

Ferdon maintained that the colonnaded gallery at Chetro Ketl mimicked **colonnades** in Mexican sites, but he misinterpreted the ladder landing at the **Talus Unit** as a **platform mound**. He focused principally, however, on three types of round buildings to support his argument: towers (in the **Mesa Verde** area), **tower kivas,** and **tri-wall structures**. He proposed that these were related to a Quetzalcoatl cult introduced into the Anasazi area by *pochteca* traders.

Ferdon's premise and his architectural evidence were later used to support similar theories proposed by Charles **DiPeso** and J. Charles Kelley. More recently, Stephen **Lekson** has cited many of the same architectural features in developing his argument for a **Chaco Meridian**.

Floodwater Farming

Rainfall provides water for both **dry farming** and floodwater farming. Whereas dry farming depends upon rainfall falling directly on fields, floodwater farming utilizes the runoff from rain falling on areas upstream from the fields. Agricultural use of this water is achieved through slowing and spreading runoff with dikes or low simple walls along natural drainages or channeling it into **canals** for distribution to fields. Slowing floodwater becomes more important as slope gradient increases and simple forms of terracing may be employed to capture both water and soil on sloping land and in the bottoms of small drainage ways.

Flotation

A process for retrieving tiny fragments of plant and animal remains from soil collected at archaeological sites. Dirt from various locations such as trash deposits, work areas, and floors is placed in tanks of water and stirred manually or moved with running water. Lightweight materials such as grain husks, plant stems, and bone splinters that float on the water are removed and dried for identification. Heavier materials that sink to the bottom of the tank can be collected, placed in a sieve, and rewashed to remove any remaining soil.

Plant and animal remains recovered through flotation are important for reconstructing past climatic conditions as well as determining the foods and plants used in ancient times. Mollie Toll, a **Chaco Project** staff member, employed flotation techniques to establish a large inventory of plants and trees used by Chacoan residents.

Foot Drums

(Figure 31)
Open, rectangular masonry vaults or boxes that were standard floor features in Chacoan **great kivas**. If covered with planks, they may have served as foot resonators for dancers. All excavated Chacoan

FIGURE 31. Foot drum in the Chetro Ketl great kiva. The masonry-enclosed seating pit for the south roof-support post is attached to the foot drum.

great kivas built in the 1000s and 1100s (with the exception of the Fort Wingate great kiva) have a pair of vaults oriented on a north-south axis. They rise about twenty-four inches above floor level and are placed between two roof beam seating pits. In some cases the vaults are divided into two compartments.

No evidence for plank covers has been found in great kivas, but wooden covers are known for single foot drums in smaller **kivas**. **Gordon Vivian**, who excavated the **Casa Rinconada** great kiva, suggested that if the vaults were not foot resonators, they may have been sudatories (sweat houses) or soil containers for the ritual sprouting of plants used in spring ceremonies, such as *Powamu* at the **Hopi** villages.

G

Gallo Canyon
(Maps 2, 3)
A major tributary side canyon of Chaco Canyon located east of the Una Vida **great house** and the National Park Service Visitor Center. Today, the National Park Service campground is located in Gallo Canyon.

There is good evidence that Chacoan farmers diverted water from this side canyon to fields near **Una Vida**. The current course of the Gallo Wash tends to follow the route of an old diversion **canal,** which may explain why water does not flow more directly into the **Chaco Wash** at the mouth of Gallo Canyon. Though a few Chacoan sites, including the **Wijiji** great house, are found east of Gallo Canyon, it forms the eastern boundary of the most intensively occupied portion of Chaco Canyon.

Gallo Cliff Dwelling
(Map 3; Figure 32)
Two small, late room blocks protected by a cliff overhang in **Gallo Canyon** adjacent to the National Park Service campground. The

FIGURE 32. Gallo Cliff Dwelling. This small building probably dates to the Mesa Verde occupation of Chaco Canyon.

central room with a high standing wall may date from a **Mesa Verde** occupation of Chaco Canyon in the 1200s. The low-walled, five-room building with an associated **kiva** at the northern end of the shelter was probably occupied in the early 1100s, when most great houses and some small house sites were built in the **McElmo style**. National Park Service excavations at the site in the 1960s produced a good collection of perishable materials such as sandals and baskets from the dry deposits in and around the rooms.

Gallup Black-on-white

(Figure 33)

A type of **Cibola White Ware** decorated **pottery** manufactured from approximately A.D. 1030 to 1150. Largely contemporary with **Escavada Black-on-white** and found throughout the **San Juan Basin**, Gallup featured more hatched designs and a larger percentage of pitchers and jars. This ceramic type was named and described by Florence **Hawley** based on research she did in Chaco Canyon, and on work by Emil Haury in the **Red Mesa Valley** near Gallup, New Mexico.

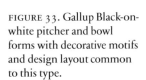

FIGURE 33. Gallup Black-on-white pitcher and bowl forms with decorative motifs and design layout common to this type.

As in earlier Cibola White Ware types, a mineral-based paint made from hematite or other iron oxides was used for Gallup designs. Archaeologists generally agree that Gallup Black-on-white is characterized by a significant increase in designs using hatching: rows of short parallel lines. These were usually combined with, and often used in opposition to, solid designs. The most common element was the triangular pennant, which may be solid, hatched, or hatched with solid tips. Wide, linked Vs were also frequently used (see Figure 15). The design field usually included the repetition of similar designs and covered most of the body of bowl interiors and jar exteriors.

Pottery decorated with similar designs but in carbon paint (from plants) was made in the **Chuska Valley,** including Chuska Black-on-white and Toadlena Black-on-white. Cooking ware was represented by several local variations of indented **corrugated.**

Gambler (or the Great Gambler)

A mythological figure in **Puebloan** and **Navajo** legends who lived at **Pueblo Alto** and, through gambling, won the possessions and great houses of the canyon population. Francisco **Hosta** recounted the story of El Capitán or El Jugador to William **Jackson** in 1877 when Jackson discovered the Pueblo Alto **great house.** A similar story involving Noqoîlpi, the Gambler, was recorded by Washington Matthews in 1889 and was told to George **Pepper** in the 1890s and Neil

Judd in the 1920s by local **Chaco Navajo**. In 2007 Taft Blackhorse and John **Stein** identified the Chetro Ketl **gridded field** as a playing field for a "golf-like game" where the Gambler, Nihwiilbiih in their version of the story, challenged Puebloan contestants.

Though several variations of the story existed, the basic themes were the same. The Gambler came from **Zuni**, Acoma, Laguna, or Jemez Pueblo and lived at Pueblo Alto, the "chief's house." He enslaved the people of Chaco and took their possessions by winning a number of different games, including foot races and stick dice. In one story a young boy won back the lives and goods of the Chacoan people; in another version, other tribes were the winners. In both stories the Gambler flew back to the Sun after his loss.

Gladwin, Harold

The founder and director of the Gila Pueblo Archaeological Foundation in Globe, Arizona, and a contributor to scientific work in the Chaco area. Gladwin was a businessman turned archaeologist who initiated important archaeological surveys and excavations throughout the Southwest and northern Mexico in the 1930s and 1940s. He was responsible for defining the **Hohokam** culture of southern Arizona and also played a role in helping Emil Haury identify the **Mogollon** culture.

Gladwin's broad interests led him to the Chaco area, and in 1934 he began an archaeological survey of the **Red Mesa Valley**. He followed this work with excavations in what he believed were six chronologically ordered sites. The results were published as *The Chaco Branch: Excavations at White Mound and in the Red Mesa Valley*, in which he outlined several "phases" of Chacoan development. Based on his own research and studies in dendrochronology, as well as University of New Mexico field school excavations at **Bc Sites** 50 and 51, Gladwin rejected arguments made by **Hawley**, Kluckhohn, and others for the coexistence of great houses and **small house sites**. He believed that **great houses** represented a later stage of development that arose from the small house tradition. Later work by several researchers proved Gladwin's theory to be incorrect.

Great Houses

(Figure 34)

The term "great house" has replaced an earlier term, "**town**." These large, usually multistoried stone buildings were constructed between A.D. 850 and A.D. 1150 on a formal plan with **core-and-veneer** walls, large rooms, high ceilings, large roofing **timbers**, enclosed plazas, and usually one or more **great kivas**. Southwestern archaeologists have debated the function of great houses for several decades. Some see them as residences of a tight-knit Puebloan community, but others believe they were ceremonial centers with a limited population of elite ritual specialists. More recently Stephen **Lekson** has proposed that they were palaces for a Chacoan royalty, the kings and queens of Chaco.

Great houses first appeared in the mid-800s in Chaco Canyon with the earliest construction at **Pueblo Bonito**, **Peñasco Blanco**, and **Una Vida**. The arced floor plan at Pueblo Bonito and Peñasco Blanco (and possibly Una Vida) may mirror contemporary buildings in southwestern Colorado, but the early canyon great houses were multistoried—the only such buildings in the Southwest at that time. Large-scale building projects at existing and new great houses during the A.D. 1000s resulted in most of the major buildings seen in Chaco Canyon today.

Construction at most of these classic great houses followed a pattern of growth that began as a core block of rooms, usually on the north side of the building, to which wings of rooms were added on the east and west. Eventually, an arced row of single rooms on the south linked the two wing room blocks, creating an enclosed plaza that often contained a number of underground **kivas**. Orientation to the south with tiered rooms stepped up to the north helped the buildings absorb solar heat in the winter. **Chetro Ketl** is an example of this classic plan.

Great kivas are present at most, but not all, of these great houses. **Veneer styles** on the core-and-veneer masonry changed over time, and additions to great houses can often be identified on the basis of different veneers.

Late in the 1000s several changes in great houses occurred. First, a number of these buildings, such as **Kin Bineola** and **Pueblo Pin-**

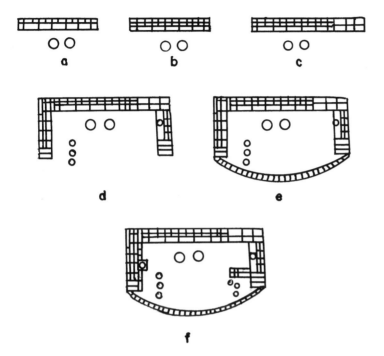

FIGURE 34. Stylized sequence of patterned growth of Chacoan great houses from approximately A.D. 920 to 1120. The left (west) wing appears to have been built first. Some great houses (such as Una Vida) do not have an east wing but do have an enclosed plaza.

tado, were constructed outside Chaco Canyon but within the **Chaco Core**. Their architecture follows the classic great house styles described above.

At approximately the same time, a very different great house plan and veneer style was introduced. These **McElmo-style** buildings were square or rectangular and enclosed one or two kivas in the middle of the building, with no great kivas or enclosed plazas. **Kin Kletso**, **Casa Chiquita**, and **New Alto** are good examples of McElmo-style buildings.

Finally, a number of great houses were constructed near the peripheries of the **San Juan Basin** in the late 1000s and early 1100s, usually within small house communities. A few of these **outlier** great houses, such as the West Ruin at **Aztec Ruins** and the **Salmon Ruin** near Bloomfield, New Mexico, followed the classic Chacoan great house plan, but most were smaller and more typical of the late McElmo plan.

Great Kivas

(Figure 35)

Large, round underground or semi-subterranean structures with relatively standard floor features used for community-wide rituals and usually associated with Chacoan **great houses**. **Basketmaker** era (A.D. 500–700) great kivas are known from Chaco Canyon (for example, **Shabik'eshchee Village**) and elsewhere, but they are often shallow and generally lack elaborate floor features. The better-known Chacoan great kivas were built in the middle and late 1000s within great house plazas (**Chetro Ketl, Pueblo Bonito**), adjacent to great houses (**Peñasco Blanco**) or as isolated great kivas (**Casa Rinconada**). These relationships to great houses were repeated at **outlier** sites.

Excavated great kivas range in diameter from about thirty-three to sixty-three feet, with estimated diameters of some unexcavated kivas exceeding eighty feet. Most of these great kivas had standard

FIGURE 35. Chetro Ketl great kiva during excavation and stabilization in 1921. (Courtesy of Palace of the Governers Photo Archives, NMHM/DCA, neg. 81714.)

floor and interior features including an encircling masonry bench; crypts or niches within the wall above the bench; a raised masonry firebox in the south central portion of the floor; four pits for roof support beams; raised masonry **foot drums** on a north-south axis between the pits; a northern entryway; and a northern antecham-ber (see Figure 9). Variations were common including north and south entryways (Casa Rinconada, **Aztec**) and peripheral rooms (Aztec, Casa Rinconada).

Great North Road

(Maps 1, 2; Figure 36)
A primary Chacoan road extending from Chaco Canyon into the northern reaches of the **San Juan Basin**. The Great North Road passes a number of sites that may have served as way stations, includ-ing Kin Indian, **Pierre's Outlier**, **Halfway House Outlier**, and **Twin Angels Outlier.** This is one of the best-documented Chacoan roads and is notable for the presence of four parallel roads in some areas.

The North Road was documented through aerial photography from **Pueblo Alto** at Chaco Canyon to Kutz Canyon in the north-ern San Juan Basin. It is presumed to follow Kutz Canyon to the San Juan River and the **Salmon Ruin Outlier** great house.

First noted by the **Wetherills** in the 1890s, the Great North Road and others were rediscovered by archaeologist **Gordon Vivian** in the 1950s. Twenty years later, **Gwinn Vivian** excavated sections of the road near Pueblo Alto, revealing the existence of low masonry "curbs" along some sections. The word "Great" was added to the term in the 1970s by National Park Service archaeologist Randall Morrison, who did preliminary work on Chacoan roads.

Gridded Fields

(Figure 37)
Formal, rectangular plots for planting **maize** (corn) and other food crops in floodwater-irrigated farms, especially on the north side of Chaco Canyon. Large fields were divided into smaller rectangular

FIGURE 36. Low masonry wall along a portion of the Great North Road in Chaco Canyon.

plots by low earth ridges that helped to contain and conserve **irrigation** water. The most critical variable for maize growth once it has sprouted is water. Standardized plots that allowed distribution of equal amounts of water to individual gardens would have significantly increased crop yields.

Based on aerial photography, limited excavations, and the presence of water control features, it is believed that most canyon bottomland on the north side of Chaco Canyon from **Mockingbird Canyon** to **Escavada Wash** was a continuous series of gridded fields.

The best-known example of this type of farming is the **Chetro Ketl** fields to the east of this great house. Approximately twenty acres of land were leveled and then divided by low soil ridges into individual plots measuring roughly seventy-five by forty-five feet, producing about thirteen fields per acre. Canals ran between sets of field grids, and masonry field gates in the ridges allowed water into each plot.

FIGURE 37. Aerial view of gridded fields near Chetro Ketl. Wide white lines (a) mark major divisions of the fields. Narrow lines (b) delineate separate fields. The Chaco Wash has cut into the field area on the south. A modern road passes through the field area. (Photo by Limbaugh Engineering and Aerial Surveys, Albuquerque.)

Some archaeologists question the identification of these features as fields and suggest that the low ridges were the foundations of a large, unfinished **great house**, the outlines of pits for mixing building mortar, or enclosed areas for raising frogs and freshwater shrimp.

Guadalupe Outlier

(Map 1; Figure 38)
The easternmost Chacoan **outlier** great house and community, located about sixty miles southeast of **Pueblo Bonito** and thirty miles northwest of Albuquerque. The **great house** at Guadalupe occupies

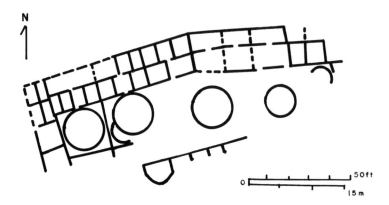

FIGURE 38. Guadalupe Outlier great house ground plan. Dashed lines represent unexcavated portions of the structure. Several open doorways are shown.

the top of a long, narrow sandstone ridge rising above the East Puerco Valley. The one-story Chacoan structure contains about twenty-five rooms and three **kivas**; additional rooms were built in the 1200s during a **Mesa Verde** reoccupation of the site. More than twenty **small house sites** in the immediate vicinity of the great house make up the outlier community. Neither **roads** nor **great kivas** are recorded for Guadalupe, but the **Chacra Face Road** is oriented in a direction that would have taken it near this outlier.

A portion of this site was excavated by Lonnie Pippin from 1973 to 1975 as part of Cynthia **Irwin-Williams**'s Rio Puerco Valley Project. The site is on Bureau of Land Management land and is protected by that federal agency.

H

Half House
(Map 3)
A deeply buried **Basketmaker** III period pithouse, located about eight miles east of **Pueblo Bonito**. This site was first discovered in

the 1920s and then excavated in 1947. One half of the pithouse was exposed when the **Chaco Wash** eroded away the river bank. The floor of the house was about sixteen feet below the present ground surface, showing the great extent of canyon bottom alluviation (filling with soil) in the past 1,300 years.

Half House was occupied in the A.D. 600s, about the same time as **Shabik'eshchee Village**. The coexistence of a pithouse on the floor of Chaco Canyon and Shabik'eshchee Village on the mesa above shows that Basketmaker peoples lived in different environmental zones within the canyon.

Halfway House Outlier

(Map 1; Figure 39)

A small **outlier** on the **Great North Road**, approximately halfway between Chaco Canyon and the **Salmon Ruin**. The only structure is a small, one-story **great house** of about twelve rooms. The **Great North Road** curves around the southern end of the building and then curves again to maintain a general north-south course. Halfway House appears to be largely road-related; because it is on a slight knoll, it may have served as a reorientation point when laying out the **road**.

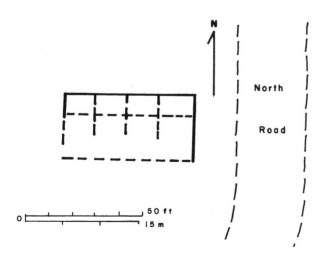

FIGURE 39. Halfway House Outlier great house ground plan. The site has not been excavated. Room locations are estimated from surface evidence. Kivas may or may not be present.

Hawley, Florence

A prominent southwestern archaeologist and ethnologist who made significant contributions to Chacoan archaeology in several research areas. Hawley received her early training at the University of Arizona as a student of Byron Cummings. She completed her M.A. at Arizona in 1928 in order to accept Cummings's offer to teach in the Department of Anthropology there. That same year, she was a student in Andrew **Douglass**'s first class in **dendrochronology**.

In 1929, she joined Edgar **Hewett** at Chaco Canyon for summer field school excavations at **Chetro Ketl,** where she initiated studies in **ceramic** dating and dendrochronology. During the following two summers, she excavated the **trash mound** at Chetro Ketl, where she demonstrated that charcoal was a viable source of tree-ring dates.

In 1933 she earned a Ph.D. from the University of Chicago. Her dissertation, "The Significance of the Dated Prehistory of Chetro Ketl, Chaco Canyon, New Mexico," showed that the refuse mound at Chetro Ketl, like that at **Pueblo Bonito**, had disturbed deposits that provided a good example of reversed **stratigraphy**. She also used data from Chetro Ketl to develop a **veneer style** sequence that differed in some respects from that proposed by **Judd**, which is more commonly accepted.

Hawley joined the Department of Anthropology at the University of New Mexico in 1934, a position she held until her retirement in 1971. She returned to Chaco in the mid-1930s, working in **small house sites**, including **Bc Sites** 50 and 51. Using her dendrochronological skills and knowledge of ceramics, she helped her fellow researchers demonstrate that **great houses** and small house sites were occupied at the same time. Her subsequent fieldwork took her to other parts of New Mexico, but she continued to lecture and write on Chaco throughout her career.

Hayes, Alden

An archaeologist with extensive southwestern experience who directed aspects of the **Chaco Project** from 1971 to 1976. Hayes's exposure to Chacoan archaeology began in 1936 when he was hired as a "camp boy" (along with Robert **Lister**) for the University of New

Mexico Chaco Field School. He returned to Chaco the following year as a field school student, having enrolled in Edgar **Hewett**'s anthropology program at the University of New Mexico.

Originally intending to become an ethnologist, Hayes did fieldwork among the Shoshone, Ute, and Goshute in Nevada and Utah. He came back into archaeology after receiving his B.A. in 1939 and did fieldwork in Texas and Tennessee. From 1941 to 1957 he took a break from archaeology and ranched in Cochise County, Arizona, and served in the U.S. Army in World War II and Korea. In 1957 he joined the National Park Service and almost immediately began long-term research at Mesa Verde National Park on the Wetherill Mesa Project. This work was followed by excavation of Spanish contact period sites in Gran Quivira and Pecos national monuments in New Mexico.

Hayes's experience on the Wetherill Mesa archaeological site survey made him ideally qualified to direct the initial Chaco Project survey in Chaco Canyon and bordering areas. This work was undertaken in 1972 and established the parameters for all subsequent surveys. In 1981 Hayes published *A Survey of Chaco Canyon Archaeology*, one of the first in a long series of volumes on Chaco Project activities. Data gathered during this survey helped Hayes to compute a maximum **population estimate** of about 6,000 for Chaco Canyon, though some later **Chaco Center** staff believed the figure was too high. In addition to directing excavations of several sites in the canyon, Hayes also investigated mesa-top **shrines** with Thomas **Windes,** and **signal stations** with other staff.

Herradura [Spanish for "horseshoe"]

A simple architectural feature with low curved walls associated with Chacoan **roads**. Herraduras consist of masonry walls up to three feet high in the shape of a "C," "D," or horseshoe. Walls are simple or compound **masonry,** and enclosure diameters range from approximately ten to thirty feet.

Herraduras are always located near Chacoan roads, and about half are oriented with their openings to the east. They are sited on elevated breaks in the local landscape that give extended views of the road route. In a few instances they occur at intersections but are more often located at slight changes in road direction. Near the herraduras, road edges are often marked with **berms**.

Though small scatters of broken **pottery** are common in the vicinity, herraduras are not believed to have been residential structures. Michael Marshall cites ethnographic evidence that identifies them as roadside shrines.

Hewett, Edgar L.

An important figure in early southwestern archaeology who directed the first archaeological field school at Chaco Canyon. Hewett became involved in Chacoan archaeology almost immediately after assuming the presidency of New Mexico Normal University in 1898.

Hewett was one of several westerners who raised concerns in the late 1890s about the wholesale removal of prehistoric southwestern artifacts to eastern museums and universities. Convinced that Richard **Wetherill** was vandalizing **Pueblo Bonito** and other Chacoan sites, he called for the U.S. General Land Office to investigate the **Hyde Exploring Expedition**. Although federal agent Stephen **Holsinger**'s 1901 report largely vindicated Wetherill, Hewett's pressure closed the project. To further protect Chaco Canyon and other southwestern sites, Hewett drafted legislation that became the federal **Antiquities Act of 1906**.

Having secured greater protection for archaeological sites, Hewett turned his attention to his second major professional goal: archaeological education. His association in 1906 with the Archaeological Institute of America led to the establishment of summer training projects in the Midwest and Southwest. In 1909 he founded the **School of American Research** in Santa Fe and at the same time organized the Museum of New Mexico, which he served as director until his death in 1946. He also founded the Museum of Man in San Diego.

Hewett used both the Museum of New Mexico and the School of American Research to initiate archaeological field projects, first in the Pajarito Plateau in northern New Mexico and then in Chaco Canyon in 1916. A five-year Chacoan research program was begun in 1919 and operated during the 1920 and 1921 seasons, but was then postponed until Neil **Judd** completed his excavations at **Pueblo Bonito**. In 1929, Hewett returned to his work at **Chetro Ketl** with students from the University of New Mexico's Department of Archaeology and Anthropology, which he had founded the previous year.

Hewett, his students, and colleagues worked primarily in the Chetro Ketl and **Kin Kletso** great houses and the **Casa Rinconada** great kiva. In 1934, he turned his attention to **small house sites,** excavating two sites in the **South Gap**. This focus was short-lived, however, and the 1935 season centered on the **Talus Unit** and **Kin Nahasbas**. Hewett ended his work at Chaco in 1935.

Numerous Chacoan scholars, including Florence **Hawley, Gordon Vivian**, Edwin **Ferdon**, and Paul Reiter, worked with or for Hewett and made important contributions to Chacoan prehistory. Unfortunately, Hewett failed to publish most of the information gained from his many years in Chaco Canyon. Ironically, there is documentation of the archaeological excavations at Wetherill's Pueblo Bonito project that he closed down, but no such record exists for Hewett's own work at Chetro Ketl, the Talus Unit, and Kin Kletso.

Hillside Ruin

(Map 4)

A large, totally collapsed **McElmo-style** house site at the base of the cliff to the east of **Pueblo Bonito**. The Pueblo Bonito trail passes just to the west of the ruin as it skirts the fallen remains of **Threatening Rock**. The site probably dates to the mid-1100s; estimates of occupation are based on the masonry **veneer style** and **ceramics,** which are typical of the McElmo tradition. The building was probably similar in layout to **Kin Kletso** and other rectangular **great houses** of this period. Neil **Judd** dug several test trenches in this site when he worked at Pueblo Bonito, but the site remains largely unexplored.

Hogan

The traditional Diné (**Navajo**) house. A hogan, or *hoghán,* is a one-room building, usually round or polygonal, with a central hearth and a doorway facing toward the east. Most are built of wood, but in areas with limited wood and abundant stone, such as the Chaco region, hogans are commonly constructed of masonry. Usually hogans were inhabited during the winter and only sporadically occupied during the summer, when families moved to more temporary homes in summer sheep herding areas.

The earliest type was the "forked-stick" hogan, which takes its name from a freestanding support structure of interlocking forked posts that formed a conical room with an elongated entryway. Smaller branches were leaned against the support timbers and then covered with layers of juniper bark and an outer layer of soil. Numerous forked-stick hogans have been found in Chaco Canyon and on the **Chacra Mesa**. Some Navajos continue to build and use this type of hogan.

The Navajos also construct hogans in several other styles. These include the "four-legged" and "eight-legged" dwellings in which four or eight three- to five- foot-high vertical posts encircle the floor at spaced intervals. Cross timbers resting on the tops of the posts serve as a base for a "cribbed roof"; short, upright wall posts set between the "legs" form the wall. Octagonal hogans made of horizontal notched logs topped with cribbed log roofs became popular in the early 1900s when plentiful metal saws and axes made it easier to cut larger timbers. All of these types retained the central fire pit, but wood-burning metal stoves eventually replaced the open hearths.

Hogans are the preferred house type for many Navajos today, and they are often built of modern materials such as wood frame walls, exterior siding, drywall, windows, and metal roofing, and are furnished with propane stoves and televisions. Typically, modern hogans or rectangular houses stand next to older log or stone homes. Today, many **Chaco Navajos** occupy some form of hogan.

Hogback Outlier

(Map 1; Figure 40)

A Chacoan **outlier** community located about fifty miles northwest of **Chaco Canyon** and possibly linked to Chaco Canyon by the **Ah-**

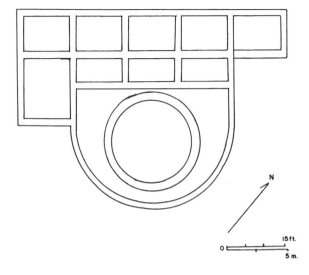

FIGURE 40. Great house ground plan at the Hogback Outlier. The great house has not been excavated; locations and sizes of rooms and the kiva were estimated from surface evidence.

shislepah Road. The community is located on a gravel terrace above the **Chaco River** near the base of the Hogback monocline, a distinctive uplift of tilted rock strata encircling much of the northern half of the **San Juan Basin.** The community is composed of a relatively small **great house**, an isolated **great kiva**, and thirty-five **small house sites. Ceramics** at the site indicate occupation from about A.D. 900 to 1050. No testing or excavation has been carried out in the community. The site is administered and protected by the Navajo Nation.

Hohokam

The prehistoric agriculturists of southern Arizona who are believed to be the ancestors of the modern O'odham (Piman-speaking) peoples of the same area. An O'odham word defined loosely as "those who have gone," the term "Hohokam" was first proposed by Harold **Gladwin** in 1931 to distinguish these people and their lifeway from the **Anasazi** culture to the north.

Two branches of the Hohokam developed differing lifeways depending upon whether they lived along flowing rivers (Riverine

Hohokam) or in less watered reaches of the desert (Desert Hohokam). Both lived in domed brush- and mud-covered pithouses with floors excavated about a foot into the ground. The Riverine Hohokam practiced canal irrigation that allowed them to farm large tracts of corn, beans, and squash. Desert Hohokam farmers planted the same crops but relied on *akchin* farming. Both groups gathered wild plant foods from the desert, and the Hohokam also hunted, especially the desert bighorn sheep.

Hohokam **pottery** differed from that of the Anasazi and **Mogollon** in manufacturing technique and color. Hohokam wares were usually red-on-buff rather than black-on-white or red-on-brown. Decorations were also quite different, most often having curvilinear designs and small repeated animal or bird motifs instead of geometric patterns. The Hohokam were long-distance traders who served as the major "shell merchants" of the Southwest.

Large ballcourts were probably the center of ritual life in Hohokam villages. These structures are comparable to the ballcourts of Mexico, and similar ritual games may have been played there. Hohokam shamans probably practiced curing ceremonies and other personal rituals.

Holsinger, Stephen

A special agent of the U.S. General Land Office who, in 1901, investigated Edgar **Hewett**'s charges that the **Hyde Exploring Expedition** was vandalizing **Pueblo Bonito.** Holsinger was the second agent sent to Chaco. The first, Max Pracht, was assigned the case in 1900 but did not visit the canyon as excavations had already begun. Pracht's report, presumably based on information gathered elsewhere, exonerated **Wetherill** and the Hydes. Hewett urged a second investigation, and Holsinger spent about a month in the canyon during the spring of 1901.

During his relatively short period in Chaco, Holsinger completed an impressive amount of work. He visited all the major ruins in the canyon and the **Chaco Core** as well as many **small house sites** throughout the area. He recorded **water control** systems in the canyon, including a large reservoir below **Peñasco Blanco** that has since been covered by sand. In addition, he described **rock art,** several **shrines,** and Chacoan **roads** within the canyon. Holsinger was not averse to digging and assisted the Wetherills in removing several burials from small house sites on the south side of the canyon. He also reported several sites outside the canyon, including the elusive **Casa Morena**, which he heard about while waiting for a train in Thoreau, New Mexico.

Holsinger essentially cleared Wetherill and the Hydes of wrong-doing, but he did question Wetherill's homestead claim on three of the largest ruins in the canyon. In a sworn affidavit attached to Holsinger's report, Wetherill relinquished these claims and recommended federal protection of all ruins in Chaco Canyon.

Holsinger's report provides a wealth of details about Chaco and Chacoan archaeology at the turn of the century. It also includes valuable information on the business enterprises of the **Hyde** brothers, who were engaged in trading with the **Navajos** on a large scale in the Chaco region. The report was so detailed that Hewett repeatedly cited it and used it in 1905 when preparing descriptions and locations of ruins to be included in what would become Chaco Canyon National Monument.

Hopi

A **Puebloan** people who live in northeastern Arizona in several villages located on or near three prominent sandstone mesas. The Hopi people have occupied the area surrounding First, Second, and Third Mesas for hundreds of years, and the remains of many historic and prehistoric villages are found throughout their reservation. Their traditional farming techniques were well adapted to their semi-arid environment, and they are famous for their deep-rooted blue, red, and white corn that is still grown in *akchin* fields. There are more than 8,000 enrolled tribal members.

The Hopi speak a **Uto-Aztecan** language, the only member of this language family found among Puebloan peoples. Their social, political, and religious systems differ in many ways from other Puebloan peoples, especially the **Tanoans**, but they do share some traits with the **Zuni.**

The **kachina religion** is highly developed among the Hopi, perhaps more so than among any other Puebloan people. This is largely due to the Hopis' resistance to the establishment of missions by Spanish priests, a process of religious conversion and social change that was common among the Puebloan peoples in New Mexico.

Hosta, Francisco

(Figure 41)
The governor of the Towa pueblo of Jemez who guided several expeditions through Chaco Canyon in the 1800s. Hosta met Lieutenant **Simpson** and Colonel Washington in 1849 when they stayed at Jemez Pueblo for several days during their westward march into **Navajo** country. He joined the expedition as a guide and, like the Mexican guide **Carravahal**, was so familiar with the route through Chaco Canyon and its sites that it is likely that he had traveled there earlier or guided **Vizcarra**'s Mexican troops through Chaco in 1823.

Simpson reported that "Hosta is one of the finest looking and most intelligent Pueblo Indians I have seen, and, on account of his vivacity and off-hand graciousness, is quite a favorite among us." These traits probably accounted for his selection as guide to **Pueblo Pintado** in 1874 by Dr. Oscar Lowe. In 1877, he led photographer William **Jackson** through Chaco Canyon. By this time he was about eighty years old and brought his grandson "for his eyes." Jackson, who was with the U.S. Geological and Geographical Survey, named **Hosta Butte** for him.

Hosta Butte

(Map 1; Figure 42)
A major landmark of the **Chacoan World** that rises from Lobo Mesa on the **Dutton Plateau** to the south of Chaco Canyon. It is easily visible from **Pueblo Alto** and other mesa-top locations in Chaco Canyon. The butte almost certainly was a sacred landmark for the Chacoans, as it is today for the **Navajo**.

Hosta Butte was named in 1877 by William **Jackson** in honor of

FIGURE 41. Francisco Hosta, civil governor of Jemez Pueblo in 1849.

FIGURE 42. Hosta Butte on the Dutton Plateau. (Photo by Tom Windes. Courtesy of National Park Service, neg. 32289.)

Francisco **Hosta**, a Jemez Indian who guided not only his expedition to Chaco Canyon but also those of José Antonio **Vizcarra** in 1823 and Colonel Washington and Lieutenant **Simpson** in 1849. According to Richard VanValkenberg, the Navajos refer to the butte as "Mountain That Sits on Top of Another Mountain." It is the home of Mirage Stone Boy and Mirage Stone Girl, mythic figures that play significant roles in the Navajo creation story.

Hosta Butte Phase

A term used by some southwestern archaeologists to refer to **small house sites** and communities. It was first used, incorrectly, to refer to an early, pre–great house period of Chacoan development dominated by small house construction.

The term was introduced in the 1930s by Harold **Gladwin,** who believed that small house sites were earlier than great houses. To prove his theory, he excavated a number of Chacoan sites in the **Red Mesa Valley** in the vicinity of **Hosta Butte**. He also studied great houses in Chaco Canyon and used **dendrochronology** to date them. Based on this research, he proposed a pre–great house period of Chacoan cultural development that he called the Hosta Butte phase, dated at A.D. 1010–1080. In Gladwin's scheme, small house populations built **great houses** after A.D. 1080. Later research proved that Gladwin's Hosta Butte phase small houses and the **Bo-nito phase** great houses were actually built and occupied at the same time.

In the 1960s, **Gordon Vivian** and Tom Mathews used the Hosta Butte phase as a term to summarize a number of traits that they believed characterized small house site communities in Chaco Canyon and the Chaco area. These included a somewhat random house plan, simple architecture, the lack of **great kivas** and **tower kivas**, and smaller amounts of "exotics" such as **copper bells**, **macaws**, and **turquoise** jewelry. They did not use the term to define a time period.

Today, Vivian and Mathews's use of the term "Hosta Butte phase" is occasionally cited as a shorthand for referring to small house site communities, but the term no longer carries any time associations.

Hubbard Site

(Figure 43)

A **tri-wall structure** in the **Aztec Ruins** community near Aztec, New Mexico. It was excavated in 1953 to bring public attention to the many different types of sites at the Aztec Ruins. It resembles a similar structure on the west side of **Pueblo del Arroyo**, the only tri-wall building in Chaco Canyon. Like the tri-wall structure in Chaco Canyon, the Hubbard Site was part of a larger building.

Huerfano Mountain (see *Tres Huerfanos*)

Hungo Pavi

(Map 3; Figure 44)

A large Chacoan **great house** located at the mouth of **Mockingbird Canyon** approximately two miles east of **Pueblo Bonito**. This completely unexcavated ruin of about 140 rooms was built in the classic D-shape and rose at least three stories in the back room block. It had an arced one-story row of rooms on the south that enclosed the plaza. Tree-ring dates suggest two stages of building: construction of

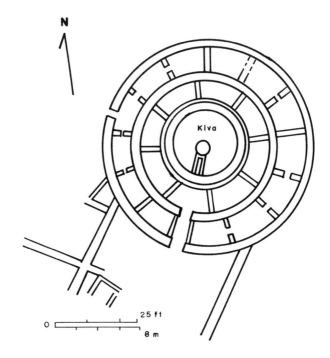

FIGURE 43. Hubbard Site tri-wall structure ground plan. Partial walls on the south side of the circular building are remnants of an additional part of the structure.

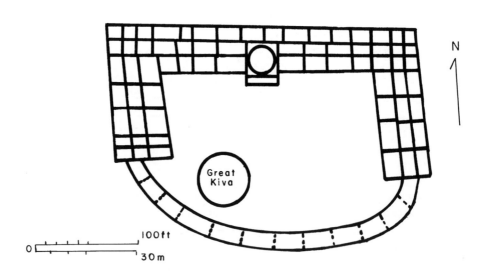

FIGURE 44. Hungo Pavi great house ground plan. This structure has not been excavated. Doorways are not shown.

many ground-floor rooms in the late 900s and early 1000s, with upper stories added in the middle 1000s.

In 1849 Lieutenant **Simpson**'s guide, **Carravahal**, gave the name "Hungo Pavie" to this great house and interpreted the name as Crooked Nose. Later, Edgar **Hewett** suggested that the name might have been a mispronunciation of "Shungopovi" or "Shongopavi," a **Hopi** village on Second Mesa.

The name "Hungo Pavi" has never been translated.

Hyde, Frederick, Jr., and Talbot (see *Hyde Exploring Expedition*)

Hyde Exploring Expedition

The sponsor of the first scientific surveys and excavations of sites in the **Chaco Core**, conducted under the leadership of Richard **Wetherill** in the 1890s. The Hyde Exploring Expedition initiated work at Pueblo Bonito and several other Chacoan sites in 1896 and continued for five summer field seasons. The discovery of four-story stone pueblos, **great kivas**, caches of dozens of ceramic **cylinder jars**, several high-status burials, **roads,** and **water control** systems touched off a wave of excitement that swept through the growing archaeological community in eastern museums and universities.

Talbot and Fred Hyde Jr., brothers and heirs to a New York soap company fortune, formed the Hyde Exploring Expedition to sponsor Wetherill's artifact collecting trips in Grand Gulch, Utah, in 1893–94. The Hyde brothers had met Wetherill in 1893 at his Colorado ranch and then again that summer at the Chicago World's Fair, where he displayed collections of prehistoric artifacts taken from **Mesa Verde** sites. Based on a trip Wetherill made to Chaco Canyon in 1895, he convinced them to fund excavations in Pueblo Bonito the following year. The Hydes requested scientific assistance from Dr. Frederick Putnam of the Peabody Museum at Harvard University, and George H. **Pepper**, a student, was assigned to assist Wetherill in the field.

Archaeological surveys carried out by the Hyde Exploring Expedition located dozens of major sites in the Chaco Core. During five field seasons, Wetherill and Pepper worked at **Pueblo Bonito, Kin Bineola, Peñasco Blanco,** and many small house sites.

All operations of the Hyde Exploring Expedition stopped in 1901 after Edgar **Hewett** requested a U.S. General Land Office investigation of the expedition's work. He believed sites were being vandalized and artifacts sold, but an investigation by Stephen **Holsinger** cleared Wetherill and the Hydes of wrongdoing. All evidence suggests that the excavations were conducted using the best scientific methods of the time.

I

Irrigation

The artificial watering of farmlands, usually involving systems of **canals** to carry water to fields or garden plots. In river irrigation, water is drawn from a perennially flowing stream and carried in fairly permanent canals to the fields. In floodwater irrigation, runoff from rainfall is diverted to fields by way of small canals, low earth borders, lines of brush, diversion **dams,** and other temporary structures. Pot irrigation involves carrying water to the fields in large jars.

Chacoan farmers developed unique forms of irrigation that involved construction of sophisticated **water control** systems to harvest runoff from rainfall. Because the volume of water could be great, the dams and canals that collected and moved water resembled the more substantial features of river irrigation. One system on the north side of Chaco Canyon from **Mockingbird Canyon** on the east to the western end of the canyon near **Peñasco Blanco** collected water from major **rincons.** Much larger systems near the **Kin Bineola** and **Kin Klizhin great houses** collected water from extensive drainage basins and channeled it in wide, deep canals from large earthen and stone diversion dams to valley bottom fields.

Irwin-Williams, Cynthia

An archaeologist who conducted significant research in the Southwest and made important contributions to Chacoan studies, stemming largely from her excavations at the **Salmon Ruin Outlier**. Irwin-Williams entered archaeology through an interest in the **Archaic** period but ultimately worked in sites of essentially every time period represented in the Southwest from the **Paleoindian** to the Spanish Colonial. She joined the faculty at Eastern New Mexico University in 1964 after receiving her doctorate from Harvard and taught there until 1982, when she became director of the Social Science Center of the Desert Research Institute of Nevada in Reno. Her broad interests and expertise in paleontology, climatology, and remote sensing were critical in developing the Anasazi Origins Project, which included fieldwork in the Arroyo Cuervo area on the eastern margins of the **San Juan Basin**. This project not only contributed to a better understanding of the Archaic and early **Basketmaker** foundations of later Chacoan culture, but stimulated Irwin-Williams's interest in the **Guadalupe Outlier**.

Irwin-Williams became more fully involved with Chacoan research in 1970 when she entered into a long-term research program with the San Juan County Museum Association at the Salmon Ruin Outlier. The association had purchased the site in 1967 to prevent possible commercial looting and to establish a research center and public interpretive facility. Irwin-Williams directed excavation at the site from 1972 through 1976, and additional studies until 1980, paralleling the research time frame of the **Chaco Center**. Irwin-Williams introduced the concepts of the **Chaco Phenomenon** and great houses as "nucleated communities."

Salmon Ruin investigations significantly contributed to outlier studies, and a member of Irwin-Williams's staff, Pierre Morenon, traced the **North Road** south toward Chaco Canyon, discovering **Pierre's Outlier** in the process. A final report on the Salmon Ruin excavation was never completed, but the Center for Desert Archaeology in Tucson took on that task in 2001.

J

Jackson, William

A professional photographer who recorded a number of southwestern archaeological sites during the 1870s while serving with Ferdinand Hayden's Geological and Geographical Survey of the Territories.

Hayden recruited Jackson in 1870 to help document western lands for the Department of the Interior through the relatively new medium of photography. The project involved recording images of Native American peoples as well as landscapes. Jackson first photographed prehistoric sites in 1874, when the survey spent time in Mancos Canyon on the eastern and southern edges of **Mesa Verde**.

Jackson arranged to return to the Southwest on his own in 1877, a trip that took him through Chaco Canyon. Because he had to travel more lightly, he took a new dry film for his 8x10 camera which, because of delays in delivery, he could not test before leaving. The film was defective, and Jackson's opportunity to produce the first images of Chacoan sites passed eventually to Victor **Mindeleff**, who photographed the canyon in the winter of 1887–88.

Despite his photographic misfortunes, Jackson contributed significantly to Chacoan archaeology. During his five-day stay at Chaco, he made the first accurate map of the canyon's major sites, took detailed notes on architecture, made the first scaled ground plans of eleven major sites, illustrated three masonry **veneer styles**, and numbered all large sites. In addition, he plotted a deeply buried old channel of the **Chaco Wash**, discovered **Pueblo Alto** and the **Jackson Staircase**, and recorded his guide **Hosta**'s story of the **Gambler** who lived at Pueblo Alto.

Jackson's considerable abilities and interest in Chaco did not fade with age. At the age of ninety-three, he spent time with the 1936 New Mexico Archaeological Field School in Chaco and even hiked the trail to Pueblo Alto, fifty-nine years after his first foray into the canyon.

Jackson Staircase

(Map 3; Figure 45)

A pair of well-preserved parallel sets of wide steps cut into a sheer cliff in a short side canyon east of **Pueblo Alto** and north of **Chetro Ketl** (Figure 45). The stairs are visible from the trail between Pueblo Alto and Chetro Ketl. Rock-cut steps are associated with Chacoan **roads** and allowed people using the roads to climb steep cliff faces. They are fairly common in Chaco Canyon; good examples can be seen behind the **Hungo Pavi** great house and near the **Casa Rinconada** small house community. One set of steps at the Jackson Staircase appears never to have been completed as the steps end a short distance from the cliff top. Though usually attributed to an engineering mistake by Chacoan road builders, archaeologist Wolcott **Toll** suggests that the lower part of this "incomplete" staircase was a wood ladder, thereby creating a parallel route over the cliff. Several parallel roads are known, so parallel stairways are possible. Photographer

FIGURE 45. The Jackson Staircase, at a canyon head north of Chetro Ketl.

William **Jackson** sketched the stairs when he discovered Pueblo Alto on his visit to Chaco Canyon in 1877.

Judd, Neil

A pioneer southwestern archaeologist who carried out the first fully scientific investigation of **Pueblo Bonito** in Chaco Canyon. Judd received a degree in archaeology at the University of Utah, where he was trained in excavation techniques by his uncle, Byron Cummings, another major figure in southwestern archaeology. He then served as a student assistant to Edgar **Hewett** in 1910 in New Mexico. He joined the **Smithsonian Institution**'s anthropology staff in 1911 and worked there until his retirement in 1949. Although his duties at the Smithsonian were primarily curatorial, he carried out fieldwork in the American Southwest and Guatemala.

Judd visited Chaco Canyon in 1920 to develop a proposal for a long-term research program for the **National Geographic Society**. He returned in 1921 as the director of this project and carried out work in the canyon each summer through 1927. His reports on excavations at Pueblo Bonito and **Pueblo del Arroyo** serve as the primary sources for information on these **great houses**.

Through his contacts with Andrew **Douglass**, Judd furthered the science of **dendrochronology** and made tree-ring collections at Chacoan sites that helped to establish a canyon chronology. His concern for multidisciplinary research led to other significant works, such as Kirk **Bryan**'s study of the geology and recent alluvial history of the canyon and **Chaco Wash**. Judd promoted important work by his student assistants, including the sequence of Chacoan **pottery** types developed by Frank **Roberts** Jr. He was also the first to recognize the importance of early sightings of Chacoan **roads** and **water control** systems by the **Wetherills** and Stephen **Holsinger**.

Judge, James

A southwestern archaeologist who headed the **Chaco Center** operations from 1978 to 1985. Judge was on the anthropology faculty at the University of New Mexico when the Chaco Center was initiated, and he oversaw the major excavations on the **Chaco Project**. He recruited a number of students from universities in the Southwest to staff the project, most of whom produced reports on this work and then established professional careers in archaeology. Judge later joined the faculty of Fort Lewis College in Durango, Colorado. He is also the coeditor of a major work on Chaco, *Chaco and Hohokam: Prehistoric Regional Systems in the American Southwest.*

Judge, along with several of his staff, developed some of the earliest theories to explain the rise of **great houses** in the canyon. They initially proposed that great houses served as collection points for stockpiling and distributing surplus food to small house populations in the canyon and that, in time, a more complex system of redistribution involved great houses throughout the **San Juan Basin**. When evidence for this level of redistribution could not be developed, Judge proposed his alternative theory that great houses served as ceremonial centers. In this scenario, they were used on a periodic basis to lodge pilgrims from throughout the San Juan Basin who came to Chaco Canyon for religious and economic reasons.

K

Kachina Religion
(Figure 46)

A **Puebloan** religion focusing on the activities of kachinas, ancestral spirits who serve as mediators between the gods and people. Kachinas play especially important roles in bringing rain and ensuring fertility for crops, animals, and people. For half the year they reside in Puebloan villages, participating in plaza ceremonies often referred to as "kachina dances." Toward the end of summer, they return to their homes in sacred places in the region. An array of dozens of different kachinas represent the spirits of ancestors, animals, and other beings in this world.

The kachina religion is represented in all modern pueblos but is most evident among the **Hopi, Zuni,** and Western **Keres** peoples. Its origin is debated among southwestern archaeologists, but most

FIGURE 46. *Awatobi Soyuk Wüqti* kachina. This kachina figure was drawn by a native artist for Jesse W. Fewkes in 1899.

agree that Mexico was the source of the concept. Theories about the routes into the Southwest and the time of arrival vary; aspects of the religion may have arrived as early as the 1100s or as late as the 1300s. Stephen **Lekson** and Catherine **Cameron** have suggested that some features of the kachina religion may have been present in Chacoan **great houses** as early as the 1000s.

Kantner, John

A Southwestern archaeologist whose interest in the **Chaco Phe-nomenon** has focused on defining the extent of the **Chacoan World**. Kantner has used architecture to define the geographic limits of this regional system of great houses and great house communities surrounding **Chaco Canyon**. His definition of an "**outlier**" requires that it have a **great house** constructed between A.D. 1020 and 1150 with **core-and-veneer** masonry, multiple stories, and blocked-in **kivas**. Other architectural features including **great kivas**, **road** segments, and **berms** in these communities further support their inclusion in his Chacoan World. Kantner argues that use of the term "outlier" has not been consistent as it includes both single structures and communities and, more importantly, implies the nature of the relationship between Chaco Canyon and communities in the greater Chaco World. He has explored that interaction with respect to roads, exchange of material goods, and **communication systems**.

For several years, Kantner has directed the Lobo Mesa Archaeological Project in the **Red Mesa Valley** and conducted excavations at the Blue J community near the **Casamero** and **Andrews** outliers. He has numerous Chaco-related publications and was coeditor of *Great House Communities across the Chacoan Landscape*. His refinement of the Chaco World concept is ongoing and can be viewed in an interactive map at his website http://greathouses.sarweb.org.

Keres (or Keresan)

One of four language groups existing today among **Puebloan** peoples in the Southwest. Keresans fall into two distinct branches in New Mexico, though all speak dialects of the Keresan family language. The Western Keres occupy the pueblos of Acoma and Laguna about fifty miles west of Albuquerque. The Eastern Keres live in several villages along the Rio Grande and its tributary, the Jemez River, including Zia, Santa Ana, San Felipe, Santo Domingo, and Cochiti. In addition to speaking a different Puebloan language, Keres ceremonies and social organization differ from those of the **Hopi**, **Zuni**, and **Tanoan** Pueblo groups. There are more than 13,000 enrolled tribal members in the combined Keresan villages.

Keres has great time depth in the Southwest. Some Chacoan peoples may have been Keresan speakers and could well be the ancestors of the people living in the Eastern and Western Keres villages today.

Kern, Edward and Richard

The cartographer and the artist for the 1849 expedition of Col. John M. Washington and Lt. James **Simpson**. Artist Richard Kern, accompanied Simpson on a full-day exploration of the lower portion of Chaco Canyon. His sketches of great houses, **veneer styles**, preserved room interiors, and **rock art** gained national attention when they were reproduced as color lithographs in Simpson's report, which was published by the Thirty-first Congress in 1850. His brother, cartographer Edward Kern, was responsible for making ground plans of several of the Chacoan **great houses**, the first maps of these structures.

Kin Bineola [Navajo for "house in which the wind whirls"]

(Map 2; Figure 47)
A large Chacoan **great house** built near the Kin Bineola Wash south of **Lake Valley** in the southwestern portion of the Chaco Core about twelve miles southwest of **Pueblo Bonito**. Several tree-ring dates and early **core-and-veneer** masonry originally were used as evidence of construction in the central wing of the structure sometime in the mid-900s. Using both **dendrochronology** and architectural evidence, Thomas **Windes** has since shown that a significant portion of the building may date from this period, though it was enlarged in the early 1100s. Like **Kin Klizhin**, this great house was almost certainly established to take advantage of the farming potential of valleys outside Chaco Canyon. A major **water control** system involving at least two large canals has been documented along the Kin Bineola Wash to the south and west of the great house.

The plan of Kin Bineola was E-shaped and differed from the more classic D-shape. There was no fronting arc of rooms around

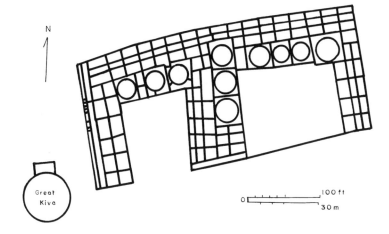

FIGURE 47. Kin Bineola great house ground plan. This structure has not been excavated; locations of rooms and kivas are based on standing walls. Doorways are not shown.

the plaza, although the east plaza was enclosed by a straight wall between room blocks. The building rose to three stories on the north and terraced down to the south. It contained almost 200 rooms and had 10 **kivas**. A **great kiva** was located just outside the southwestern corner of the building.

Numerous **small house sites** are located to the south along the Kin Bineola Wash, but only a few are close by the great house. Although the **Coyote Canyon Road** has not been documented for this area, its route would have taken it close to Kin Bineola. The site is a detached unit of Chaco Culture National Historical Park and is protected by the National Park Service.

Kin Kletso [Navajo for "yellow house"]
(Map 4; Figures 48, 49)
This **McElmo-style** great house in Chaco Canyon is located about one-half mile west of **Pueblo Bonito**. The building's rectangular ground plan combines two typical square McElmo buildings, each with two central **kivas** surrounded by room suites. Construction

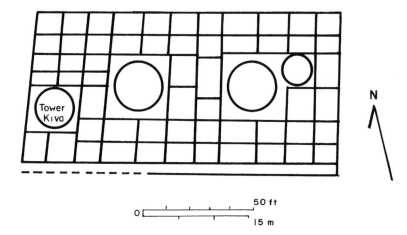

FIGURE 48. Kin Kletso great house ground plan. The structure has been excavated; doorways are not shown.

evidence suggests that the west unit was built first and the east unit was added shortly thereafter.

The building rose to three stories on the north, terracing down to two stories in the rest of the structure. A two-story kiva at the edge of the west unit has been identified as a **tower kiva**. Like all McElmo buildings, there was no associated **great kiva**, no enclosed plaza, and the **veneer style** was of squared soft yellow sandstone blocks with a dimpled surface. Tree-ring dates from the site show a very short construction span of about A.D. 1125–30.

Edwin **Ferdon** excavated at least two kivas and three rooms in the site in 1934 for the New Mexico State Museum–**School of American Research.** In 1951 **Gordon Vivian** completed excavation of the entire structure for the National Park Service prior to major **stabilization** of the building. Vivian's final site report, *Kin Kletso: A Pueblo III Community in Chaco Canyon, New Mexico*, was published in 1965.

Kin Kletso is often called "yellow house," the translation of this **Navajo** name. The prehistoric trail that serves as the primary visitor access to **Pueblo Alto** and the Pueblo Bonito overlook begins at Yellow House.

FIGURE 49. Kin Kletso from the cliff top. (Arizona State Museum, University of Arizona; Helga Teiwes, photographer.)

Kin Klizhin [Navajo for "black house"]

(Map 2; Figure 50)

A small Chacoan **great house** located on the western edge of the Kin Klizhin Wash about ten miles southwest of **Pueblo Bonito**. The most striking aspect of this building is the three-story **tower kiva**, a massive masonry structure rising above the adjacent room block. There is no **great kiva** at Kin Klizhin or in the immediate vicinity. Tree-ring dates indicate the great house was built in the late 1080s.

Although the great house was small, containing only about sixteen rooms and two **kivas**, it may have had a significant role in providing food for people in Chaco Canyon. A large masonry and earthen **dam** built across the Kin Klizhin Wash diverted floodwaters into canal and ditch systems that watered large fields just downstream from Kin Klizhin. Portions of the dam and a spillway are still visible in the valley bottom. The yields from such a large

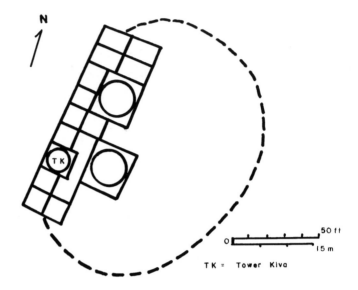

FIGURE 50. Kin Klizhin great house ground plan. The structure has not been excavated; locations of rooms and kivas are based on standing wall. Dashed lines represent the estimated location of an enclosed plaza. Doorways are not shown.

farm would have exceeded the needs of the local residents, and **maize** (corn) and other crops were probably carried into Chaco Canyon.

The **Coyote Canyon Road** probably passed by this site, though no traces of it have been found. Kin Klizhin is visible from the **road** as it leaves Chaco Canyon through the **South Gap,** and the tower kiva may have served as a beacon for the road and as a **signal station** for sending information to Chaco Canyon. The mesa-top site of **Tsin Kletsin** in Chaco Canyon is also visible from Kin Klizhin.

Kin Klizhin is a detached unit of Chaco Culture National Historical Park and is protected by the National Park Service. A National Park Service archaeological survey near the great house in the 1980s identified a number of **small house sites** and resulted in an expansion of the boundaries of the protected area.

Kin Nahasbas [Navajo for "round house"]

(Map 3)

A **great kiva** located a few hundred yards west of the **Una Vida** great house and about three miles east of **Pueblo Bonito**. Like **Casa**

Rinconada, this great kiva is elevated above the valley floor, standing on an eroded sandstone ridge extending out from the terraced edge of the canyon wall. From the canyon floor the site appears only as a long, flat-topped rubble slope below the ridge.

Kin Nahasbas was remodeled at least two times, and the interior diameter of the final stage was almost fifty-one feet. Most of the standard great kiva architectural features are present, including seating pits for the roof supports, **foot drums**, a central fire box, and an antechamber on the north side.

For years, Kin Nahasbas was thought to be an "isolated" great kiva, like Casa Rinconada, and not associated with any **great house**. This interpretation was based on information collected from the site when it was excavated in 1935 as a University of New Mexico field school project. In 1983 Joan **Mathien** and Thomas **Windes**, National Park Service archaeologists, tested the site and concluded that Kin Nahasbas was actually an early great house with two small room blocks and an associated great kiva.

Kin Ya'a Outlier [Navajo for "tall house"]

(Map 1; Figure 51)

A Chacoan **outlier** great house located on the northern slopes of the **Dutton Plateau** near the modern community of Crownpoint, New Mexico, approximately twenty-five miles south and slightly west of Chaco Canyon. As at **Kin Klizhin**, the massive spire of a four-story **tower kiva** signals the presence of this **great house** from miles away. The rectangular building, with at least thirty-five rooms and four **kivas**, may have been three stories in height, terracing to second-story rooms on the east (Figure 49). Tree-ring samples yield dates from the late 1080s through the first decade of the 1100s.

Kin Ya'a was the center of a large **outlier community**. More than a hundred sites, mostly small house buildings, have been recorded in a four-square-mile area. An unexcavated isolated **great kiva** is located within one cluster of **small house sites** to the northwest of Kin Ya'a. The community is linked to Chaco Canyon by the **South Road**, which passes on the east side of the great house and creates a swale between the building and a large **trash mound**.

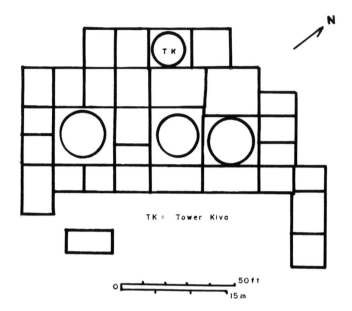

TK = Tower Kiva

FIGURE 51. Kin Ya'a Outlier great house ground plan. The structure has not been excavated; doorways are not shown. Rooms and kivas are estimated from surface evidence.

Although the great house and community are not located near a major drainage, they are on the edge of a large, wide valley that received runoff from the Dutton Plateau to the south, making it especially suitable for farming. Kin Ya'a is a detached unit of Chaco Park and is protected by the National Park Service.

Kiva

(Figures 52, 53)

A special room used by **Puebloan** peoples for many purposes, most of which are related to ritual and the performance of religious ceremonies. First appearing among Puebloan peoples during the **Basketmaker** period, these underground chambers have been a hallmark of Puebloan religious life for about 1,500 years.

Among modern Puebloan peoples, kivas are centers of religious and social life for the men of a village. The number of kivas within a village varies. **Hopi** and **Zuni** villages have several kivas, **Keresan**-speaking pueblos generally have two, and **Tanoan** villages have one or two. Men may join a kiva in their village and work together to perform selected rituals and to prepare costumes and paraphernalia for upcoming ceremonies. While primarily used by the men of the pueblo, women and, in some villages, even outsiders are invited to attend ritual performances in the kivas.

Prehistoric kivas share many features. They are usually underground, but may be only partially underground or even built above ground. This subterranean aspect may represent physical ties to the earlier pithouses and conceptual links to the underworld. Roof entries were common in prehistoric kivas. Other features include an encircling bench, a floor hearth, a ventilator for drawing fresh air into the room, and a stone or wood screen (deflector) between the hearth and ventilator. A *sipapu*, a small floor pit representing an opening to the underworld, may also be present. Kivas are generally oriented with the ventilator on the south side. In Chaco Canyon and other Eastern Puebloan sites, kivas are round; in Western Puebloan sites, they are rectangular or square.

Chacoan peoples built several types of kivas that can be identified by their architectural features and their placement in a building. **Tower kivas** may not have been kivas as defined here, and **great kivas** almost certainly served different functions than the smaller kivas, which occur in much greater numbers.

Architecturally, there are two styles of smaller kivas in Chacoan sites. "Chaco-style" kivas are most common in **great houses,** and good examples can be seen in the eastern portion of **Pueblo Bonito** (Figure 52). The Chaco-style kiva is round, usually larger (up to twenty-five feet in inside diameter) and has a low, wide masonry bench rising above the floor. A short break in the bench on the south side may be a token remnant of a southern recess found in many early Anasazi kivas. A ventilator shaft built into the south wall runs beneath the floor to an opening in front of the hearth, eliminating the need for a deflector to block a draft. Many of the Chaco-style kivas had **foot drums** built into the floor west of the hearth. Neil **Judd** discovered intact kiva roofs in Pueblo Bonito that showed the enormous number of **timbers** used to cover a single structure. The cribbed log roof began at bench level, thereby eliminating the bench as a place for seating or storing goods. Six to ten short, horizontal logs were spaced evenly around the bench and

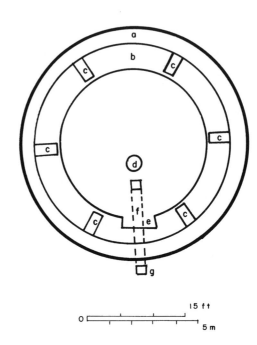

FIGURE 52. Chaco-style kiva plan. Common attributes include (a) thick outer wall, (b) bench, (c) log base for cribbed roof, (d) hearth, (e) southern recess, (f) ventilator, (g) ventilator shaft opening.

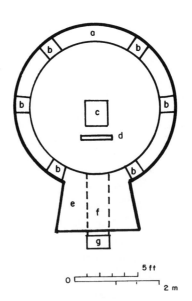

FIGURE 53. San Juan–style kiva plan. Common attributes include (a) bench, (b) masonry columns for cribbed roof, (c) hearth, (d) deflector, (e) southern recess, (f) ventilator, (g) ventilator shaft opening.

served as the base for as many as 350 overlapping logs laid horizontally to form the roof.

"San Juan-," "Mesa Verde-," or "keyhole-style" kivas are generally more common in **small house sites**, though occasional examples are found in excavated great houses (Figure 53). These kivas are usually smaller, seldom exceeding twenty feet in diameter. They have a rather high, narrow bench and a deep recess or alcove in the south wall that forms the keyhole shape. A ventilator shaft is built into the south wall but enters the kiva through an opening at the base of the alcove. Because this air drafts directly into the kiva, a deflector placed before the hearth is standard. Four to eight masonry columns are built on the bench and extend nearly to the top of the wall, forming the base for a cribbed roof similar to the Chaco-style kivas. However, the San Juan–style roofs required much less timber because the roof started much higher. Both great houses and small house sites also have "hybrid" kivas in which features of both Chaco-style and San Juan–style kivas are present.

In Chacoan great houses, subterranean kivas are located in the plaza and are called "court kivas." Kivas are also found within great house room blocks and may be either "surface/blocked in," when they rest on ground level, or "elevated/blocked in," when built above ground level. Examples of all types are present in Pueblo Bonito. In all cases, entry was through the roof, giving the impression that the kivas were below ground.

L

Lake Valley
(Map 1)
A wide, fertile valley on the lower five miles of the **Kin Bineola** Wash (also known as the Kim-me-ni-oli Wash), just above its confluence with the **Chaco River**. Lake Valley was named after "Juan's Lake," which was constructed in the 1930s to provide water for local **Navajo** farmers but dried up in the mid-1990s. The Kin Bineola **great house** is located in the valley. Historically, Navajo farming

attested to the agricultural potential of Lake Valley. Neil **Judd** described and O. C. Havens photographed Chischilly-begay's large **corn** and melon fields in upper Lake Valley in 1925, and Glenn Pablo, a contemporary Navajo farmer, planted the same area in the 1990s. Both men depended on overbank or floodplain watering from the Kin Bineola Wash and the shallow depth of the water table. However, they also diverted some water from the wash into the fields. The Kin Bineola great house is located near the southern head of the valley where there is evidence that water from the Kin Bineola Wash was diverted to agricultural fields via large **canals**. Corn from these fields may have been transported into **Chaco Canyon** from Lake Valley.

La Plata Black-on-white
(Figure 54)
The earliest of several types of **Cibola White Ware** pottery. La Plata Black-on-white pottery was made throughout the **San Juan Basin** and its peripheries from about A.D. 600 to 850. Like most Cibola White Wares, the vessels featured simple black geometric designs executed in mineral paints made from ground stones such as hematite, an iron oxide. La Plata Black-on-white was named by Harold **Gladwin** for early decorated pottery found by Earl **Morris** in the La Plata River valley of northwestern New Mexico. Florence **Hawley** published the first thorough description of the type in 1936.

The most common vessel shape was an open bowl, but globular jars were also produced. La Plata bowl interiors were usually deco-

FIGURE 54. La Plata Black-on-white bowl with decorative motifs and design layout common to this type. Contemporaneous Kana'a Neck-banded pitcher.

rated with designs composed of solid triangles, zigzag lines, lines with attached barbs or hooks, fringed triangles, and concentric lined triangles and diamonds. Many of these designs were similar to those found on baskets and sandals. Occasionally, anthropomorphic and geomorphic motifs were used. Designs on bowl interiors often started at the rim and extended toward the bottom of the bowl. These pendant designs frequently were repeated around the bowl interior in quadrants or as bipartite or tripartite panels. Jars had similar designs on the exterior. Pottery decorated with similar designs but in carbon paint (made from plants) was produced outside the Chaco area, the most common being Lino Black-on-gray.

The major cooking ware used with La Plata Black-on-white was Lino Gray. These simple cooking pots, also known as *ollas*, were the precursors of later **corrugated** cooking jars. La Plata Black-on-white pottery type was succeeded by **Red Mesa Black-on-white**.

Lekson, Stephen

A prominent Southwestern archaeologist who has published extensively on Chacoan archaeology. Lekson began his Chacoan investigations as a research archaeologist for Cynthia **Irwin-Williams** at the **Salmon Ruin Outlier** and then served for a decade as an archaeologist with the National Park Service **Chaco Project**. Several books and articles resulted from this work including *Great Pueblo Architecture of Chaco Canyon, New Mexico*, a landmark in Chacoan architectural studies and a primary source on the subject. He subsequently edited *The Architecture of Chaco Canyon* and *The Archaeology of Chaco Canyon: An Eleventh-Century Pueblo Regional Center*, a synthesis of and commentary on the **Chaco Project** studies.

Lekson continually has urged his colleagues to "think outside the Pueblo box" and be more critical of long-held assumptions about Puebloan and Chacoan prehistory. His **Chaco Meridian** theory is an example of his promotion of a broader perspective on Southwestern prehistory. This approach was considerably expanded in one of his most recent books, *A History of the Ancient Southwest*. Here, Lekson argues that geopolitical events in the Southwest were far more complex than those described in many current interpretations.

He proposes that Chacoan royal families, "kings and queens," played a pivotal role for at least four centuries in the evolution of the **Anasazi**, **Hohokam**, Mimbres, and **Paquimé** worlds (see "Explaining Chaco"). Lekson is the husband of Chacoan scholar Catherine **Cameron**.

Leyit Kin [Navajo for "way down deep house"]
(Map 3; Figure 55)
A partially excavated small house site on the south side of Chaco Canyon about one mile southeast of **Pueblo Bonito.** The rectangular building has at least three **kivas** and about twenty-seven rooms.

There may have been three periods of occupation at Leyit Kin. A cluster of tree-ring dates in the mid-1000s probably represents a second occupation as this part of the building covers earlier structures. Ceramic styles and a few later tree-ring dates also point to an occu-

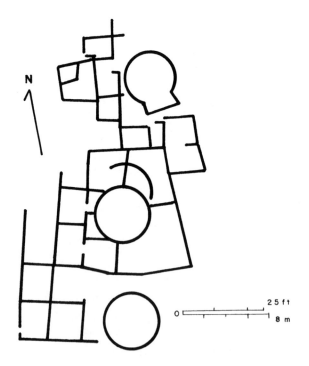

N

25 ft
0
8 m

FIGURE 55. Leyit Kin ground plan. Open doorways are shown.

pation in the middle to late 1100s. Most excavated **small house sites** in Chaco Canyon show evidence of extended occupation, pointing to the contemporaneous evolution of small house sites and **great houses** from about A.D. 850 to the mid-1100s.

Leyit Kin was excavated in 1934 and 1936 by Bertha Dutton for the **School of American Research** and the Museum of New Mexico. **Backfilling** of the excavated rooms and erosion have eliminated most visible traces of the structure.

Lister, Robert and Florence

Southwestern archaeologists and authors of numerous books dealing with southwestern prehistory and the archaeologists who worked in the region. Robert (Bob) Lister started his Chacoan career in 1936 as a staff "camp boy" for the University of New Mexico Archaeological Field School. Florence began her long association with ceramic studies at the field school in 1940. That same year she met Bob, who by then was working in Chaco for the National Park Service. They were married in 1942. After a long teaching career, Bob returned to Chacoan studies in 1971 when he rejoined the National Park Service, and he directed the **Chaco Center** until 1978.

The Listers are especially well known for their many books on southwestern prehistory. Those dealing with Chacoan archaeology and archaeologists include *Chaco Canyon, Archaeology and Archaeologists; Earl Morris and Southwestern Archaeology;* and *Aztec Ruins on the Animas: Excavated, Preserved, and Interpreted.* Florence's long history as a ceramic specialist is recounted in *Pot Luck: Adventures in Archaeology,* and her most recent book is *Chaco's Vanished Past: Hogans, Tents and Ruins.*

Lithics

A term used by archaeologists to refer to all stone tools and the waste materials from their production. Commonly, archaeologists divide lithics into "ground stone" and "flaked and chipped" stone, depending on how they were made. Ground stone tools, made by cutting and smoothing, include grinding implements such as manos, metates, mortars and pestles, as well as paint palettes, arrow shaft smoothers, mauls, and stone ornaments. Flaked and chipped tools, such as projectile points, knives, scrapers, and flake axes, were made by flintknapping. Flintknapping involves the removal of a flake from a stone nodule, or "core," with a wooden striker or hammerstone. The flake is then shaped through the removal of smaller stone chips through "percussion" or "pressure" flaking.

Lizard House

(Map 3; Figure 56)

A small building on the north side of Chaco Canyon about one mile east of **Pueblo Bonito**. The structure, built against a cliff face in a short canyon east of **Chetro Ketl**, had at least two stages of construction. Based on a single tree-ring date, the first building phase is estimated to be in the early 1100s. Three kivas and more than a dozen rooms were defined during a National Park Service salvage excavation at the site.

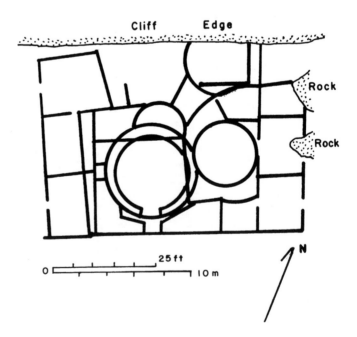

FIGURE 56. Lizard House ground plan. Doorways are shown. Multiple remodeled kivas are shown in the center of the building.

This site, along with a number of similar sites in Chaco Canyon, is important because it helps to show the dramatic change in the size and layout of habitation sites in the early 1100s. Throughout the 1000s, Chacoans lived either in **great houses** or clusters of small houses. Beginning sometime in the late 1000s or early 1100s, it appears that people living in great houses began to move into smaller buildings. Many of these had architectural features identified as **McElmo-style**. Others, like Lizard House, had some McElmo features, such as **core-and-veneer** masonry, but did not totally fit the standard pattern. Moreover, these new buildings occur on both sides of Chaco Canyon, whereas great houses were built almost exclusively on the north side. During this period, people living in the **small house sites** seem to have continued their settlement and dwelling traditions with fewer major changes.

Lowry Ruin Outlier

(Map 1; Figures 57, 58)
A Chacoan great house **community** and **great kiva** located approximately 120 miles northwest of **Pueblo Bonito** in southwestern Colorado, northwest of Cortez. This **great house** was on the far northern limits of the **Chacoan World**, about 35 miles farther from the canyon than its neighbor, the **Chimney Rock Outlier.**

The great house was begun in the 1090s as a four-room structure (possibly five) with a kiva in front of the room block. Based on tree-ring evidence, the great kiva was built at the same time, if not a few years earlier. Two more construction phases at the great house were carried out in the early 1100s, creating a rectangular building with at least two additional **kivas.** The great kiva was used throughout these Chacoan construction activities. At least one Chacoan **road** has been traced between the great house and the great kiva, and other short road segments have been reported in the vicinity. More than a dozen **small house sites** are located on nearby ridges. Non-Chacoan additions to the great house were made in the middle to late 1100s and again in the 1200s.

This site was excavated in 1930–31 and 1933–34 by Paul **Martin** for the Field Museum of Natural History in Chicago as part of the

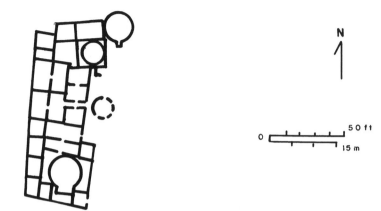

FIGURE 57. Lowry Ruin Outlier great house and great kiva ground plan. The structure has been excavated, and open doorways are shown.

FIGURE 58. Great kiva at Lowry Ruin.

museum's ongoing research in the Southwest. Martin chose this site because Chacoan ceramics and the great kiva suggested strong Chacoan influence, if not actual residence, at a considerable distance from Chaco Canyon. Martin's work here and Frank **Roberts** Jr.'s excavations at the **Village of the Great Kivas** near Zuni, New Mexico, were among the first to identify sites now known as Chacoan outliers. Lowry Ruin is interpreted and protected by the U.S. Bureau of Land Management.

M

Macaws

Large, brightly colored tropical and temperate forest birds of the **parrot** family that were traded from southern Mexico to **Puebloan** peoples for use in rituals. More than thirty macaws were recovered from sites in Chaco Canyon, primarily at **Pueblo Bonito**, where they were probably kept for their feathers. Neil **Judd**, who excavated the **great house** in the 1920s, presented the Macaw clan at **Zuni** Pueblo with a macaw in 1924, as their last captive bird had died many years before. In his monograph, *The Material Culture of Pueblo Bonito*, Judd reported that when he saw the bird again in 1939, it had been "pretty thoroughly plucked."

All but one of approximately 150 macaws found in prehistoric southwestern sites, including Chaco Canyon, were the Scarlet Macaw, a species with blue, yellow, and red feathers that is native to the humid lowlands of Mexico, the same region for **cacao** production. It is not known why the green, red, and blue Military Macaws, which range into northwestern Mexico, were not traded into the Southwest, especially since there is excellent evidence of breeding of both species at **Casas Grandes** (**Paquimé**) in Chihuahua.

Maize

The primary domesticated food crop of the **Puebloan** peoples of the Southwest. Maize (*Zea mays*) is more commonly known as corn. The sweet corn we eat today is the result of a long and continuing evolution of a tropical grass known as *teosinte* that probably originated in southern Mexico and northern Central America.

Archaeological evidence indicates that maize was brought into the Southwest almost 3,500 years ago. By 1,000 years later, several different "races" had emerged as the plant adapted to various southwestern environments with different soils, rainfall, and length of growing season. These many adaptations suggest that it had become an increasingly important food crop to peoples throughout the region.

Corn kernels, cobs, husks, and **pollen** have been recovered from many Chacoan sites in quantities that confirm its importance in the Chacoan diet. Archaeologists have also identified several races of corn in Chacoan sites.

Marcia's Rincon

(Map 3)

A **rincon** near **Fajada Gap** with four **small house sites** excavated by the **Chaco Project.** Named for Marcia Truell Newren, a Chaco Project staff member, this wide rincon is located about one mile east of the National Park Service Visitor Center in the east-facing cliffs of the **Chacra Mesa.** The **Three-C Site** lies a short distance to the south of the excavated structures. These sites and other unexcavated structures are part of what has been termed the Fajada Gap **Community.**

Martin, Paul

A southwestern archaeologist who made significant contributions to early Chacoan studies. Martin joined the Field Museum of Natural History in Chicago as chief curator of anthropology in 1929 after having worked briefly for the Carnegie Institute and the Colorado Historical Society.

Martin's association with the Historical Society alerted him to the research potential of prehistoric sites in southwestern Colorado. During the 1930–31 and 1933–34 field seasons of the Field Museum's Archaeological Expedition to the Southwest, he excavated a large portion of the **Lowry Ruin** northwest of Cortez, Colorado. While the site would not be identified as a Chacoan **outlier** for several decades, Martin was ahead of his time in noting its strong architectural similarities to the **Aztec Ruin** and sites in Chaco Canyon. He also observed that some Lowry Ruin ceramics were Chacoan in character. In his 1936 report on the site, Martin concluded that "certain cultural elements" from the Chaco area appeared to have moved northward sometime during the 1000s.

Masonry Types

(Figure 59)

Three different techniques used by Chacoan masons for building a stone wall. Chacoan masons used various **veneer styles** at different times.

The Simple wall was laid with a single row of building stones, often set with abundant mud mortar. Sometimes the wall was "chinked," with small stones pressed into the surface of the mortar joints to create a smoother finish. A variation on this type was the Double Simple wall, in which two simple walls were placed against one another but were not bonded with interlinking stones.

The second type, the Compound wall, was similar to a double simple wall, but the two rows of building stones were tied together with interlinking stones for greater strength and stability. The outer surfaces of both rows of building stones were carefully finished to present a more pleasing appearance.

The third type, the **core-and-veneer** wall, had either a solid core of stone or a rubble core of small broken stone and soil. This core was faced on both sides with a row of finished building stones. Mud mortar was used in laying up these walls, but the outer layer of veneer stones was pressed into a backing layer of mud so that no mortar was visible on the surface.

Although all three types of walls are found in Chacoan **great houses**, by far the most common building technique in these sites was the core-and-veneer wall. Small houses, on the other hand, seldom have core-and-veneer walls; the simple or compound wall was standard for these sites.

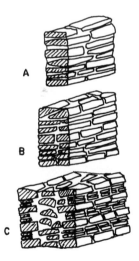

FIGURE 59. Cross sections of Chacoan masonry types: (A) simple; (B) compound; (C) core-and-veneer with fill core.

Mathien, Joan

An archaeologist who has spent her career making substantial contributions to Chacoan research. A long-term member of the **Chaco Project**, Mathien was responsible for the organization and editing of many of the twenty-plus volumes of the Chaco Canyon Studies Publications in Archaeology. During this time she also assisted in developing database management systems for the Chaco Project. This work triggered her deep interest in **turquoise,** leading to numerous publications identifying the sources of turquoise found at **Chaco.** The work led her to investigate possible Chacoan connections with **Mesoamerica**, regional exchange systems, and the social and economic implications of turquoise and other jewelry. She also investigated the **Kin Nahasbas great kiva** community with Thomas **Windes.**

Drawing on her detailed knowledge of the Chacoan natural environment, prehistory, and archaeology, Mathien wrote the synthesis volume of Chaco Project research, *Culture and Ecology of Chaco Canyon and the San Juan Basin*. In this 2005 publication, she effectively summarized nearly four decades of research on the environmental and culture histories of the region and also outlined a broad research framework for further evaluation of Chacoan data.

McElmo Phase

A term used to describe a period in Chacoan prehistory, approximately A.D. 1090–1150, that was marked by the distinctive **McElmo-style** buildings and **community** type. The **great houses** of the period depart radically from the earlier **Bonito phase** buildings and represent the last major construction phase before the canyon was abandoned by the Chacoans. "McElmo Phase" is also occasionally used as shorthand for referring to the McElmo-style great house and its associated attributes.

The term was introduced in the 1960s by **Gordon Vivian** and Thomas Mathews based on their work at **Kin Kletso.** They dated the McElmo phase from approximately A.D. 1050 to 1125, a period that overlapped the Bonito phase. Vivian and Mathews believed the McElmo phase was marked by the movement of immigrants from the **Mesa Verde** area into Chaco Canyon. These new people introduced the McElmo-style masonry typical of the Kin Kletso, **Casa Chiquita,** and **New Alto** great houses, as well as a new ceramic type, McElmo Black-on-white. Thomas **Windes** later redefined this type as **Chaco-McElmo Black-on-white.**

Later research suggested that McElmo-style great houses were a final expression of the Chacoan great house within the canyon and were not introduced by migrants from the north. This research also indicated that the dates for the introduction of the McElmo-style masonry are later than proposed by Vivian and Mathews, and do not begin until the last decade of the A.D. 1000s. McElmo-style buildings were probably built as late as the middle 1100s.

McElmo Style

A term used to identify a number of new architectural and ceramic features that appeared in Chaco Canyon and at some Chacoan **outliers** in the late 1000s and early 1100s. The name comes from the McElmo Valley in southwestern Colorado where similar architecture and ceramics appeared at about the same time. Because of minor differences in the two areas, "style" is added to distinguish Chacoan architecture and pottery.

McElmo-style **great houses** are strikingly different from their earlier counterparts such as **Pueblo Bonito.** McElmo buildings consist of either one or two compact structural units, each of which contains one or two central kivas surrounded by several rows of rooms. Single-unit buildings are basically square (for example, **Casa Chiquita, New Alto**); double-unit buildings are rectangular (for example, **Kin Kletso**). McElmo-style great houses do not have enclosed plazas or associated **great kivas.** Rooms are often smaller than in classic great houses, and there is less terracing of rooms from the back to the front of the dwelling.

The McElmo-style **masonry type** can be either **core-and-veneer** or compound. Core-and-veneer walls are more common in Chaco Canyon; compound walls occur frequently in southwestern Colorado. The building stones were usually cut from a soft, light-colored sandstone and were more squarish or "blocky" than the hard, dark, tabular stones used in earlier Chacoan veneers. The exposed faces of McElmo building stones were lightly pecked with a hammerstone to produce a "dimpled" surface—possibly a means for ensuring that clay plaster would stick to the wall.

McElmo-style ceramics in Chaco Canyon are called **Chaco-McElmo Black-on-white**. They were decorated with black carbon paint derived from plants, rather than the mineral paints used in earlier Chacoan pottery types.

Archaeologists **Gordon Vivian** and Tom Mathews believed that Kin Kletso and other McElmo-style buildings in Chaco Canyon represented the movement of peoples from southwestern Colorado into the canyon in the late 1000s and early 1100s. Stephen **Lekson** suggested, however, that these structures were a late form of Chacoan great house that served specialized purposes. Ruth **Van Dyke** agrees that the buildings were late great houses. But she argues that they were constructed to reinforce confidence in a Chacoan worldview that was important for social and ritual organization at a time when some Chacoans were moving to new settlements on the San Juan and Animas Rivers.

The jury is still out on this question, a problem that poses intriguing possibilities for future research.

Mesa Verde [Spanish for "green tableland"]
(Map 1; Figure 60)
A term used to designate both a large uplifted landform in southwestern Colorado and the prehistoric culture of the people that inhabited the mesa and the valleys surrounding it. The occupation of the Mesa Verde area closely coincides with that of Chaco Canyon but extends for at least an additional one hundred years, into the late 1200s. Although Mesa Verde is most famous for its cliff dwellings—such as Cliff Palace, Spruce Tree House, and Long House—most of the occupation in this area was in mesa-top or valley-bottom sites.

Mesa Verde and Chacoan peoples shared common **Puebloan** cultural roots, but in time they developed distinctly different cultural systems, architecture, and ceramics. There is some evidence that in the early 1100s Chacoans built **outliers** in the general Mesa

FIGURE 60. Long House cliff dwelling at Mesa Verde. (Arizona State Museum, University of Arizona; Helga Teiwes, photographer.)

Verde area (for example, **Lowry Ruin**) and possibly even on Mesa Verde itself (for example, Far View House). After Chacoan peoples abandoned their **great houses** in the northern **San Juan Basin** (for example, **Aztec** West Ruin) and the **Chaco Core** in the mid-1100s, some of these structures were reoccupied and remodeled about a hundred years later by people making **Mesa Verde Black-on-white**. It is thought that some of these people came from the Mesa Verde area. The relationship between Chacoans and Mesa Verdeans is not clear at this time and presents a need for further research.

Mesa Verde Black-on-white

(Figure 61)

A late type of San Juan/Mesa Verde pottery found in limited quantities in Chaco Canyon. Mesa Verde Black-on-white was produced from about A.D. 1200 to 1300 and is found only in Pueblo III sites that post-date the Late Bonito phase. Archaeologists have not included it in the **Cibola White Ware** group because its origins are more firmly tied to the northern **San Juan Basin**. Like **Chaco-McElmo Black-on-white**, this type was decorated in carbon paint, reflecting a general regional trend away from mineral paints at this time. Alfred Kidder wrote the first full description of the type in his classic 1924 publication, *An Introduction to the Study of Southwestern Archaeology*.

Mesa Verde Black-on-white has been found in a number of Chacoan outlier great houses in the northern San Juan Basin and in lesser quantities in some **great houses** and later structures in Chaco Canyon and on the **Chacra Mesa**. The presence of this distinctive ceramic type in Chacoan sites about A.D. 1200, five decades after most sites in the **Chaco Core** were abandoned, has been interpreted by a number of archaeologists as evidence of the reoccupation of Chacoan great houses by peoples from the **Mesa Verde** region in southwestern Colorado. Other archaeologists point out that the material used as a ceramic **temper** in Mesa Verde Black-on-white varies throughout the region, supporting the argument that it was made locally by potters in many areas. Though the production of this type by a specific people cannot be proven, it is clear that its manufacture was associated with a strong cultural tradition centered in the Mesa Verde region.

A variety of container forms was produced in Mesa Verde Black-on-white pottery, including bowls, jars, dippers, and pitchers. Two forms are highly characteristic of the type. The first is a mug that closely resembles a small German beer stein, and the second is the kiva jar. Kiva jars—low, fairly broad containers with a very short neck—were distinguished from other jars by having a slight ledge within the open neck to hold a lid or cover, much as in a modern teapot. Most of these vessels were found in **kivas,** hence the name. Design motifs of Mesa Verde Black-on-white are primarily geometric,

FIGURE 61. Mesa Verde Black-on-white mug and bowl forms with decorative motifs and design layout common to this type.

though zoomorphic and a few anthropomorphic figures occur, usually on bowls. Decorative elements include opposed stepped triangles, interlocking scrolls, zigzag lines and frets, multiple combinations of parallel lines, and abundant dots. Dots appear most frequently as "ticking" on the flattened rims of bowls. Designs commonly are painted in a band layout parallel with the rim of a bowl or around the upper circumference of jars. In contrast to those of Cibola White Ware, the exteriors of Mesa Verde Black-on-white bowls are often decorated with band designs. The exteriors of mugs are usually totally covered with design elements.

Cooking ware associated with Mesa Verde Black-on-white includes several varieties of indented **corrugated** pottery. Red and orange wares often found with this type were mostly imported from areas to the south and west of Chaco Canyon.

Mescalito, Rafael

A **Chaco Navajo** who took part in early excavation and ruins **stabilization** projects in Chaco Canyon. Rafael Mescalito was a regular employee on **Judd**'s excavations at **Pueblo Bonito** from 1921 through 1925. In 1929, he was one of several Navajos hired by **Hewett** to assist a field school student, Janet Tietjens, in compiling a list of local Navajo place names. Though his family held lands along the **Escavada Wash**, they had another **hogan** in Rafael's Rincon, a major side canyon on the south side of the **Chaco Wash** approximately a mile west of Pueblo Bonito. He moved off national monument lands in the 1930s and settled along the Escavada Wash, though he continued to maintain a winter sheep camp on the **Chacra Mesa** to the south of the **Wijiji** great house. This camp was on land held by the **Atencio** family; Rafael's daughter had married into the family and gained use of grazing land. David **Brugge** references Rafael and the Mescalito family several times in *A History of the Chaco Navajos*.

Mesoamerica

A prehistoric culture area as defined by archaeologists that includes Mexico and the northern portion of Central America. A number of archaeologists believe that the lifeways of **Puebloan** peoples in the Southwest were directly or indirectly affected by the movement of ideas, food crops, and material items from the high cultures of Mexico. The **kachina religion, maize, pottery,** and **copper bells** are examples of these influences. The rapid emergence of Chacoan culture in the 1000s has been explained by some archaeologists as a result of direct involvement by Mesoamerican peoples, particularly the Toltec. Charles **DiPeso**, Edwin **Ferdon** and Jonathan Reyman are major proponents of this theory.

Mexican Springs Road

A possible Chacoan **road,** identified solely on the basis of aerial photography, that closely parallels the **Coyote Canyon Road** running from the **South Gap** of Chaco Canyon into the southwestern sector of the **San Juan Basin**. Although this road is shown on a number of Chaco area maps, its existence has never been confirmed by physical evidence on the ground. It is most likely that the lines traced on the aerial photographs do not represent a Chacoan road because no **Chacoan communities** have been identified along its proposed path.

Midden

A mound of prehistoric household trash and other refuse, usually part of a residential archaeological site. Archaeologists tend to use the terms "refuse mound," **trash mound,** and "midden" interchangeably, although midden is more common outside the Southwest. Middens are a source of important archaeological information because their contents reflect the daily lives of past peoples. In addition, stylistic changes in tools, **pottery,** and other items can be traced in the **stratigraphy** of a midden.

Mindeleff, Victor and Cosmos

Self-trained architectural historians who recorded **Puebloan** lifeways in the Southwest and took the first photographs of sites in Chaco Canyon. Victor Mindeleff and his younger brother, Cosmos, joined the second southwestern expedition of the **Smithsonian Institution**'s Bureau of Ethnology in 1881. They were assigned the task of measuring the pueblo of **Zuni** in order to construct a scale model of the pueblo for the new U.S. National Museum. Continuing their association with the Bureau of Ethnology, they spent several field seasons mapping, sketching, recording, and photographing southwestern pueblos. Cosmos produced numerous models of contemporary, historic, and prehistoric structures, and Victor wrote most of the reports, including his monumental contribution, *A Study of Pueblo Architecture in Tusayan and Cibola.*

In 1883 they shifted their focus to prehistoric sites, apparently visiting Chaco Canyon and Canyon de Chelly. Victor returned briefly to Chaco in the late summer of 1884, and in the winter of 1887–88 the brothers spent six weeks recording sites in Chaco Canyon and the **Chaco Core.** During this trip they became the first to photograph sites in Chaco Canyon following William **Jackson**'s unsuccessful photographic venture in 1877.

Mockingbird Canyon

(Maps 2, 3)
A large canyon on the north side of Chaco Canyon approximately

midway between **Pueblo Bonito** and **Una Vida.** Large quantities of runoff flowing down this canyon probably were a major factor in the decision to build the **Hungo Pavi** great house near the mouth of this tributary. If **water control** structures were built in Mockingbird Canyon, they have been washed out or buried by alluvium. Several early **Navajos** reported the presence of small stands of pine in this canyon. Richard **Wetherill**'s first entry into Chaco Canyon in 1895 was via Mockingbird Canyon.

Mogollon

An archaeological term referring to the prehistoric people who occupied the high mountainous country angling from central Arizona into southwestern New Mexico. A desert branch of the Mogollon has been identified in southern New Mexico.

The Mogollon people, like their **Puebloan** neighbors, were sedentary farmers. However, living in the mountains where game was plentiful, they depended on hunting to a much greater extent. The cold mountain winters probably accounted for their long-standing tradition of living in **pithouses,** dwellings that could be heated more efficiently than surface rooms. After about A.D. 1000, they began building stone surface pueblos that resembled those of their Puebloan counterparts. Multiroom cliff-dwelling communities appeared in steep mountain canyons during the 1300s.

Mogollon potters used the coil and scrape method of manufacture to produce brown ware ceramics decorated with reddish paint. Later, some Mogollon groups used a white slip on their vessels and painted them with black geometric designs in an apparent attempt to copy the black-on-white **pottery** of their Puebloan neighbors. A regional branch of the Mogollon, the Mimbres, are famous for their pictorial bowls showing realistic animals and humans, and detailed portrayals of daily activities such as hunting, fishing, and weaving.

Despite their location between the **Hohokam** to the south and the **Anasazi** to the north, the Mogollon do not seem to have been as deeply involved in trading as their neighbors. Some shell and **turquoise** jewelry is found, but usually in limited quantities. Most

Mogollon settlements, which are often small, have a large communal pithouse that is interpreted as a religious structure. The term **kiva** has been applied to these buildings.

The term "Mogollon" was adopted in 1931 at an archaeological conference in Globe, Arizona, to distinguish this culture from the Anasazi and the Hohokam, the latter being defined at the same conference. "Mogollon" was taken from the Mogollon Mountains, named in turn for an early governor of New Mexico, Don Juan Ignacio Flores Mogollón.

Morris, Earl

One of the primary figures in the early development of southwestern archaeology who excavated several Chacoan **outliers**. Morris's exposure to the prehistory of the **San Juan Basin** began early because his father, Scott, partially supported his family in the 1890s through the sale of antiquities excavated from sites along the San Juan River near Farmington, New Mexico. Scott Morris preceded the **Wetherills** in Chaco, spending part of the winter of 1893 trenching the **Pueblo Bonito** refuse mound in an unsuccessful search for whole ceramic vessels.

Earl Morris chose an academic approach to archaeology and obtained his M.A. from the University of Colorado in 1915. The following year he assisted Nels Nelson in doing some of the first **stratigraphic** analyses of **trash mounds** in the Southwest, including the Pueblo Bonito mound. In 1916 he began excavation of the West Ruin at the **Aztec Ruins** group for the American Museum of Natural History, a project that lasted until 1921. His last major excavation at the site was clearing the **great kiva**, which he later restored. Based on his work at Aztec, Morris believed his data demonstrated conclusively that while much of the West Ruin had been built by Chacoans, it was reoccupied by peoples of the **Mesa Verde** cultural tradition. Morris later excavated two Chacoan **outliers** in the La Plata Valley as well as the **Twin Angels Outlier**.

Morris's archaeological contributions went far beyond Chacoan culture. He helped to establish the presence of **Basketmaker** II sites in southwestern Colorado, excavated important Basketmaker III sites in northeastern Arizona, and carried out some of the earliest work in historic **Navajo** sites in the Dinetah, the Navajo homeland. Morris also spent a number of years working in the Yucatán. In addition, he collected tree-ring samples for early **dendrochronological** work, described and defined many ceramic wares, produced architectural studies, and did important **stabilization** work at several sites. His legacy is marked by numerous scholarly publications and many popular articles.

Morrison Chert (see *Chert*)

N

NAGPRA

The Native American Graves Protection and Repatriation Act (NAGPRA), passed by the U.S. Congress in 1990 to provide proper care and treatment of prehistoric and historic human remains and certain objects associated with native peoples of the United States, including Alaska and the Hawaiian Islands.

Under the act, human remains and all items placed with the deceased are protected on federal and tribal lands. Such materials currently in museums may be returned to native peoples who can demonstrate a legitimate claim to them. Most archaeologists now avoid excavating burials, but those discovered in construction projects or other inadvertent situations may need to be removed for return to the appropriate tribal peoples. Procedures for the return of human remains and funeral objects are often complicated. For example, several tribal groups claim affiliation with ancient Chacoan peoples.

NAGPRA also provides for the protection and return of sacred items necessary for the ongoing practice of native religion as well as items of "cultural patrimony." The latter are objects owned by an entire group, such as **Zuni** war god figures and some items used in **Hopi** kachina ceremonies. The law also forbids sale and trade of these objects, including such items as pottery, baskets, and stone tools that were placed in burials.

Narbona Pass Chert (see *Chert*)

National Geographic Society

A scientific and educational organization promoting research and exploration, best known for its publication, *National Geographic Magazine*. In 1920 the society's research committee recommended an archaeological reconnaissance of the Chaco area to investigate the possibility of the long-term excavation and preservation of a canyon **great house**. Neil **Judd**, a curator of archaeology at the National Museum in Washington, undertook the survey and outlined a five-year program of excavation at **Pueblo Bonito** with additional work at **Pueblo del Arroyo**. The project was approved, and Judd worked in Chaco Canyon from 1921 through 1927, spending the last season completing reports on the previous six years of excavation. A number of articles on the work at Chaco appeared during this time in *National Geographic Magazine*. The society played an important role in the developing young science of **dendrochronology** as Judd collected hundreds of tree-ring samples for analysis by Andrew **Douglass.**

Navajo

A non-Puebloan tribal group that inhabits a large part of the Four Corners area of New Mexico, Colorado, Utah, and Arizona. The Navajo (known in their language as "Diné") and neighboring Apache are Southern Athabaskan speakers who probably separated from Northern Athabaskan speakers in northwestern Canada about A.D. 700. Originally nomadic hunters, they moved slowly southward and arrived in the Southwest about 500 years ago.

The earliest evidence for Navajo occupation in the Southwest is in the Dinetah, or Navajo homeland, in the northwestern corner of the **San Juan Basin**. When the Navajos arrived, they were a nomadic hunting and gathering people. They soon began raiding **Puebloan** villages in the Rio Grande Valley for **corn**, textiles, and slaves. With the arrival of Spanish colonists in the Southwest in the 1600s, the Navajos added these settlements to their raiding inventory and quickly accumulated large herds of horses, sheep, and goats.

Their wealth attracted the attention of Comanche and Ute peoples, and the Navajos in turn became the object of raiding. This pressure forced them to abandon the Dinetah in the early 1700s and to move south through the Chaco area, where they resided primarily on the **Chacra Mesa**. By this time, the Navajos had became pastoral herders and had adopted a number of crafts, including weaving, from their Puebloan neighbors. Those who settled in the immediate vicinity of Chaco Canyon came to be known as the **Chaco Navajo**.

By the early 1800s, the Navajos began moving west from the Chacra Mesa and Mount Taylor regions. They had crossed the **Chuska Mountains** by the mid-1800s, when Lieutenant **Simpson** and Colonel Washington encountered them in the Narbona Pass area. They eventually extended their territory to the Black Mesa and Monument Valley regions in north-central Arizona. There are more than 175,000 enrolled tribal members.

Navajo social, political, and religious systems differ in many ways from those of their Puebloan neighbors, though they have borrowed some ritual elements used in their ceremonies. Some Navajos believe they are related to the **Anasazi** and that their ancestry can be traced back into the Puebloan past. These claims are based on the fact that some Navajo clans were derived from Puebloan women who married Navajo men.

Navajo Springs Outlier

(Map 1; Figure 62)
A Chacoan **outlier community** located about 120 miles southwest of Chaco Canyon, notable for having a **great house** surrounded by several **berms**. Navajo Springs is one of several outlier communities in the West Puerco Valley and one of the more westerly of Chacoan communities south and west of Chaco Canyon. Analysis of ceramic

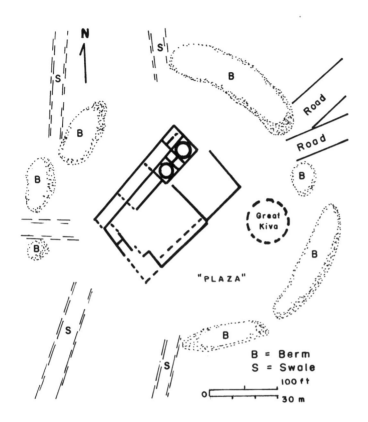

FIGURE 62. Navajo Springs Outlier great house site plan. The site has not been excavated; locations of rooms and kivas have been estimated from surface evidence and some standing walls. Berms, swales, and roads around the great house are shown.

styles found at the site indicate that it was occupied from about A.D. 975 to 1125.

The Navajo Springs Outlier community included the great house and associated features; a nearby cluster of at least three smaller house mounds with associated **trash mounds**, called the "North Complex"; and several **small house sites**. The great house has about forty rooms, rises to two stories in some areas, and is fronted on the east by two enclosed courtyards. A **great kiva** lies just outside the courtyards on the east.

These features are surrounded by at least seven **berms** that may create an additional plaza area. Two prehistoric **roads** enter this zone on the east through a break in the berms. One of the roads appears to link the great house with the North Complex. Other breaks in the berms have been termed "swales."

The Navajo Springs Outlier **community** is protected by the Navajo Nation.

New Alto

(Map 4; Figure 63)

A small **McElmo-style** great house located on the mesa to the north of **Pueblo Bonito** and a few hundred yards west of **Pueblo Alto** (also known as Old Alto). This building follows the typical plan of single-unit McElmo buildings, having one kiva in the center surrounded by two or three rows of rooms on all sides. New Alto had thirty-two ground-floor rooms, all of which were two-story except for the front row of six one-story rooms facing to the south. The masonry veneer is McElmo-style. There is no associated **great kiva**. No Chacoan **roads** lead to New Alto; however, several roads converge on nearby Pueblo Alto. Three tree-ring dates in the early 1060s are almost certainly from reused beams, because construction of McElmo-style buildings has been firmly pegged to the early 1100s. The site has not been excavated.

The relationship of McElmo-style **great houses** to the earlier classic great houses such as Pueblo Bonito has not been well studied, but the proximity of New Alto and Pueblo Alto provides an en-

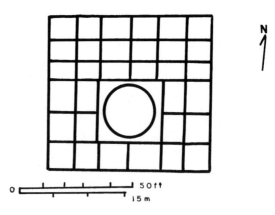

FIGURE 63. New Alto great house ground plan based on standing walls. Doorways are not shown.

ticing research opportunity. Their relationship is made even more intriguing by the presence of a long, low wall that connects the rear of both buildings and extends well beyond them to the east and west. This unusual feature suggests that the buildings not only were linked, but that they stood within a defined great house precinct.

Newton, Roy

A member of a well-known **Chaco Navajo** family who often served as an interpreter and field assistant to early archaeologists working in Chaco. Newton attended the Albuquerque Indian School, and his language skills were invaluable on excavation projects that employed Navajo crew members. He was employed by Neil **Judd** at **Pueblo Bonito** in 1925 and in later years often referred to his experiences with "Mr. Judd." He was the primary informant on Francis H. Elmore's Navajo ethnobotany project in 1935 and frequently worked with students in the University of New Mexico field school in Chaco. He was employed by the National Park Service in the 1940s and 1950s in various capacities. Roy Newton's descendants and other family members still live along the **Escavada Wash** just north of Chaco Canyon. Roy's son David worked in Chaco for the National Park Service, and his granddaughter Ramona Begay Martinez is also a Park Service employee.

North Road (see *Great North Road*)

O

Obsidian

A hard, dark volcanic glass that forms when rhyolitic lava cools extremely rapidly. It was the most popular prehistoric raw material for chipped and flaked stone tools such as knives and arrow points because it fractured in a predictable manner with razor-sharp edges. Obsidian is commonly found in areas with volcanic activity.

This "volcanic glass" was one of four "exotic" stones traded into Chaco Canyon for making **lithic** tools and projectile points. Like the three imported **cherts** that increased or decreased in use over time in the canyon, the popularity of obsidian fluctuated. Obsidian imports are also of interest to archaeologists because sources changed from early to late periods. Moreover, there is some evidence that obsidian tools were imported during some periods, but obsidian nodules for chipping were brought in at other times.

Ojo Alamo [Spanish for "cottonwood spring"]
(Map 1)
An area in the northern portion of the De-Na-Zin/Bisti Wilderness Area surrounding the Ojo Alamo spring, located approximately twenty miles north of Chaco Canyon. It is marked by **badlands** formations, exposures of petrified wood, and a relict stand of ponderosa pine. Chacoan peoples collected petrified wood, quartz, and **chert** from this area for use in making cutting tools and hammerstones. It is possible that they also harvested pine timbers here, although current stands contain few suitable trees. Richard **Wetherill** established a short-lived trading post at the spring in the early 1900s, an extension of his trading business in Chaco Canyon. Today the area is protected by the Bureau of Land Management.

Old Alto (see *Pueblo Alto*)

Organic Materials

(Figure 64)
An archaeological term referring to objects made from plant and animal products, such as fiber baskets and sandals, wooden bows and arrows, leather bags, and bone tools. Organic materials are perishable and are usually found only under extremely protected conditions such as in rock shelters or collapsed rooms. Fragmentary pieces of organic materials are often collected for archaeological analysis through the process of **flotation**.

FIGURE 64. Child's sandal from a Basketmaker period site in northern Arizona. (Arizona State Museum, University of Arizona.)

Unlike **pottery** and **lithics**, organic materials contain carbon, and their age can be determined by **carbon-14 dating**.

Outliers (or Outlier Communities)

Prehistoric sites in the **San Juan Basin** that share some architectural and ceramic traits with sites in Chaco Canyon. "Outlier" generally has been used to designate a **great house** located outside the **Chaco Core**, usually on the periphery of the San Juan Basin. The term "outlier community" has been used to define the great house along with associated small house villages, **great kivas**, connecting **roads,** and other features clustered around the great house. Archaeological surveys have shown that these communities are dense occupation zones surrounded by land with few if any prehistoric sites. Individual communities were separated from others by open "buffer zones."

Between seventy and one hundred sites have been identified as Chacoan outliers, but the status of some sites is in question, thereby clouding the outlier "count." The identification of outlier communities is often difficult. Most of the great houses have no standing walls, and their Chacoan features may not be evident. The size of the ruin mound has become a gauge for assigning outlier status. The presence of a great kiva or a Chacoan road at the outlier is a significant factor, but not all outliers have great kivas or roads.

Dating of outliers is also difficult because most have not been excavated, and tree-ring samples are not available. Many outliers are dated solely on the basis of associated ceramics. A few (for example, **Guadalupe Outlier**) suggest dates in the A.D. 900s and early 1000s, but most well-dated outlier sites, particularly in the northern San

Juan Basin, were established in the late 1000s or early 1100s.

Explaining the presence and function of outliers and outlier communities has become a major focus of archaeological research. Some archaeologists believe they were established by people from Chaco Canyon seeking trade contacts or new farmlands outside the Chaco Core. Others think local leaders at existing **small house sites** built great houses to imitate the buildings they had seen in Chaco Canyon as a means of enhancing their status within their communities.

Two important surveys were carried out in the 1970s to locate, describe, and interpret Chacoan outliers. The **Chaco Project** initiated a reconnaissance of outliers mostly to the north of Chaco Canyon in 1976, and the New Mexico State Historic Preservation Office and Public Service Company of New Mexico started work primarily to the south of Chaco Canyon in 1977. Robert Powers, William Gillespie, and Stephen **Lekson** produced a thorough report on Chaco Project results in 1983; Michael Marshall, John **Stein**, Richard Loose, and Judith Novotny published their equally detailed synthesis in 1979. In 2000, Chacoan scholars John **Kantner** and Nancy Mahoney edited a volume analyzing outlier information and descriptions of new studies on these sites.

P

Padilla, Tomas

The patriarch of a large Navajo family who provided researchers with important information about Chaco Canyon in the mid-1800s. Tomas Padilla was hired by Richard **Wetherill** in 1897 for work at **Pueblo Bonito**. In 1910 he was accused of participating with **Chis-chilling-begay** in the killing of Richard Wetherill, but never convicted. Years later he worked for Neil **Judd** at Pueblo Bonito and was interviewed by him in 1927. He recalled Chaco Canyon as having more vegetation when he was a youth in the 1860s. By that time the **Chaco Wash** was beginning to cut down or become entrenched. Padilla spoke of several Chacoan **roads** and remembered **canals** in the canyon, particularly near the confluence of the Chaco and Escavada washes.

The Padilla family had large landholdings on the Chaco Wash below the confluence with the **Escavada Wash,** and Padilla Well is still an important landmark in the area. They also lived in **South Gap.** Information on Tomas Padilla and other family members was recorded by Judd, and the Padilla family is included in David **Brugge**'s *A History of the Chaco Navajos.*

Paleoclimate

(Figure 65)

A reconstruction of the climate during a past time, estimated through various scientific means. In the Chaco area, paleoclimatic reconstruction has been used to chart long-term cycles of wetter and drier years as well as annual shifts in rainfall. This information also is used to explain changes in human culture. There is some indication

FIGURE 65. Average annual precipitation in the San Juan Basin, A.D. 900–1000, showing cycles of wetter and drier periods.

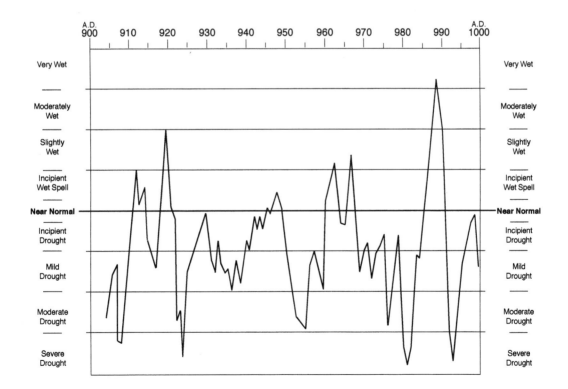

that surges in great house construction may be related to periods of increased moisture and assumed greater crop yields.

Increasingly, archaeologists in the Southwest are using tree rings from prehistoric beams to chart variations in rainfall and temperature over time, a technique known as dendroclimatology. **Palynology** is less precise for measuring short-term changes in temperature and moisture but can be used to record larger-scale shifts in vegetation susceptible to climatic change. For example, a decrease in pine pollen could reflect a warmer and drier period. Similar changes in animal life also serve as a gross measure of climatic change. Southwestern archaeologists also study changes in erosion or soil deposition along streambeds as an indication of total available moisture and related rises or drops in water tables.

Paleoindian

A term used by archaeologists to refer to a way of life throughout North, Central, and South America that lasted from at least 12,000 years ago to 7,500 years ago. The Paleoindian lifestyle was based on gathering wild plant foods and hunting a wide range of animals, many of them now extinct (for example, early bison, mammoth, giant sloth, and tapir). Paleoindian groups were mobile, following herds and collecting seasonal plants as they matured. As a result, they built only simple shelters and did not have a large inventory of tools and other possessions.

Paleoindians are well known for their fine-chipped stone spear points, and many regional varieties are now recognized. The earliest and best-known is the Clovis point, which was first identified at a site near Clovis, New Mexico. Clovis points are associated with mammoth hunting. The first evidence for the later Paleoindian "Folsom" hunters was discovered near the small town of Folsom, New Mexico. They concentrated on taking an early, now-extinct species of bison.

Some archaeologists now believe that human groups may have been in the Americas as early as 30,000 years ago. Recent archaeological finds in several South American sites have well-dated deposits at 12,000 years ago, suggesting that Clovis may not be the earliest Paleoindian presence in the New World.

Paleoindian hunters may have followed herds of mammoth and large bison in the **Chuska Valley**, but the evidence for their presence is limited to a few finds of their spear points. There is no archaeological support for Paleoindian use or occupation of Chaco Canyon or the **Chaco Core**.

Palynology

The identification and analysis of pollen grains in soil. Archaeologists collect old pollen from prehistoric sites to reconstruct past environments and the diets of ancient peoples. Soil samples are taken from a site, and a "pollen count" is made of each type of pollen found in the sample. Different quantities and types of pollen from sites spanning a long time period in one area reflect changes in the vegetation. Those changes, in turn, may point to past shifts in temperature and moisture.

While plants and their flowers are rarely preserved in archaeological sites, pollen grains have very hard outer shells that are almost indestructible. The outer shells of different plant pollens have very distinctive shapes and markings, and are easily identified when viewed under a microscope.

Pollen studies carried out in the Chaco area have shown high counts of **maize** (corn) in almost all sites, making it clear that Chacoan peoples depended on this crop for many centuries. Palynology also has demonstrated that the vegetation and climate in the **Chaco Core** has not changed much over the past 2,000 to 2,500 years.

Paquimé

(Map 5)
The Nahuatl word for **Casas Grandes**. According to Charles **Di-Peso**, the archaeologist who carried out major excavations at this site in northern Chihuahua from 1958 to 1961, the word is translated as

"big houses." The Nahuatl included several groups in central Mexico, including the Aztec, who spoke a **Uto-Aztecan** language. Early Spanish accounts of this site sometimes used the Hispanicized term "Amaqueme."

Parrots

Tropical, brightly colored birds of medium size with short, hooked bills. The thick-billed parrot is an occasional migrant into the pine forests of southeastern Arizona and southwestern New Mexico, and its feathers may have been used in religious rituals at Chaco Canyon because of their attractive green color.

Neil **Judd** recovered two examples of this species in his excavations at **Pueblo Bonito**. While the thick-billed parrot may have been more common in these areas in the past, they occur less frequently in Chacoan sites than the Scarlet **Macaw**, which was traded into the area from Mexico.

Pecos Classification

A system for describing periods of development in Ancestral Puebloan (**Anasazi**) culture. The classification is based on the division of the Anasazi lifeway into two broad time periods: the earlier **Basketmaker** period and the later **Pueblo period,** which was marked by aboveground architecture, white-slipped pottery, and the introduction of cotton. Cultural traits, rather than dates, are used to separate the Basketmaker and Pueblo periods because the cultural changes were not abrupt and occurred at different times throughout the Anasazi region.

The two broad periods were divided into smaller units identified by Roman numerals: Basketmaker I, II, and III were defined, and five subperiods were established for the Pueblo period, with Pueblo V representing the recent historic Pueblo period. Certain traits were also used to distinguish these shorter-term periods.

Initially, dates were applied to each of the subperiods, but the actual dates when many of the traits first appeared differ considerably. For example, Chacoan **great house** architecture is Pueblo III in form and style but appears at a time generally considered to be Pueblo II. These differences are a result of rapid cultural development in some Anasazi areas with lags in other areas.

The Pecos Classification, first developed by Alfred Kidder, is still used by many southwestern archaeologists as a form of "shorthand" for quickly identifying general date ranges and the level of cultural development at a site. It was "officially" accepted at the first **Pecos Conference** held in 1927 at Pecos Pueblo in New Mexico.

Pecos Conference

An annual meeting of professional, amateur, and student archaeologists working in the Southwest, held to review and discuss recent archaeological discoveries and problems. The first Pecos Conference was convened in 1927 by Alfred Kidder, an early dean of southwestern archaeology, following several years of work at Pecos Pueblo in New Mexico. Kidder's goals were to discuss current problems and find ways to resolve them, and to reach agreement on "a unified system of nomenclature": the resulting **Pecos Classification**. Neil **Judd** and Earl **Morris** were among those who attended this conference.

Peñasco Blanco [Spanish for "white rock point"]

(Map 3; Figure 66)

An early Chacoan **great house** situated about three miles west of **Pueblo Bonito** on the **Chacra Mesa** overlooking the confluence of the Chaco and Escavada washes. The third largest great house in Chaco Canyon, Peñasco Blanco stands apart from other canyon great houses in several ways. Other than **Tsin Kletsin**, it is the only great house located on the south side of Chaco Canyon. The oval ground plan is unlike any other great house and contrasts with the classic D-shape of canyon great houses such as **Pueblo Alto** and **Chetro Ketl**. Its four **great kivas**, two in the plaza and two outside the building, are one more than at any other great house. A small **McElmo-style** building with a ground plan similar to the west **Rabbit Ruin** is located to the north of the great house.

Several tree-ring dates in the early A.D. 900s show that the building began as an arced room cluster near the center of the building. The back row of rooms rose to two stories, stepping down to a single story on the plaza side. Major construction in the middle and late 1000s added a third rear story, additional rooms, and an arced row of rooms that enclosed the plaza.

Although this site was never excavated, several Navajos dug a number of rooms in the building when Richard **Wetherill** was working at Pueblo Bonito, reportedly because they believed large quantities of turquoise had been found there. Frank **Roberts** Jr. trenched the **trash mound** to the east of the building as part of his attempt to develop a ceramic sequence for Chaco based on stratigraphic tests in various great house **middens**.

A Chacoan **road** passes to the south of the great house, closely skirting one of the great kivas situated just outside the building. The **Ahshislepah Road**, which crosses the mesa to the west of Peñasco Blanco and descends the cliffs near the junction of the **Chaco** and **Escavada washes**, may also be linked to Peñasco Blanco.

The site was named by Lieutenant **Simpson** during his brief survey of the canyon in 1849. The translation of the Navajo name for the site is "house around which the wash bends."

Pepper, George H.

The field director of the **Hyde Exploring Expedition** investigations at Chaco Canyon. The Hyde brothers originally requested that Frederick Putnam of Harvard University direct the project. His responsibilities at Harvard and the American Museum of Natural History did not permit his extended absence, and he selected Pepper, an inexperienced student, to direct the excavations at **Pueblo Bonito**. Richard **Wetherill** had assumed he would oversee the work, and the men often had a testy working relationship.

Pepper's notes on the excavations at Pueblo Bonito were published by the American Museum of Natural History in 1920. He also published several short papers on ceremonial objects and a burial room at Pueblo Bonito. Pepper later worked for the University of Pennsylvania Museum and Gustav Heye's Museum of the American Indian in New York.

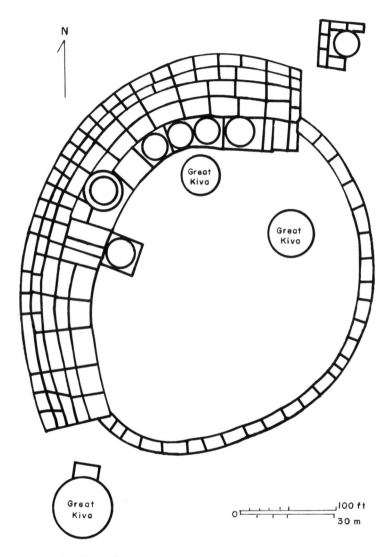

N

Great
Kiva

Great
Kiva

Great
Kiva

100 ft

0

30 m

FIGURE 66. Peñasco Blanco great house ground plan. The site has not been excavated; locations of rooms and kivas are based on standing wall and surface evidence. Doorways are not shown. A fourth great kiva (not shown) is northwest of the structure.

Perishables (see *Organic Materials*)

Petroglyph

(Figure 67)

A form of rock art created by pecking, scraping, grinding, or incising a design into a rock surface. Petroglyphs were commonly made by the **Ancestral Puebloans** and are found at many locations in Chaco Canyon. In the Southwest, petroglyph and **pictograph** designs and their subject matter changed over time and varied by region. Rock art specialists have developed regional classifications for petroglyphs of various time periods.

Within the Chaco area, the most common petroglyphs are from the late **Basketmaker** and **Pueblo periods** and are regarded as a generalized Anasazi style. They commonly include geometric designs

FIGURE 67. Incised Navajo Ye'i petroglyph at Chaco Canyon.

along with depictions of humans, mountain sheep, birds, and insects made with thick pecked lines. Those made by the later **Navajos** usually consist of much thinner scratched lines and often show historic scenes, including group dances and men on horseback. Early Navajo rock art frequently depicts Ye'i, Navajo deities.

Pictograph

(Figure 68)

A rock art design that is painted onto a rock surface. Like **petroglyphs,** the motifs in the designs changed over time and varied by region in the Southwest. Because paint can be eroded by wind and water, pictographs are generally less common than **petroglyphs**, although they do occur in protected locations such as rock shelters.

The **Supernova pictograph**, located on a protected section of cliff wall below **Peñasco Blanco,** is one of the few pictographs to have survived in Chaco Canyon. A number of **Archaic** period pictographs, often of sticklike human figures, are found in the Chaco area.

FIGURE 68. Late Archaic period pictographs at Atlatl Cave, Chaco Canyon.

Pierre's Outlier

(Map 1; Figure 69)

A Chacoan outlier located about fifteen miles north of Chaco Canyon on the **Great North Road**. The outlier community consists of three small great houses, eleven **small house sites**, several isolated rooms, and a probable signal station. Two of the **great houses** are located on the top of a steep-sided mesa called the Acropolis; the third is at the base of **El Faro**, a cone-shaped hill topped by a probable **signal station**.

All three great houses are essentially rectangular with one or two interior kivas and approximately fifteen rooms. No **great kivas** are present. Several tree-ring dates were obtained from the site, and all

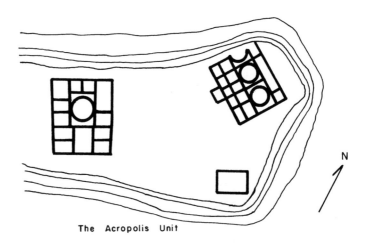

The Acropolis Unit

FIGURE 69. Pierre's Outlier. Ground plans of buildings on the Acropolis and at the base of El Faro. The physical relationship of the two units is not shown. The buildings have not been excavated; locations of rooms and kivas are based on standing wall and surface evidence. Dashed lines represent estimated rooms. Doorways are not shown.

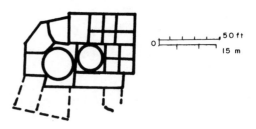

El Faro Unit

dated in the early 1100s. Trees represented in these **timbers** include not only ponderosa pine but also white fir, a species that today is found no closer than the La Plata Mountains some sixty-five miles to the north.

Pierre's Outlier is one of several **outliers** along the Great North Road between Chaco Canyon and the **Salmon Ruin** on the San Juan River. It may have served as a way station, but the settlement's size suggests that farming was also carried out in the nearby valleys.

The **Navajo** name for the site is Flint Striking Stones. The site is named for Pierre Morenon, who discovered it in 1974 while surveying the Great North Road for the San Juan Archaeological Program. It is protected by the Bureau of Land Management.

Pintado-Chaco Road

(Map 2)

A Chacoan **road** also known as the East Road, extending about three miles from the **Pueblo Pintado** great house to the head of Chaco Canyon. The depression of the roadbed is visible on the west side of the **great house** as it curves from the southwestern corner of Pueblo Pintado and then heads in a direct line to the west. Other traces of the road are distinctly visible on aerial photographs. The road ends today at a set of rock-cut steps where it descends into Chaco Canyon. It may have connected with the **East Community** and almost certainly ran along the bottom of the canyon to other great houses in the lower canyon.

Pithouse

(Figure 70)

A mud-plastered house, usually one room, with floor and lower walls excavated into the earth. Pithouses were used throughout the prehistoric Southwest in the earlier phases of the **Anasazi, Mogollon,** and **Hohokam** cultures, and each developed its own distinctive style.

Pithouses in **Basketmaker** and early **Pueblo period** sites in Chaco have features that are common throughout most of the

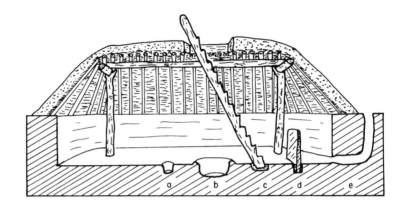

FIGURE 70. Cross-section view of late Basketmaker pithouse. Features include: (a) ash pit; (b) hearth; (c) seating pit in floor for notched log entry ladder; (d) stone slab air deflector; and (e) a ventilator shaft for bringing fresh air into the room.

Anasazi area. In Basketmaker times a fifteen- to twenty-five-foot-diameter house pit was dug about three feet into the ground. The base of the walls were often lined with sandstone slabs. The flat roof was supported by four upright posts set into the floor in a square. Short **timbers** laid around the top edge of the pit were angled inward and rested against the framework of the square roof. These sloping walls and the roof were then covered with reeds, juniper bark, or brush and plastered over with mud. A narrow entrance passageway on the south led first into an antechamber, a small circular room that may have served as a storage place, and then into the main room of the pithouse. An opening in the center of the roof allowed smoke from a central hearth to leave the building. Other interior features often included depressions in the floor to hold pots, and stone slab wingwalls that marked off areas for storage and special use.

In late Basketmaker and early Pueblo period pithouses, pits were much deeper, with the walls completely underground and the pit topped only by a mud-plastered roof framework. The antechamber was remodeled and served only as a ventilator for bringing fresh air into the room. A stone slab deflector moved incoming air away from the central hearth and ash pit. Entry into the house was through an enlarged smoke hole in the roof. The shift to deeper pithouses has been interpreted as a reaction to colder cycles of climate; heating was more efficient in structures with roof-high earthen walls.

Most archaeologists believe that as the transition was made to above-ground living rooms with masonry walls in the Pueblo period, the pithouse was kept as a place for ritual activities, evolving into the **kiva**.

Platform Mounds

(Figure 71)

Raised, flat-topped earth (or masonry and earth) religious structures common in **Mesoamerica** and at some **Hohokam** sites. Usually rectangular, they range in size from fifty feet on a side to as large as a city block. They may reach from six feet to more than fifty feet high. Steep-sided versions of these mounds in Mesoamerica are often called pyramids, but they differ from Egyptian pyramids in having a level surface at the top that was usually the base for a ritual building. Hohokam platform mounds are usually smaller, more simple, and may be circular.

Based upon Neil **Judd**'s excavation data, Stephen **Lekson** and John **Stein** believe that the two **trash mounds** fronting **Pueblo Bonito** on the south are platform mounds. They point to the fact that

FIGURE 71. Hohokam platform mound at the Snaketown site, Arizona. (Arizona State Museum, University of Arizona; Helga Teiwes, photographer.)

a masonry wall surrounded them, and that the east mound had two narrow sets of steps rising to the mound top. In addition, they believe an adobe surface covered the trash fill within the walls. Were the Pueblo Bonito mounds only walled trash deposits or intentionally constructed platform mounds? Wirt "Chip" **Wills** and Patricia **Crown** may resolve this significant question following detailed reanalysis of the mound **stratigraphy** that was exposed when they reopened Judd's trenches through the mounds. If the mounds were used for public ceremonies, it is a departure from the normal **Puebloan** practice of conducting rituals within **kivas** and enclosed plazas.

Pochteca (or Puchteca)

The Nahuatl (**Uto-Aztecan** speaking groups in central Mexico) word for traveling merchants who specialized in precious goods such as **parrot** feathers, **turquoise**, jade, and **cacao**. They were also believed to have served as spies for their rulers.

A number of archaeologists (for example, Charles **DiPeso**, J. Charles Kelley, Jonathan Reyman) have proposed that some southwestern cultures, especially the **Hohokam** and Chacoan, were directly influenced by members of the *pochteca* who entered the Southwest and established trading centers at sites such as **Pueblo Bonito.** These scholars have suggested that many of the architectural traits of Chacoan **great houses** have close **Mesoamerican** parallels. The evidence supporting these theories is limited, and it is not certain that a pochteca-like class was present in pre-Aztec Mesoamerican society at the time Chacoan culture was in full development.

Pollen (see *Palynology*)

Population Estimates

Estimates of the number of people who may have inhabited prehistoric sites. Archaeologists use various techniques for making these estimates. Some multiply the total number of room **suites** by an average family size (usually five). Others use the square footage of floor space required by a family rather than the number of rooms. A different approach estimates the number of people that could be supported by available agricultural land. This technique requires assumptions about what the land could have produced and the caloric output of the projected yields.

Archaeologists have arrived at dramatically different population estimates for Chaco Canyon from A.D. 850 to 1150, when **great houses** were occupied. Some who believe that great houses were primarily ceremonial centers rather than residential buildings estimate a total canyon population of between 2,000 and 3,000 people. Others propose a canyon population of 5,000 to 6,000. Early estimates of 10,000 persons in the canyon have little support today.

Pottery

Objects, usually containers, made of moist clay that is hardened by firing in some type of kiln. Some archaeologists distinguish "pottery," fired at less high temperatures, from "ceramics," fired at very high temperatures; however, most use the terms interchangeably.

Potters in Chaco Canyon produced some local ceramics, but the lack of large quantities of wood needed for firing probably stimulated the brisk trade into the canyon of thousands of vessels. Archaeologists usually can identify the area in which pots were produced by examining the **temper,** crushed and ground rock or other materials added to the clay to add strength and make the clay more workable. The rock fragments in the pottery can be matched to samples from specific areas in the **San Juan Basin.**

Precipitation

Water, as rain or snow, falling to the earth's surface. The total amount of precipitation in an area, especially summer **rainfall,** is critical to agriculture. The annual precipitation in the **San Juan Basin** (snow and rain) varies from somewhat less than eight inches in parts of the interior basin to almost twenty inches in the northern mountainous region. Chaco Canyon averages little more than eight inches per year. Estimates of past precipitation and **paleoclimate**, made on the basis of tree-ring records, have been helpful in charting fluctuations in moisture in the **Chaco Core** and the San Juan Basin.

Pseudo-cloisonné

(Figure 72)

A decorative technique used at Chaco Canyon in which designs were carved out of a base coat of paint on an object and parts of the design were then filled with contrasting colors of paint. It is somewhat similar to the Old World process of cloisonné in which wire strips are welded to a metal backplate to form a design. The separate areas of the design are then filled with different colored enamel. The Chacoan process did not involve the use of metal, enamel, or welding.

Three pieces of pseudo-cloisonné painted on sandstone were found in **Pueblo Bonito**. Careful analysis suggests that they were probably made in Chaco Canyon, but the process may have been learned from similar objects made in the **Hohokam** area or northern Mexico. The presence of pseudo-cloisonné in Chaco Canyon has been cited by several archaeologists to support their belief that Chacoan culture was strongly influenced by, or even derived from, **Mesoamerican** high cultures such as the **Toltec**.

Public Architecture

(Figure 73)

Buildings and other structures used for activities that involve large segments of a local population. Modern examples include cathedrals, churches, market squares, government buildings and theaters. Public architecture in the prehistoric Southwest included **Hohokam** ballcourts and **platform mounds,** and Puebloan **great kivas**.

Michael Marshall, John **Stein**, and Richard Loose were some of the first archaeologists to propose that Chacoan **great houses** were built as public architecture rather than for residential use. They based this belief on the lack of domestic "furniture" in ground-floor rooms (such as fire hearths and corn grinding bins), the large size of the rooms, and the small number of **burials** at these sites.

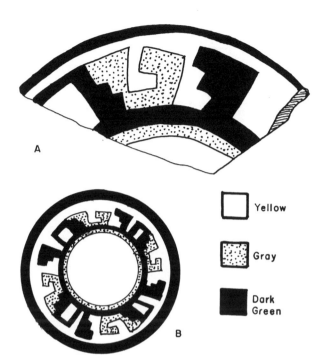

A

B

Yellow

Gray

Dark Green

FIGURE 72. Pseudo-cloisonné from Pueblo Bonito: (A) fragment of pseudo-cloisonné covered sandstone disc; maximum width of fragment is about 3.5 inches (9 cm); (B) hypothesized reconstruction of the entire disc.

FIGURE 73. Pyramid at Monte Albán. An example of public architecture in Mexico. (Arizona State Museum, University of Arizona.)

Generally, these archaeologists interpret great houses in one of two ways. Some argue that they were used for only brief periods of time each year by groups of related people who came together for ceremonies to celebrate their unity. Others believe that the great houses were staffed by a small group of religious elite who conducted rituals for pilgrims who visited Chaco Canyon for periodic ceremonies and trading fairs.

More archaeological work needs to be done to determine if great houses served only public needs. In many historic pueblos, residents did not occupy the ground-floor rooms, reserving them instead for storage. In addition, information on burial practices at Chaco Canyon is too limited to assume that great houses were not residential structures.

Pueblo Alto [Spanish for "high town"]
(Map 4; Figure 74)
A late Chacoan **great house** on the mesa above the canyon approximately one-half mile north of **Pueblo Bonito**. Pueblo Alto is also known as Old Alto to differentiate it from **New Alto,** a **McElmo-style** great house about one-quarter mile to the west and connected to Old Alto by a low wall. A similar wall extends east of the great house and then turns south toward the canyon.

Construction of this classic D-shaped great house began around A.D. 1020 and continued into the late 1000s through several additions. The front arc of rooms was added in the early 1100s. Today the structure has almost no exposed standing walls, a result of its windswept mesa-top location and the fact that it was never more than one story high.

Pueblo Alto is the sixth largest of canyon great houses in total area and has about 120 rooms and 18 kivas. Unlike most other great houses of the same time, Pueblo Alto does not appear to have a **great kiva**.

Pueblo Alto's mesa-top location may have been purposefully selected for communication with other great houses. **Una Vida, Tsin Kletsin,** and **Peñasco Blanco** can be seen from Pueblo Alto, and

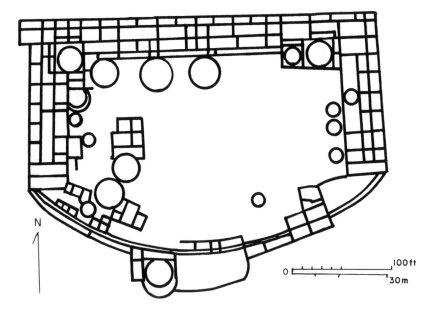

FIGURE 74. Pueblo Alto great house ground plan. The site has not been completely excavated; room and kiva wall tops were defined by the Chaco Project. Doorways are not shown. No great kiva is known for this site.

Peñasco Blanco, in turn, is visible from a number of canyon bottom great houses.

Pueblo Alto was also the focal point for a number of Chacoan **roads** leading toward the canyon from the north, including the **Great North Road**. Several of these roads converged on a narrow opening in a wall extending from the northeast corner of the great house, while another road passed just to the west of the building.

The site was selected for partial excavation by the **Chaco Center**, and major work was carried out there from 1976 to 1978 by Thomas **Windes** and several other **Chaco Project** archaeologists. This undertaking included trenching the enormous refuse mound at the structure's southeast corner. The same mound was trenched in 1927 by Frank **Roberts** Jr., who was attempting to establish a Chacoan ceramic sequence based on the **stratigraphy** of great house **trash mounds**.

Puebloan

A term used to designate a broad cultural tradition or lifeway present in the Southwest from at least A.D. 500 to the present. Chacoan culture is part of the Puebloan tradition.

Puebloan culture is characterized by a sedentary agricultural lifestyle with limited seasonal movement. Sedentism probably resulted from a commitment to subsistence farming based on **maize**, beans, and squash. Early agricultural technology was simple, but in late prehistoric and historic periods, Puebloan peoples developed a variety of **water control** practices, including **irrigation**.

Sedentism also promoted more-permanent architecture, and by the A.D. 1200s most Puebloan peoples were building multiroom, multistory stone or adobe buildings with specialized rooms for living, storage, ritual, and other purposes. Ritual activities were often carried out in circular, square, or rectangular underground rooms called **kivas**.

Puebloan peoples are known for their well-developed ceramic tradition, which featured predominantly black-on-white geometric designs and coil-and-scrape production. Gray cooking wares and decorated orange and red wares (black-on-orange, black-on-red) were also common. Polychrome (usually red, black, and white) wares were rare during the early prehistoric periods but more common after A.D. 1300.

Puebloan social organization is based on the extended family, often linked through clans or through a structure of dual social units within a community. Political organization was centered at the village level, though loose and shifting confederacies of several villages were known from the historic period and probably existed in prehistoric communities, including those in the Chaco area. Trade was important to all Puebloan groups and often involved partnerships with other Puebloan and non-Puebloan peoples.

Ritual was conducted by trained priests who usually operated through specialized religious societies of initiated men. Ritual activities focused on both individual healing and community concerns such as weather control, healing, hunting, and war.

The **Pecos Classification** of stages of Puebloan development differentiates between **Basketmaker** and **Pueblo periods**, but many of the attributes distinguishing Puebloan culture were present late in the Basketmaker period.

Pueblo Bonito [Spanish for "beautiful town"]
(Map 4; Figure 75)
The best known of all Chacoan great houses, located at the center of **Downtown Chaco,** less than a half mile from **Pueblo Alto, Chetro Ketl, Pueblo del Arroyo**, **Kin Kletso,** and **Casa Rinconada**. Though it covers somewhat less ground space than Chetro Ketl, this D-shaped great house is the largest of all Chacoan great houses with almost 700 rooms, 32 **kivas**, and 3 **great kivas**.

Pueblo Bonito rose four stories on the north back wall and terraced down toward the plaza on three sides, taking advantage of passive solar heating as the winter sun sank low on the southern horizon. The plaza was closed on the south side by a row of rooms, and two walled trash mounds lay just outside the plaza enclosure. At least one Chacoan **road** approaches the building from the north, and there is good evidence for a road linking Pueblo Bonito with Casa Rinconada, the isolated great kiva on the opposite side of the canyon.

Pueblo Bonito was the object of two major excavation programs and, with the possible exception of Kin Kletso, is the most completely excavated of any great house in Chaco Canyon. As a result, its 300-year construction history is known in great detail. Beginning in the mid-800s as a large arced room block that rose three stories on the north, the structure was remodeled and enlarged at least seven times. Pueblo Bonito architects retained the original arced ground plan even while construction of most great houses in the early 1000s became more rectangular. However, the wings added to Pueblo Bonito at that time did conform to the new order. Final construction at the site occurred in the late 1000s and early 1100s.

Pueblo Bonito was the first Chacoan **great house** to be excavated. Richard **Wetherill** and the **Hyde Exploring Expedition** carried out seasonal work at the site from 1897 to 1900, opening 189 rooms and several kivas in the process. Neil **Judd** then conducted work in other parts of the building from 1921 to 1927. Minor work

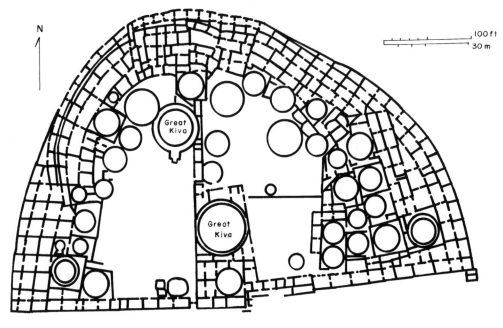

FIGURE 75. Pueblo Bonito great house ground plan. The structure has been completely excavated. Doorways are shown.

has been done at the site since that time by the National Park Service, some of the most significant being the collection by Thomas **Windes** and several colleagues of new tree-ring samples. This work proved that the building had been started in the 850s, almost seventy years earlier than previously thought.

Pueblo del Arroyo [Spanish for "town by the arroyo"]
(Map 4; Figure 76)
A Chacoan **great house** located a few hundred yards west of **Pueblo Bonito** in the heart of **Downtown Chaco.** In contrast with other canyon great houses, Pueblo del Arroyo was built in the middle of the canyon rather than against the north cliff, and faces east rather than south. The great house's location near **Chaco Wash**, for which it is named, placed it in danger from erosion as the wash shifted its course over the centuries.

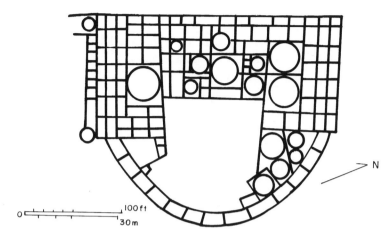

FIGURE 76. Pueblo del Arroyo great house ground plan. The site has not been completely excavated; locations of rooms and kivas in unexcavated portions are based on standing wall evidence. Doorways are not shown.

Pueblo del Arroyo is the fourth largest of the canyon great houses. It rose to four stories in the southern wing and had almost 300 rooms. The ground plan is the classic D-shape, with southern and northern wings and an enclosing arc of single rooms. It contains fourteen kivas, but no **great kiva** has been discovered at the site.

Construction of the central room block began in the 1060s, and the two wings were added about thirty years later. After the building was completed, a **tri-wall structure** was built to the west of the pueblo in the early 1100s. A number of small rooms were tacked onto the south side of the building sometime later.

About half of the site was excavated by Neil **Judd** between 1923 and 1926, along with the tri-wall structure. Judd believed the building may have been founded by a group from Pueblo Bonito when that great house could no longer hold its growing population. There is good evidence for a spur **road** coming to this site from the vicinity of **Pueblo Alto.**

Pueblo Period

A period of time in the Ancestral **Puebloan** culture that follows the

Basketmaker period and is characterized by a number of common traits, primarily the occupation of above-ground pueblos. In general, the broad period is marked by refinement of ceramics, greater dependence on agriculture, improvements in farming and storage technologies, increasingly sophisticated multiroom architecture using stone, and more trade with neighboring groups.

The Pueblo period was defined in the **Pecos Classification** and consists of five subperiods extending from Pueblo I (approximately A.D. 750–900) through Pueblo V, which includes historic and modern times. Although the original Pecos Classification established broad dates for each subperiod, those dates vary by region within the Puebloan (**Anasazi**) area. This is because each subperiod is identified by certain traits, and a lag in the appearance of one or more of those traits in some areas may delay the beginning of that subperiod.

Pueblo Pintado [Spanish for "painted town"]
(Map 2; Figure 77)
A Chacoan **great house** located about three miles east of the head of Chaco Canyon and about sixteen miles east of **Pueblo Bonito.** Built on the summit of a rounded ridge, the site is visible for miles from most directions and was the first great house encountered by all of the early expeditions that approached Chaco Canyon from the east. It is sometimes called a Chacoan **outlier** but is actually within the **Chaco Core.**

Pueblo Pintado is L-shaped with a central room block and a west wing, but no east wing. The arc of rooms that encloses the plaza on the south continues to the east, thereby creating an east "side" to the structure. It covers less ground area than most canyon great houses but has slightly more rooms (135 total) than **Pueblo Alto.** The pueblo rose to three stories, and possibly four. Unlike most great houses, the plaza contains a large mound that probably represents the remains of a room block. A later **Navajo** corral was also built into the northwest corner of the plaza. A **great kiva** was built southeast of the structure in the vicinity of a large **trash mound.**

Construction appears to have started at Pueblo Pintado in the

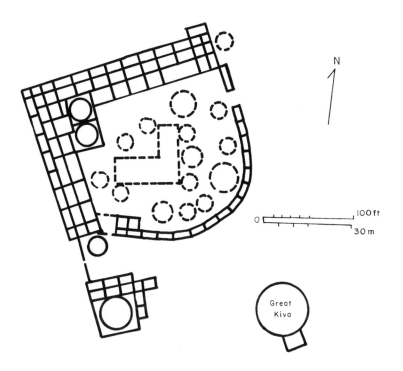

N

0 ⊢⊢⊢⊢⊢⊢⊢⊢⊢ 100 ft
⊢⊢⊢⊢⊢⊢⊢⊢⊢⊢ 30 m

Great
Kiva

FIGURE 77. Pueblo Pintado great house ground plan. The structure has not been excavated; locations of rooms and kivas are based on standing wall evidence. Locations of rooms and kivas in the plaza are based on limited surface evidence. Doorways are not shown.

1060s and probably continued through the late 1000s. The site has not been excavated, and few tree-ring dates have been collected. A **community** of more than thirty **small house sites** encircles the great house. At least one Chacoan **road** is present, the East or **Pintado-Chaco Road,** which begins near the southwest corner of the great house and runs west to the head of Chaco Canyon.

R

Rabbit Ruin
(Map 4; Figure 78)
Two **McElmo-style** buildings located on the mesa above the canyon, about a mile north of **Pueblo Bonito** and 300 yards north of **Pueblo Alto.** Only mounds of rubble are visible today, but test excavations

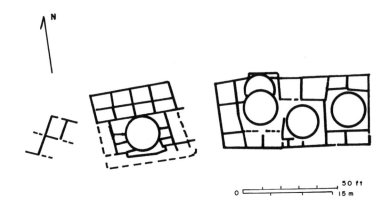

FIGURE 78. Rabbit Ruin ground plan. The east and west units are shown. Locations of rooms and kivas have been estimated based on surface evidence. Doorways are not shown.

by the **Chaco Center** revealed two buildings very similar to **New Alto**. The ruins are near the **Great North Road** but were probably not associated with it.

The eastern building is rectangular, containing about thirteen ground-floor rooms and three **kivas**. It is constructed of McElmo-style **core-and-veneer masonry** and may have been two stories high. The western building is smaller in area, with fourteen rooms and a central kiva, nearly duplicating the floor plan of New Alto. It was probably only one story high. A few rooms are present to the west of this building. One tree-ring date in the late 1080s from the eastern structure indicates a probable construction date in the late 1000s or early 1100s.

Radiocarbon Dating (see *Carbon-14 Dating*)

Rainfall

Precipitation that falls as rain, as opposed to snow, hail, or other forms of moisture. Rainfall, mostly from thunderstorms in July, August, and September, contributes at least half of the total annual **precipitation** in Chaco Canyon and the **San Juan Basin**. These summer storms were critical to prehistoric agriculture in the Chaco area. Summer rainfall at Chaco Canyon is extremely unpredictable because local thunder showers are produced by tropical storms pushing northward from the Gulf of Mexico or the Pacific Ocean. The San Juan Basin is on the northern fringe of these storm paths, and when moisture is not carried far enough, there is no rain in Chaco Canyon. The storm clouds must also pass over the mountains that border the basin on the south, dropping part, or all, of their rain before they reach Chaco, a classic example of the "rain shadow" effect.

While spring snowmelt provided moisture for germination of seeds and the growth of young plants, summer rainfall was necessary for the later development of **corn**, beans, and squash. However, because the thunderstorms were often so intense, much of the water would run off into washes. **Water control** systems were necessary to take advantage of the summer rains for farming.

Ramada [from the Spanish *enramada*, meaning "shade" or "bower"] *(Figure 79)*
An open, brush-covered shade structure supported by upright wooden posts. In historic southwestern pueblos, ramadas were typically placed in front of buildings and served to protect work areas

FIGURE 79. Contemporary Tohono O'odham ramada similar to prehistoric southwestern structures. (Arizona State Museum, University of Arizona; Helga Teiwes, photographer.)

from the summer heat. Other native groups in the Southwest also used ramadas. Post holes found in front of room **suites** in Chacoan **great houses** and **small house sites** have been interpreted as evidence for use of ramadas.

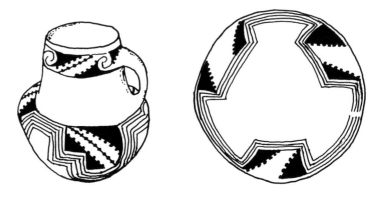

FIGURE 80. Red Mesa Black-on-white pitcher and bowl forms with decorative motifs and design layout common to this type.

Red Mesa Black-on-white

(Figure 80)

A **Cibola White Ware** decorated **pottery** type commonly found at Pueblo I period sites in the **San Juan Basin**. Red Mesa Black-on-white was produced from about A.D. 875 to 1040, making it one of the longest-lived Cibola White Ware pottery types. Like the earlier **La Plata Black-on-white**, Red Mesa pottery featured black geometric designs painted with mineral pigments of iron oxide. It was named and described by Harold **Gladwin** based on his work in the **Red Mesa Valley**.

Bowls are the predominant Red Mesa container form, but pitchers, dippers, effigy duck pitchers, and globular jars, often with lug handles on the shoulder, were also made. Design motifs are almost exclusively geometric. The most frequent elements include solid triangles, with or without ticked edges, interlocking scrolls, dotted lines (also called "barbed wire lines"), and wavy or straight lines. Elements are often combined. Line work is usually fine, and the use of parallel lines to frame other motifs was a common practice. Bowl designs generally encircle the top half of the bowl interior, leaving the bottom undecorated. Bowl rims are always painted black. Pottery with similar designs, but executed in carbon paint (from plants), was made outside the Chaco area, including Cortez Black-on-white in the **Mesa Verde** region.

The undecorated cooking ware used during early production of Red Mesa Black-on-white was Kana'a Neckbanded, which featured coils of clay around the neck of the vessel that were flattened, but not smoothed. This was gradually replaced by narrow neckbanded, and by the 1000s, indented **corrugated** was the primary cooking pottery type. As production of Red Mesa Black-on-white declined in the early 1000s, **Escavada Black-on-white** and **Gallup Black-on-white** became the dominant Cibola White Ware types.

Red Mesa Valley

(Map 1)

A large valley on the southern edge of the **San Juan Basin** that was densely populated in prehistoric times. It was the location of several Chacoan **outlier communities.** Harold **Gladwin** conducted intensive surveys of the area in the 1930s and excavated a number of sites that represented early developmental stages of Chacoan culture.

The valley is drained by the West Puerco River and extends from near Thoreau, New Mexico, on the east to Gallup, New Mexico, on the west. It is bordered on the north by dramatic red sandstone cliffs.

Remote Sensing

The location of prehistoric buildings, **roads, canals,** and other features from a distant vantage point using aerial photography and other scientific techniques. Several kinds of aerial photography—including infrared, stereoscopic, and high altitude imaging—have been employed in the Chaco area, especially for tracing roads. Aerial photography can detect both surface and subsurface remains, and is an effective aid in mapping these features. The **Chaco Project** Remote Sensing Division carried out much of this work.

Reservoirs (see *Dams*)

Rincon [Spanish for "inside corner"]

Short side canyons that drain into Chaco Canyon from both the south and north. Larger side canyons on the north, extending a mile or more into the mesa, are generally named and are not considered "rincons" (for example, **Cly's Canyon**, **Mockingbird Canyon**, **Gallo Canyon**).

Water from almost all the rincons on the north side of the canyon between **Escavada Wash** and Mockingbird Canyon was collected prehistorically in a system of diversion **dams** and **canals** associated with **great houses** and diverted to **gridded fields** in the canyon bottom. Few **water control** systems are found on the south side of the canyon among the **small house sites.**

Roads

(Figure 81)

Engineered roadbeds, approximately thirty feet wide, that extend in several directions from **great houses** in Chaco Canyon, frequently linking **outlier communities** to the canyon great houses. At least eight roads lead from Chaco Canyon, and some have been traced for up to 35 miles. Several, such as the **Great North Road**, have projected distances of more than 50 miles. Approximately 130 miles of road have been verified through aerial photographs and ground surveys, but it is estimated that more than 250 miles existed. Structures are sometimes associated with Chacoan roads, including **berms** and **herraduras.**

Chacoan roads run in nearly straight lines for miles, passing over hills and ridges or across canyons rather than detouring around them. They often dogleg at high points to correct course, and herraduras are frequently present in these locations. In open country the roadbed is excavated a foot or more below ground surface, with the soil banked along the edge of the road. Where sandstone is present, the roads are often cleared to bedrock and edged with a low stone wall. Roads entered canyons by way of ramps or wide steps cut into the rock, such as the **Jackson Staircase**.

Several puzzling details suggest that the roads were more than mere thoroughfares. In some areas, short stretches of two or four parallel roads were built no more than sixty yards apart. In a few instances, grooves cut into the sandstone separate roadways that converge for short distances. Near Chaco Canyon, several roads divide into spur roads approximately nine feet wide that lead to different great houses in the canyon.

The **Wetherills** and Stephen **Holsinger** identified several of these roads near Chaco Canyon at the turn of the century, and Neil **Judd** documented their existence in the 1920s. In the 1950s, **Gordon Vivian** used aerial photography to trace features of a number of roads but misidentified a few as irrigation canals. **Gwinn Vivian** and Robert Buettner made the same mistake in the 1970s, but after recognizing their error they traced the routes of most roads in Chaco Canyon. The **Chaco Project** Remote Sensing Division used multiple techniques for refining road identification and ground-truthing. These procedures were helpful for various project staff who reported on roads at canyon great houses and at **outliers**. Two major road studies conducted by Chris Kincaid, Fred Nials, John **Stein**, and John Roney for the Bureau of Land Management in the 1980s further documented roads leading into Chaco Canyon. Gretchen Obenauf and Gwinn Vivian have summarized and interpreted road studies.

Why Chacoans, who had no wheeled vehicles or pack animals, would build roads remains a mystery. Various answers have been proposed. Transportation of **pottery**, food, stone for chipped tools, and building **timbers** is a viable explanation, but human transport would not require such a wide road. David Wilcox, a southwestern archaeologist, has suggested that they were used to move soldiers to **outlier communities**, but there is no good evidence for a Chacoan military force.

Based on examples of roads in **Mesoamerica** and South America,

FIGURE 81. Groove cut in sandstone on a section of the road from Pueblo Alto to Chetro Ketl.

archaeologist Gwinn Vivian suggests most of the roads were long-distance routes that served some transportation needs but were primarily symbolic links between great houses in Chaco Canyon and the outlier communities. He maintains that the width and direct route of roads was necessary to make them visible for long distances and to underscore their symbolic function as a link between a "mother" great house in Chaco Canyon and a "daughter" outlier community. John Roney, an archaeologist with Chacoan experience, believes that only the **North** and **South Roads** were long-distance routes. In his scenario, all others were short segments built near great houses to promote social cohesion of the local community. Other archaeologists believe that their purpose was purely practical.

Roberts, Frank, Jr.

A southwestern archaeologist who carried out important fieldwork at a number of Chacoan sites. Roberts began his career in southwestern Colorado in 1921 as a student on field projects that included the investigation of the **Chimney Rock Outlier**. In 1926 he joined Neil **Judd** at **Pueblo Bonito** and used ceramic collections from several **great house** refuse mounds for his Ph.D. dissertation on the development of a Chacoan ceramic sequence. His work, along with studies by Florence **Hawley**, served as the basis for identification of Chacoan **pottery** types.

Roberts returned to Chaco in 1927 as an employee of the Bureau of American Ethnology to carry out excavations at **Shabik'eshchee Village**, a **Basketmaker** site. His report stood for decades as the primary source on the San Juan Basketmaker culture, and his knowledge of this time period was useful to Alfred Kidder in drafting the **Pecos Classification**. From 1929 to 1933 he worked in the **Zuni** area and excavated the **Village of the Great Kivas Outlier** in 1930. His interest in Chaco continued with teaching stints at the University of New Mexico Chaco Field School in 1940 and 1941.

Roberts had many other archaeological interests, including conducting fieldwork in Paleoindian sites, assisting Gila Pueblo on **Hohokam** excavations, and directing the extensive River Basin Survey program for the National Park Service.

Rock Art

Painted, pecked, or incised geometric and figural designs on rock surfaces. Painted images are usually called **pictographs**; designs cut into the surface are **petroglyphs.** Rock art is an ancient tradition that occurs worldwide.

Rock art in the Chaco area falls into three time periods, each with a distinctive style: Late **Archaic, Puebloan**, and **Navajo**. The few Late Archaic images are mostly human stick figures painted in dark red ochre, often on the ceilings or back walls of rock shelters.

Most of the petroglyphs found along the canyon walls date from the **Pueblo period**. The images, normally pecked into the surface in broad lines, include spirals, mazes, blanket or textile designs, and various animals such as mountain sheep and birds. Stylized human figures are also commonly portrayed, occasionally in groups. One of the best known set of spirals is the **Sun Dagger** solstice marker.

Navajo rock art is almost always incised with thin, shallow lines. Occasionally they are ground into the rock surface. Unlike earlier rock art, the Navajo images are often narrative, portraying humans hunting, riding horseback, or joining in a social dance. Horses, with or without riders, are commonly depicted, as are more modern forms of travel such as trucks and trains. More esoteric images include panels of Ye'i, the Navajo deities.

Though technically not rock art, numerous historic travelers, livestock herders, and local residents have left inscriptions on the canyon walls. Unfortunately, this practice still occurs today, a violation of the laws protecting the park.

Room-Wide Platforms

(Figure 82)

Large shelves made of beams set into the walls across one or both ends of rooms in Chacoan **great houses**. These platforms are about midway between the floor and ceiling, and average 4½ feet in width. As in roof construction, the beams were covered with shorter cross timbers and brush or juniper bark, then topped with packed mud to create a flat surface. When platforms were built in both ends of a room, they left only a narrow space between them.

These platforms have been found in several Chacoan great houses, including **Pueblo Bonito, Chetro Ketl, Pueblo Alto,** and the **Aztec Ruins**. They are also present at **Paquimé** in northern Chihuahua, Mexico. Although Neil **Judd** found the remains of five **macaws** on one platform at Pueblo Bonito, he believed the shelves were for storage and not just macaw perches. Charles **DiPeso** called the shelves at Paquimé "bed platforms," and some Chacoan archaeologists believe they may have served this function. Stephen **Lekson** cites room-wide platforms as one of the architectural attributes supporting his **Chaco Meridian** theory.

FIGURE 82. Room-wide platform in Pueblo Bonito. (Courtesy of Palace of the Governors Photo Archives, NHMH/DCA, neg. 66875.)

S

Salmon Ruin Outlier
(Map 1; Figure 83)

A Chacoan **great house** and **outlier community** located on the San Juan River approximately three miles west of Bloomfield, New Mexico, and forty-five miles north of Chaco Canyon. Archaeological surveys in the area of the great house have revealed a number of **small house sites**, but the limits of the community have not been defined.

Salmon Ruin was probably connected to Chaco Canyon via the **Great North Road**. Some archaeologists believe the most northern section of the **road** ran westward along the bottom of Kutz Canyon to its confluence with the San Juan River near Salmon Ruin. Others think that after leaving Chaco Canyon, it ended at the edge of Kutz Canyon about fifteen miles southeast of the Salmon outlier community.

The ground plan of the great house was bracket-shaped, but erosion and flooding from the San Juan River to the south of the great house may have removed or buried an arced row of rooms that enclosed the plaza. If they were present, the ground plan would have followed the classic D-shape of Chacoan great houses. The building had about 150 ground-floor rooms and approximately 100 second-story rooms. The site is noteworthy for apparently having only two Chaco-era kivas: an elevated **kiva** in the central room block and a **great kiva** in the plaza. In this respect, the site is similar to **Hungo Pavi** in Chaco Canyon.

Most of the great house construction took place between A.D. 1088 and 1100, a very short time span compared to many of the great houses in Chaco Canyon. Minor additions and remodeling were made until approximately A.D. 1130, when the Chacoan occupation may have ended. A major reoccupation and remodeling of the site by probable **Mesa Verde** immigrants started in the late 1180s and continued into the mid-1200s. The building was abandoned by the late 1200s.

Approximately 30 percent of the great house was excavated by Cynthia **Irwin-Williams** from 1972 to 1978 for the San Juan

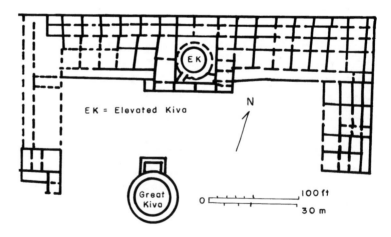

FIGURE 83. Salmon Ruin Outlier great house ground plan. The site has not been completely excavated; dashed lines represent unexcavated portions. Late Mesa Verde remodeling is not shown.

EK = Elevated Kiva

Great Kiva

N

0 100 ft
   30 m

County Museum Association, which was created specifically to purchase, preserve, and interpret the Salmon Ruins. Irwin-Williams prepared a number of annual reports on the excavations at Salmon Ruin, but final data analysis was delayed until 2001 when the Center for Desert Archaeology in Tucson initiated a multiyear program with the Museum Association to prepare and publish a final report. *Thirty-five Years of Archaeological Research at Salmon Ruins, New Mexico*, a three-volume report edited by Paul F. Reed, was published in 2006. The great house, a museum, and interpretive walks are open to the public.

San Juan Basin

(Map 1)

A large, relatively level basin in the northwestern corner of New Mexico that takes its name from the San Juan River, which drains its northern edge. Most of the 12,000-square-mile basin is drained by the **Chaco Wash**, which flows toward the west through the center of the basin and then turns northward to meet the San Juan River near Farmington, New Mexico.

The San Juan Basin is closely associated with Chacoan culture. Surrounded by mountains on four sides, it was a sphere of contact and social interaction even before the rise of the **Chaco Phenomenon**. As the Chacoan cultural system evolved, it spread throughout the region. Only a few confirmed Chacoan **outliers** have been found outside the basin.

The San Juan Basin is defined on the north by **Mesa Verde** and the La Plata and San Juan mountains. The San Pedro and Nacimiento mountains form the eastern border. Mount Taylor and the Cebolleta mountains anchor the southeastern corner and extend toward the **Dutton Plateau**. The Zuni Mountains mark the southern edge of the basin. The western border is created by the continuous chain of the **Chuska**, Lukachukai, and Carrizo mountain ranges. The most prominent landform within the basin is the **Chacra Mesa,** which is cut through in part by Chaco Canyon.

School of Advanced Research (see *School of American Research*)

School of American Research

A research facility in Santa Fe, New Mexico, that was founded in 1909 by Edgar **Hewett** to conduct archaeological projects in the Southwest and Mexico. Hewett served as the director of the institution until 1946. During much of this time the SAR, as it is commonly called, operated archaeological field schools at various southwestern sites, including Chaco Canyon. It sponsored much of Hewett's work at **Chetro Ketl** and continues to support anthropological research. As a result of increased worldwide research in anthropology, the facility's name was changed to the School of Advanced Research in 2007.

Sebastian, Lynne

A prominent Southwestern archaeologist with specializations in Chacoan prehistory and historic preservation. Sebastian is known primarily for her 1992 book, *The Chaco Anasazi: Sociopolitical Evolution in the Prehistoric Southwest*, in which she argued against the prevailing dependence in Chacoan studies on environmental causes for triggering social and political change and growth. In numerous publications, including her "The Chaco Synthesis" chapter in *The Archaeology of Chaco Canyon: An Eleventh-Century Pueblo Regional Center*, Sebastian has urged fellow scholars to move beyond the question of whether Chacoan society was politically based or ritually based and the use of analogies to modern pueblo societies. Instead, she recommends that archaeologists consider organizational models in the international ethnographic literature including sub-Saharan Africa.

Sebastian served for a number of years as the Historic Preservation Officer for the state of New Mexico and now provides similar preservation expertise for the Statistical Research Foundation in New Mexico.

Shabik'eshchee Village

(Map 3; Figure 84)

A **Basketmaker** village located about nine miles east of **Pueblo Bonito** on a flat-topped arm of the **Chacra Mesa** that overlooks the **Chaco Wash**. For many years, Shabik'eshchee was considered the type site for the **San Juan Basin** Basketmaker III period. A portion of the site was tested by Frank **Roberts** Jr. during the **National Geographic Society**'s 1926 field season in Chaco, and he continued work there in 1927 for the Bureau of American Ethnology.

Roberts excavated nineteen pithouses, forty-five storage cists, a **great kiva,** a stone- and adobe-paved courtyard, and a later **Pueblo** I period **pithouse** that he called a "proto-kiva." Two of the pithouses and the proto-kiva were located to the south of the main cluster of structures. Later work at the site by the National Park Service determined that as many as forty additional pithouses were probably present to the south of Roberts's excavations.

Two Chacoan researchers, Thomas **Windes** and Wirt **Wills**, have proposed that all of the pithouses were actually clustered in three areas. They believe the village may have served as a seasonal gathering place for Basketmaker families who lived in smaller hamlets scattered through the region the rest of the year.

Tree-ring dates from the site place construction of the great kiva and probably many of the pithouses in the mid-500s. Occupation may have lasted into the early 700s. The proto-kiva, courtyard, and a few pithouses may represent a Pueblo I reoccupation of the site sometime after A.D. 700.

Shrine

A place of special significance in **Puebloan** religion used for prayer, offerings, or other acts of reverence and respect. They are commonly placed at sacred points on the landscape such as springs, other water sources, and mountain peaks and can mark the cardinal directions. Often consisting of a small structure placed at a landscape feature, shrines may range from a single large stone to a pile of rocks or a small walled enclosure.

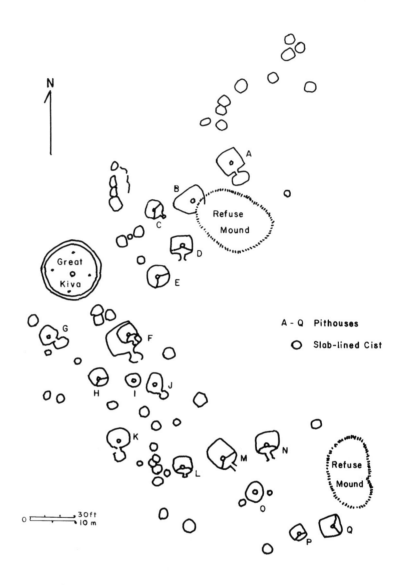

FIGURE 84. Shabik'eshchee Village site plan. The excavated portion of the site is shown.

A number of shrines and features believed to be shrines have been found in Chaco Canyon. Several of these are located at high points on the Chacra Mesa that provide a view of several **great houses.** One such shrine near the **Peñasco Blanco** great house consisted of a low, curving masonry wall protecting an enclosure of upright sandstone slabs that contained a carved sandstone bowl. A number of **turquoise** beads and several turquoise fragments were found in the bowl. From this location it is possible to see seven great houses.

Two similar shrines farther east on the **Chacra Mesa** are visible from the Peñasco Blanco location. All of the canyon great houses can be seen from these shrines, suggesting that they may have served as points for observing celestial phenomena such as solstices, and as **signal stations** for conveying that information to the canyon population.

Signal Stations

(Figure 85)
High points on the landscape or tall buildings that may have been used for sending simple messages across long distances through use of fires, smoke, or reflected sunlight. The presence of burned stone and charcoal at hilltop sites, including one west of **El Faro** at **Pierre's Outlier,** suggests they were used for signaling. **Tower kivas** at **Kin Klizhin** and **Kin Ya'a** may have served a similar purpose.

Some Chacoan sites, including **shrines,** may have been placed in certain locations to aid in sending signals. All of the great houses in Chaco Canyon can be seen from three shrines spaced along the **Chacra Mesa**. The appearance of the sun at horizon markers for the solstices and equinoxes may have been signaled to all canyon great houses from these viewing stations.

Similarly, the three Chaco great houses located above the canyon—**Pueblo Alto, Peñasco Blanco,** and **Tsin Kletsin**—have lines of sight to one another and to most canyon great houses, making them excellent points for transmitting messages. A number of **great houses** outside the canyon also are visible from the mesa-top buildings.

With the establishment of **outlier** great houses and communities in the middle to late 1000s, the need for signaling may have become greater, and messages probably could have been relayed across the **San Juan Basin** in several directions. Several nighttime tests of this theory carried out by National Park Service staff using flares were partially successful. In 2003 **Gwinn Vivian** and Douglas

FIGURE 85. Possible signal station butte in the Pierre's Outlier area.

Palmer, using small, hand-held mirrors, accomplished relatively short-distance signaling between **Tsin Kletsin** in Chaco Canyon and **Pierre's Outlier** on the **Great North Road**—a distance of about seventeen miles. Their later attempts to use selenite, a crystalline form of gypsum, for signaling were not successful. In 2007 the Colorado Archaeological Society used much larger mirrors to relay signals from the **Chimney Rock Outlier** to Chaco Canyon via **Tres Huerfanos** mesa. This experiment was moderately successful.

Simpson, James

One of the first Americans to explore Chaco Canyon and the first American to publish a report on the prehistoric sites found there. Lieutenant Simpson, of the Army Corps of Topographical Engineers, was a member of an 1849 military reconnaissance to the **Navajo** country led by Brevet Lieutenant Colonel John M. Washington, the chief of the ninth military department and governor of the Territory of New Mexico.

After leaving Jemez Pueblo with guides Francisco **Hosta** and **Carravahal** on August 22, the company arrived at **Pueblo Pintado** on August 26 and then traveled into Chaco Canyon on the 27th. Simpson and the **Kern** brothers sketched, mapped, and made surface collections at **Wijiji** and **Una Vida** before camping in the vicinity of **Fajada Butte**. On the 28th, Simpson, Richard Kern,

Carravahal, and several militia men left the main company, which moved out of the canyon at **Fajada Gap**, and traveled down canyon to the confluence of the **Chaco** and **Escavada** washes. Simpson and Kern spent the day recording Chacoan great houses, including **Hungo Pavi**, **Chetro Ketl**, **Pueblo Bonito**, **Pueblo del Arroyo**, and **Peñasco Blanco**.

Simpson's detailed notes and the Kerns' maps and drawings of potsherds, **rock art**, **masonry types**, and room interiors stood as the primary source on Chacoan sites for almost fifty years. The contemporary views and artist's reconstructions of the great houses in Simpson's report sparked considerable interest among eastern archaeologists and scholars.

Sipapu

A **Hopi** word for the place where people emerged from an earlier underworld into this world. In **Puebloan** religion, the Earth as we know it is the most recent of four worlds in which humans have lived. Events in each of the former worlds forced some people to move to a new world above, usually by climbing a hollow reed to a hole in the sky. The original *sipapu* is thought by many Hopi to be in the Little Colorado River near its confluence with the Grand Canyon.

Today this point of emergence is often commemorated in Puebloan **kivas** by a small pit in the floor. This pit, also called *sipapu*, is highly sacred and serves as a shrine by providing a connection with earlier worlds and the ancestors and spiritual beings who still live there.

Archaeologists often interpret small holes or pits in kiva floors at Chaco and elsewhere as *sipapus*, and in some instances they may be correct. But Puebloan peoples have a number of types of *sipapus*, such as plank-covered pits that may also be used as resonators or **foot drums**. Furthermore, it is not certain that all kivas had *sipapus*.

Skunk Springs Outlier

(Map 1; Figure 86)
One of the largest Chacoan **outliers** in the **Chuska Valley**, located

about fifty miles northwest of **Pueblo Bonito**. This large outlier community is in one of the major valleys draining the **Chuska Mountains** and occupies the top of a broad natural terrace and part of the valley below. The **great house**, which is on the terrace, is notable for having an irregular ground plan and two **great kivas** in a fronting plaza. The building seems to partially cover an earlier structure on the west side that also had a great kiva. The great house has not been excavated, but four elevated **kivas** and thirty-two rooms have been estimated for the structure, including some second-story rooms. Multiple **small house sites** are located west of the great house, but far greater numbers of these sites are on the valley floor. Mike Marshall and John **Stein** reported that these small house sites appear to be "lined in irregular streets" and constituted one of the most dense population centers in the prehistoric Southwest.

A possible Chacoan **road** is located to the south of the great house in the terrace edge. Harold **Gladwin** reported in 1928 that the **Navajos** described a "clay road" between the Skunk Springs Outlier and **Pueblo Bonito** that was used for carrying pine logs to Chaco Canyon.

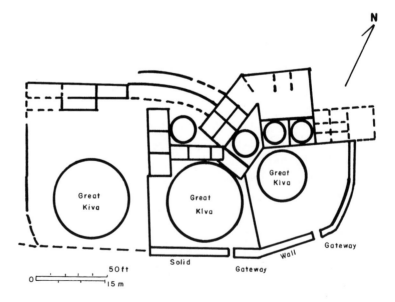

FIGURE 86. Skunk Springs Outlier great house ground plan. The site has not been excavated; locations of rooms and kivas have been estimated from ground surface evidence. Doorways are not shown.

Small House Sites

Small masonry pueblos that were built at the same time as Chacoan **great houses,** but which differ architecturally in many respects. These buildings seldom contain more than twenty rooms. Construction was almost always single-story, and **core-and-veneer** masonry was rare. Rooms were less than half the size of most great house rooms, roof lines were lower, and shorter roof timbers were cut locally from nearby stands of pinyon, juniper, and cottonwood. Although small houses had a standard floor plan that changed somewhat through time, there is no evidence for the planned growth and large-scale additions seen at great houses. Typically, several small house sites were clustered to form a **community.**

Enclosed plazas are rare at these sites, and **great kivas** are not found at individual small houses. However, community great kivas such as **Casa Rinconada** were sometimes built to serve several small houses. The term "small house site" generally has replaced the earlier use of "village."

Small houses first appeared in the late A.D. 700s and early 800s, predating Chacoan great houses by fifty to seventy-five years. Early small house sites usually consisted of a slightly arced row of rooms, two to three rooms deep, fronted by one or more **pithouses** or **kivas.** In time the structures became rectangular, with kivas usually incorporated into the room block. **Masonry types** also grew more sophisticated: early walls were usually built using simple masonry a single block wide; later structures often used compound masonry.

There are hundreds of small house sites in Chaco Canyon, mostly on the south side of the canyon opposite several of the great houses. Archaeologists generally agree that small house sites were used as residences by groups of people linked through kinship or marriage. Many archaeologists also believe that small house sites were associated with one or more great houses to form distinct communities within the canyon. This concept of a community is best illustrated in Chacoan **outlier** sites where a great house is often surrounded by small house sites. If such communities were present in Chaco Canyon, it is difficult to draw boundaries between them because of the dense placement of small house sites.

Clyde Kluckhohn, a noted American anthropologist, codirected the 1937 University of New Mexico Archaeological Field School excavations at **Bc Sites** 50 and 51, small house sites near Casa Rinconada. His resulting report, published in 1939, included the proposal that inhabitants of great houses and small house sites may have been different ethnic populations who spoke different languages. Kluckhohn's suggestion was further explored by both **Gordon** and **Gwinn Vivian** in several of their published interpretations of Chacoan prehistory.

Systematic investigation of small house sites did not begin until the 1930s. Based on his work in the **Red Mesa Valley**, Harold **Gladwin** assigned small house sites to his **Hosta Butte phase**. The practice of associating these sites with this phase designation was continued by Gordon Vivian. The **Chaco Project** excavated a number of small house sites, especially in **Marcia's Rincon**. An excellent synthesis of small house studies, including later work conducted by the **Chaco Center**, was prepared by Chaco Center archaeologists Marcia Truell and Peter McKenna.

A number of small house sites have been excavated in Chaco Canyon, and several examples in the Casa Rinconada area are interpreted for the public.

Smithsonian Institution

The national museum of the United States in Washington, D.C. The Smithsonian was the scientific cosponsor of research carried out in Chaco Canyon by Neil **Judd** from 1920 to 1927 for the **National Geographic Society**. The artifact collections from these excavations are now held by the Smithsonian's Museum of Natural History.

Sofaer, Anna

An artist who discovered the **Sun Dagger**, a petroglyph on **Fajada Butte** that records the solstices and equinoxes. Sofaer and Jay Crotty found the Sun Dagger in 1977 while volunteering on a long-term project to record **rock art** in Chaco Canyon. Sofaer, Rolf Sinclair, and others later researched not only the solar aspects of the site, but the potential for it to record major and minor lunar standstills. Sofaer has devoted the past fifteen years to a study of the solar and lunar aspects of Chacoan **great houses** and believes that their orientations, locations, internal geometry, and geographic relationships are linked to the cycles of the sun and the moon. She and Sinclair have published several articles on this research, and she has produced two video documentaries, *The Sun Dagger* and *The Mystery of Chaco Canyon*.

Southeast Road

A hypothetical Chacoan road believed by some to have extended from **Fajada Gap** in Chaco Canyon to the eastern end of the **Red Mesa Valley** near Grants, New Mexico. Short segments of Chacoan **roads** located near **outlier** great houses in the valley such as Kin Nizhoni and Haystack were thought to be branches of this longer road. However, based on intensive analysis of aerial photographs and partial ground surveys carried out in the 1980s by the Bureau of Land Management, it has been determined that this road probably did not exist. Connections between known segments of roads within the Red Mesa Valley area have not been confirmed.

South Gap

(Maps 2, 3, 4)

A broad, low-lying break in the **Chacra Mesa** opposite **Pueblo del Arroyo** and **Pueblo Bonito**. Water flows into Chaco Canyon through this gap, creating an especially well-watered zone where it meets the **Chaco Wash**. This may account for the establishment of Pueblo Bonito at this location in the mid-800s.

The **Coyote Canyon Road** enters Chaco Canyon through the South Gap, running along the base of the cliff on the western side of the break. The **South Road** is also thought to enter this gap on the east side. Travel through South Gap continued in historic times, when it was the route to Crownpoint and Gallup, New Mexico.

South Road

(Map 2)

A Chacoan road that has been traced from a point about seven miles south of Chaco Canyon to the **Kin Ya'a Outlier** near Crownpoint, New Mexico. Another short segment of the road runs south of Kin Ya'a and climbs the **Dutton Plateau**. If it continues over the plateau, it would enter the **Red Mesa Valley,** an area that was heavily populated during Chacoan times.

It is uncertain where this road enters Chaco Canyon. It is believed that the South Road may have split somewhere in the Kin Klizhin Valley, with one branch entering the canyon through the **South Gap** and another through the **Fajada Gap**. A short segment of road known as the Rincon or Latrine Road in the Fajada Gap is assumed to be a part of the South Road. While traces of the **Coyote Canyon Road** can be seen on the west side of the South Gap, no evidence of the South Road on the east side has been found.

Continuous segments of the South Road can be traced for about twenty-five miles, making it only slightly shorter than the **Great North Road**. Like the Great North Road, there also is some evidence for two parallel roads in some places.

Spalls

Small flakes, chips, or fragments of stone pressed into the plaster or mortar of Chacoan walls in Type I and Type II **veneer styles**. They may have served as a kind of lath to help hold plaster to the walls.

Stabilization (or Ruins Stabilization)

The use of various construction techniques to strengthen and stabilize walls and other features of a building. At Chaco Canyon, ruins stabilization has been used on **great houses, small house sites, great kivas,** and other archaeological features with exposed architecture. This work does not include reconstruction of rooms.

A number of stabilization procedures have been used at Chaco through the years, including capping the tops of walls, filling holes in walls, replacing mortar in exposed wall faces, bracing slumping walls, and **backfilling**. Most exposed walls in the canyon have been capped with about eighteen inches of stone laid in a hard cement mortar to protect the walls below from erosion.

Ruins stabilization was practiced by the early archaeologists in Chaco Canyon, including Neil **Judd** and Edgar **Hewett**. A National Park Service Stabilization Unit was created in the 1930s by **Gordon Vivian** and staffed by local **Navajos**, some of whom had worked for Judd and Hewett. A number of Navajo families, such as the **Weritos, Clys,** and Trujillos, have produced several generations of expert masons, and their descendants work today for the National Park Service Stabilization Unit.

Standing Rock Outlier

(Map 1; Figure 87)
A Chacoan **outlier** great house and **community** located approximately thirty miles southwest of Chaco Canyon near the present-day Standing Rock Trading Post, about ten miles west of Crownpoint, New Mexico. One of several outliers in this sector of the **Chacoan World,** it is believed to be linked to Chaco Canyon by the **Coyote**

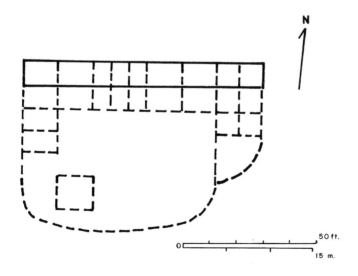

FIGURE 87. Standing Rock Outlier great house ground plan. The site has not been excavated; locations of rooms and kivas have been estimated from surface evidence.

Canyon Road, a segment of which passes by the **great house**. At least one other well-defined **road** segment approaches the Standing Rock outlier from the north.

The Standing Rock community consists of a great house, an associated **great kiva,** and as many as forty **small house sites**. The great house is a small-scale D-shaped structure with about twenty-five ground-floor rooms. Mound height suggests a second story in some areas with as many as a dozen additional rooms. There are no tree-ring dates from this site. Ceramic evidence suggests that the small house sites were occupied as early as the A.D. 800s; the great house was probably constructed and occupied in the late 1000s and early 1100s. The site is protected by the Navajo Nation.

Stein, John

An archaeologist with a long history of Chacoan-related research and publication who has served for years as an archaeologist for the Navajo Nation. Stein's earliest work, from 1977 to 1979, focused on the comprehensive documentation of Chacoan **outlier** sites in the **San Juan Basin** in advance of ongoing and proposed coal, oil, natural gas, and uranium development. The survey and subsequent report, *Anasazi Communities of the San Juan Basin*, prompted federal agencies and the Navajo Nation to protect many of the located sites. Stein later assisted in a Bureau of Land Management study of Chacoan **roads** designed to protect these features from land development. Some of his most comprehensive work was carried out as an archaeologist for the Navajo Nation and included a survey of Chacoan and post-Chacoan sites in the Manuelito region west of Gallup, New Mexico. He has been instrumental in the ongoing efforts of the Chaco Sites Protection Program.

Stein's interest in Chacoan architecture has centered on his interpretation of **Chaco** as a highly evolved ritual center and the evolution of what he terms "Anasazi ritual landscapes." While he views small house sites as domestic structures, he sees great houses as thresholds "to the existential realm" and ritual landscapes as the focus of the "**Anasazi** nation."

FIGURE 88. Stone basin on mesa top near Pueblo Bonito.

Stone Basins

(Figure 88)

Shallow man-made basins cut into the bedrock on the cliff tops above Chaco Canyon. The round basins average about three inches deep and range from seven to twenty inches in diameter. Usually the sides and bottom are slightly curved. Three of the almost fifty known basins in Chaco Canyon are rectangular. Most are found within **stone circles**, and several can be seen on the backcountry walk to **Pueblo Alto**.

After studying these basins, Thomas **Windes** determined that they were not for collecting water, supporting posts, or holding water jars. There also was no evidence that they had been used for fires. Because so many of the basins were associated with stone circles, which Windes believes had a ritual function, he concluded that they probably held materials related to ceremonies carried out in the circles.

FIGURE 89. Stone circle on mesa top west of Pueblo Bonito. South Gap is in the background.

Stone Circles

(Figure 89)

Circular, oval, or occasionally rectangular stone enclosures found on the cliff tops above Chaco Canyon. While many of these circles consist only of scatters of loose stones today, they were originally low masonry walls.

Of the twenty known sites, almost all are on the north side of the canyon. They range from 30 to 105 feet long, and 23 to 65 feet across. They contain almost no archaeological features other than **stone basins,** and very few artifacts have been found in the circles.

Gwinn Vivian originally interpreted the stone circles as **water control** devices designed to slow water as it moved over the bedrock cliff to terraced gardens below. Thomas **Windes**'s analysis of stone circles suggested to him that they probably had a ritual function associated with canyon **great houses.** He pointed out that **great kivas** and **shrines** were observable from every stone circle, and suggested that the circles may have been used for ceremonial events or dances.

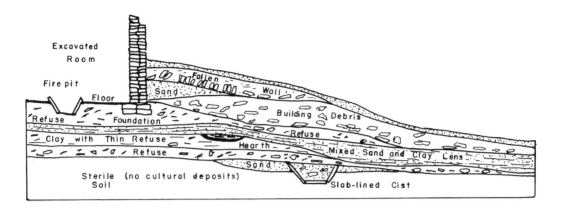

FIGURE 90. Stratigraphic profile. Cross section of stratigraphy showing cultural and noncultural deposits before, during, and after construction and occupation of a pueblo room.

Stratigraphy

(Figure 90)

The graphic representation of the layering of soils and cultural materials in archaeological sites, usually studied to determine the relative ages of the layers. Under normal circumstances, when one layer of materials lies below another, the lower layer was deposited first, making it older than the layer above (the law of superposition). However, the identification of different layers and the interpretation of disturbed deposits can often be a complex and difficult process.

Stratigraphy was originally developed by scientists studying geological deposits, but the practice was quickly adopted by archaeologists who realized that they could trace the history of a room, a **trash mound**, or a site by charting and analyzing different layers of deposits. This **dating technique** has been especially useful in the relative dating of ceramic styles because fragments of **pottery** found in the various layers of a site often have different design motifs. Similar changes in other kinds of tools can also be analyzed and dated.

The use of stratigraphy in the Southwest was first introduced by archaeologist Nels Nelson in the early 1900s. Along with his young assistant, Earl **Morris**, Nelson trenched the **Pueblo Bonito** trash mound in 1916 to record its stratigraphy. Neil **Judd** and Frank

Roberts Jr. later trenched this same mound but found the ceramic sequence very confusing. They eventually determined that the ancient Chacoans had moved the trash mound several times and in doing so had placed older deposits on top of more-recent refuse, creating what archaeologists call "reverse stratigraphy."

Suites (or Chacoan Room Suites)

(Figure 91)

A series of connected rooms that served as a living unit in prehistoric pueblos. Room suites were found in both Chacoan **great houses** and **small house sites**. Early suites in these structures are similar, consisting of one or more living rooms backed by two small horizontally connected storage rooms. The rooms were linked front-to-back by doorways. **Ramadas** were usually built in front of the living rooms.

Room blocks at early great houses and small house sites consisted of several room suites built side by side. Each ran the depth of

FIGURE 91. Temporal changes in great house room suite patterns. All dates are approximate, and some patterns overlap time periods: (a) A.D. 920–1000; (b) 1020–1040; (c) 1050–1060; (d) 1060–1075; (e) 1095–1105; (f) 1105+

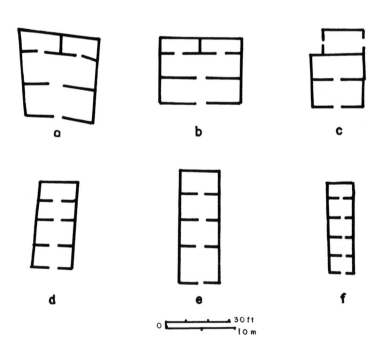

the building. Usually a plaza containing several **kivas** fronted the room block. Room suite patterns changed over time in Chacoan great houses. In general, they maintained a linear orientation, with room size decreasing from the front, or plaza side, of the building to the rear rooms. The small paired storage rooms at the rear of the suite were replaced by a single room sometime after A.D. 1020.

Room suites are not as easily defined in early 1100s buildings such as **Kin Kletso**; Stephen **Lekson** believes that the room suite pattern was discontinued at this time in favor of many interconnected rooms.

Sun Dagger

(Figure 92)

A set of petroglyphs at the top of **Fajada Butte** that indicates annual solstices and equinoxes. Located approximately three miles southeast of **Pueblo Bonito**, the site consists of two spiral **petroglyphs** pecked on a cliff face and three large sandstone slabs that lean against the cliff. Spaces between the slabs permit light to strike the cliff face at different times during the day. In 1977, Anna **Sofaer** discovered that a shaft of light, which she called a "sun dagger," struck the cliff and moved down through the center of the larger spiral on the day of the summer solstice.

Sofaer's later work on Fajada Butte, produced with assistance from Rolf Sinclair, revealed that with the sun's movement through the year, the winter solstice and the spring and autumn equinoxes were marked by sun daggers moving through one or both spirals on the cliff face. Sofaer, Sinclair, and L. Doggett have since proposed that the spirals also record the far northern rising positions of the moon at its major and minor "standstills."

Access to the site is closed because of its fragile nature and out of respect for Native American religious beliefs.

Supernova Pictograph

(Map 3; Figure 93)

A **pictograph** with three design elements that some archaeologists

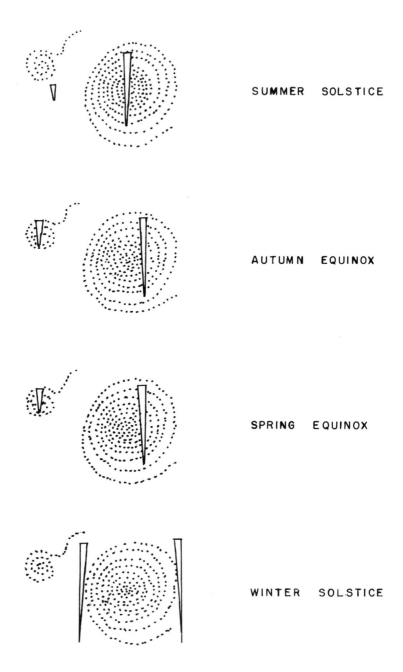

SUMMER SOLSTICE

AUTUMN EQUINOX

SPRING EQUINOX

WINTER SOLSTICE

FIGURE 92. Sun Dagger solstice and equinox markings.

FIGURE 93. Supernova pictograph.

believe is a depiction of a supernova event in A.D. 1054. The picto-graph consists of a ten-pointed reddish "star" (the assumed super-nova), a dark red crescent (believed to be the moon in crescent phase), and a white handprint (possibly the sign of the person re-cording the event). It is painted on the ceiling of a small natural cliff overhang at the western end of Chaco Canyon below **Peñasco Blanco.**

Based on Chinese accounts of the appearance of this supernova during a crescent phase of the moon, some archaeoastronomers have interpreted this rock art panel as a Chacoan recording of the celestial event. A supernova is a star that grows very bright for a short period and then returns to its normal size. The remnant of this supernova is now called the Crab Nebula in the constellation of Taurus the Bull.

Others who have studied **Puebloan** rock art believe the picto-graph may only represent Venus in the night sky at the time of a crescent moon, with a white hand serving as a clan symbol.

Though seldom noted, a large, light red and yellow pictograph on the cliff face just below the supernova pictograph appears to represent a comet. If this is true, some believe it may be a depiction of Halley's Comet.

T

Talus Unit

(Map 4; Figure 94)

A small building at the base of the cliff several hundred feet west of **Chetro Ketl** and less than a quarter mile east of **Pueblo Bonito**. The structure consists of two buildings joined by two rooms. The east building has eight rooms, two of which enclose **kivas**. The west building is larger, containing about twenty ground-floor rooms and five kivas.

The east building of the Talus Unit apparently served as the access point to a Chacoan **road** on the cliff above. The two largest rooms were filled with earth and may have served as a landing for a timber ladder extending up to steps cut in a cleft in the sandstone

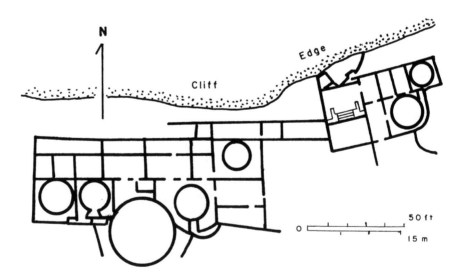

FIGURE 94. Talus Unit ground plan. Masonry steps and ladder platform are located in the east unit of the site.

cliff face. Above the steps, a spur road led to the **Pueblo Alto** great house. Masonry steps in the front room gave access to the landing.

The floor plan of the west building of the Talus Unit is typical of the early stages of **great houses**. Two short wings, now mostly filled with kivas, were added to a central rectangular room block. Several of the kivas are constructed of **McElmo-style** masonry and are considered late additions. Like most Chacoan great houses, the rear rooms rose to three stories and terraced down toward the front (south) of the building. Tree-ring dates from both buildings fall mostly within the A.D. 1060–70 period, though lintels from one door in the east building date from the early 1030s.

The site was partially excavated in the 1930s by Edgar **Hewett**. More limited work by the National Park Service was done in the late 1950s, and Stephen **Lekson** summarized all information on the site in 1985. The presence of freestanding "piers" (large solid blocks of masonry) in the buildings and a platform landing have caused considerable speculation about the function of the Talus Unit. The earth-filled landing has been interpreted by some archaeologists as a **platform mound,** but its purpose appears to be largely related to providing access up the cliff face. The west building seems to be an early stage in great house development and may represent an off-shoot from Chetro Ketl.

Tanoan

One of four **Puebloan** language groups in the Southwest. Tanoan speakers, who belong to the larger Kiowa-Tanoan language family, live in the northern and central Rio Grande Valley of New Mexico. Tanoan religion and social organization differ from those of their Puebloan neighbors, the **Keresan** speakers in the Rio Grande Valley and the **Hopi** and **Zuni** peoples. Oral history, pottery, and architecture suggest that some Chacoans may have been Tanoan speakers.

Tanoan speakers are divided into three language subgroups: Towa, Tiwa, and Tewa. The sole Towa-speaking pueblo today is Jemez; Pecos Pueblo was a Towa village, but its few remaining residents moved to Jemez in 1838. Tiwa speakers live at Taos and Pícuris pueblos in the northern Rio Grande Valley, and at Isleta and Sandia pueblos about a hundred miles to the south. In between are the Tewa villages of San Juan, Santa Clara, San Ildefonso, Pojoaque, Tesuque, and Nambe. A colony of Tewa speakers moved to First Mesa at Hopi in historic times, and their Tewa-speaking descendants still live in the village of Hano. There are more than 10,000 enrolled tribal members in the combined Rio Grande villages.

Temper (or Ceramic Temper)

A substance added to clay when producing **pottery** to make it easier to work and to prevent breakage during the firing process. Temper reduces the stickiness of the clay and makes it more porous so that steam can escape when it is heated. **Organic materials** (such as grass and tree bark) and inorganic materials (such as sand and crushed rock) can be used as temper.

Puebloan ceramics traditionally were tempered with sand, crushed rock, or crushed potsherds. Analysis of pottery found at Chaco Canyon has shown that most was tempered with minerals found only in areas outside the **Chaco Core**. This indicates that most of the pottery was traded into Chaco, much of it from the **Chuska Valley** to the west.

Threatening Rock

(Figure 95)
A 150-foot-long section of sandstone cliff behind **Pueblo Bonito** that fell into the **great house** on January 22, 1941. When the 30,000-ton rock collapsed, it crushed the tallest part of the back wall and destroyed or damaged about sixty-five rooms.

The Chacoans showed their concern for this threat by building a massive masonry buttress beneath the rock and wedging large support timbers into cracks at the bottom. For a final measure of protection, they also placed ritual prayer sticks into crevices in the rock.

"Threatening Rock" is the name given to the stone by the National Park Service; it was known during **Wetherill**'s time as

FIGURE 95. Threatening Rock in 1901. Forty years later it collapsed onto Pueblo Bonito. (Courtesy of Palace of the Governors Photo Archives, NMHM/DCA, neg. 6153.)

"the Elephant." The Navajo name for Pueblo Bonito translates roughly as "the house where the rocks are propped up."

Three-C Site
(Map 3; Figure 96)

A **small house site** located in **Marcia's Rincon** in the **Fajada Gap** about three miles east of Pueblo Bonito. The nine-room, single-story room block was fronted by two **kivas** and a **trash mound**. No tree-ring dates were collected from the site, but associated **ceramics** suggest an occupation between about A.D. 870 and 950. The site was occupied during the initial construction phases of the **Pueblo Bonito** great house.

Early salvage excavations of the room block were made in 1939 by **Gordon Vivian** when a Civilian Conservation Corps camp was built on the site. He returned in 1949 to excavate the two kivas. The **Chaco Project** later excavated several small house sites just north of the Three-C Site.

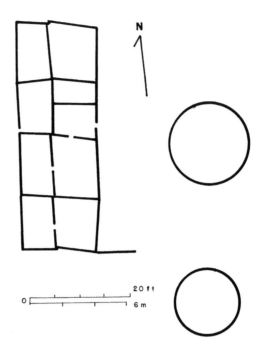

N

20 ft
0
6 m

FIGURE 96. Three-C Site ground plan. Doorways are shown.

Timber

Wood used for construction purposes, primarily as beams and lintels. Chacoan builders used enormous quantities of timber in their **great houses.** Because of the local scarcity of suitable trees, most of this wood was imported from forests up to a hundred miles from Chaco Canyon. Archaeologists have estimated that as many as 200,000 trees were cut and carried into Chaco for use in great houses. Many of these beams probably came from the **Chuska Mountains** to the west of Chaco Canyon and the Zuni Mountains to the south. Recent experimental work involving chemical analyses of trace elements in trees and the associated rocks and soils they grow in holds promise for identifying more precisely the source of many timbers.

A remarkable quantity of original wood, including complete intact roofs, was preserved in Chacoan great houses. As a result, archaeologists such as Jeffrey Dean and Thomas **Windes** have been able to determine the species used and, through **dendrochronol-**

ogy, the year the logs were cut. By studying the outermost growth ring, they have even been able to tell the time of year that logs were harvested.

Timbers used in great houses contrasted markedly with those in **small house sites**, especially in the 1000s. Wood in the small houses was obtained locally and consisted of juniper, pinyon, and cotton-wood. Most of the wood used in great houses was ponderosa pine, but spruce and fir were also collected in distant mountains.

The large-scale building projects at great houses undoubtedly called for stockpiling timber and for coordinating work groups to cut and transport the beams. They were cut to predetermined lengths, barked, dried, and then transported to Chaco. Most of the cutting was apparently done in the spring. However, the details of the timber industry remain a matter of conjecture. The specific tools used, the exact locations of the timber camps, and the amount of labor required for cutting and transportation are largely a matter of speculation. The question of whether Chacoans or the people living closer to the mountains did the cutting also remains unanswered.

Toll, Wolcott

A primary member of the **Chaco Project** archaeological team and Chacoan **ceramic** scholar. Toll's early analysis of refuse deposits in the **Pueblo Alto** trash mound significantly influenced the "pilgrim-age fair" model developed by James **Judge** and his Chaco Project staff to explain the function of **great houses** (see "Explaining Chaco"). Toll interpreted ceramic deposits exposed in the **stratigraphy** of the Pueblo Alto **trash mound** as remains of periodic feasting events rather than the remains of daily cleaning of individual households. He proposed that great house religious leaders organized occasional gatherings of groups from many areas of the **San Juan Basin** to participate in religious ceremonies, including the ritual destruction of pottery. The events also served as a means for reinforcing **Chaco Canyon**'s importance in the region and enabled the exchange of many items including pottery, stone tools, and jewelry. Toll postulated that some pilgrim groups might have contributed labor toward the construction of new units in great houses.

Much of Toll's Chacoan research focused on ceramics in both Chaco Canyon and the **Totah** region. In addition, he and his wife, Mollie—a Chaco Project archaeobotanist—and several other Project staff conducted farming experiments in Chaco Canyon producing valuable information on the agricultural potential of various zones in the Canyon. With Catherine **Cameron** he directed the Organization of Production seminar for the Chaco Synthesis project and wrote the subject chapter for *The Archaeology of Chaco Canyon: An Eleventh-Century Pueblo Regional Center.*

Toltec

One of the major political and cultural systems operating in **Mesoamerica** during the Early Postclassic period, about A.D. 900–1200. From their capital at Tula, about fifty miles northeast of modern Mexico City, the Toltecs exerted their influence over much of central and southern Mexico, extending as far southeast as Chichen Itza in Yucatán.

A number of southwestern archaeologists, including Charles **DiPeso,** believed that Toltec influence reached northward to the **Hohokam** in southern Arizona and the Chacoan peoples of the **San Juan Basin**. Trade was an important aspect of Toltec expansion, and DiPeso proposed that Toltec merchants, the ***pochteca***, were instrumental in advancing and controlling Chacoan culture. The evidence for such contact and control is limited.

The Totah [Navajo for "rivers coming together"]

(Map 1)

An archaeological zone surrounding the confluences of the Animas and La Plata rivers with the San Juan River in the northwestern **San Juan Basin**. The Totah was defined by Peter McKenna and Wolcott **Toll** to distinguish this region's prehistoric development from the **Mesa Verde** culture to the north and Chacoan culture to the south.

Though permanent rivers in this area made it highly attractive for **Puebloan** farmers, population density was not great until the late 1000s. Groups in the Totah had some cultural ties with Chaco

Canyon in the early and mid-1000s, and the establishment of the **Salmon Ruin Outlier** at about A.D. 1080 marked a surge in local building activity. Many archaeologists believe this represents a shift of Chacoan cultural power northward from Chaco Canyon. This heightened building activity, which included the large **Aztec Ruins** building complex, continued to about A.D. 1150 but then ceased for almost fifty years.

About A.D. 1200 a number of Chacoan **great houses** in the Totah region were remodeled, and residents built many other large new buildings, possibly intended as **public architecture**. Ceramics at these new structures include **Mesa Verde Black-on-white**, which has prompted some archaeologists to suggest that cultural influence and possibly groups of people were coming into the Totah from the Mesa Verde region to the northwest. This area was almost totally abandoned by the mid-1200s.

Tower Kiva

(Figure 97)

A specialized type of Chacoan structure with a room-sized cylindrical open space extending upward through a solid square masonry block. While their walls may have risen to forty feet, it is uncertain whether they had multiple floor levels. Tower kivas occurred late in Chacoan prehistory—the late 1000s and early 1100s—at the same time that **tri-wall structures** and other new architectural forms appeared. They are found at **Kin Kletso** and **Chetro Ketl** in Chaco Canyon, and at the **Kin Ya'a** and **Kin Klizhin** outlier **great houses**.

All of these tower kivas had one or more "benches" or step-backs around the inner walls of the round space. These ledges were likely supports for the beams of multiple floors within the building. However, some archaeologists have suggested that there were no floors and that the "benches" were used to hold temporary scaffolding while the walls were being raised.

The two excavated tower kivas, at Kin Kletso and Chetro Ketl, do not show typical kiva floor features. In both cases, there is a **T-shaped door** at the first floor level. The Kin Kletso tower had a central fire pit. At Chetro Ketl, a masonry cylinder filled with stone rubble was

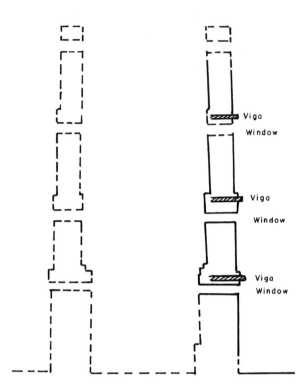

FIGURE 97. Profile of the Kin Ya'a tower kiva. Only a portion of the building remains intact.

set near the inner wall. The function of this feature, which was about six feet high and six feet in diameter, is unknown. A rare T-shaped window is located on the second level of the tower kiva at **Kin Ya'a**.

Although they have been called "kivas," the function of tower kivas is not well understood. Their use as **signal stations** has been suggested, but there is little evidence to support this theory, and lines of sight have not been tested. Jesse Fewkes, an early southwestern archaeologist, proposed that the Kin Ya'a tower kiva may have been an enlarged *sipapu* in which four stacked kivas represent the worlds into which the Puebloans had emerged.

Towns

A word used to refer to Chacoan **great houses**. The term was coined by Edgar **Hewett** and then used by **Gordon Vivian, Gwinn Vivian,** and others when comparing great houses (towns) and small house sites (villages). The preferred term is "great house."

Trash Mound

A large pile of prehistoric household trash and other refuse, usually part of a residential archaeological site. Archaeologists use the terms "refuse mound," "midden," and "trash mound" interchangeably, although **midden** is more commonly used outside the Southwest. Trash mounds are a source of important archaeological information because their contents reflect the daily lives of past peoples. In addition, stylistic changes in tools, **pottery,** and other items can be traced through **stratigraphy** of a trash mound's layers. Contemporary **Puebloan** peoples view trash mounds as sacred places because they contain the spirits of broken objects, food plants and animals, and other items in the mound.

Trash mounds are a common feature at Chacoan sites, but a number of archaeologists interpret the large mounds at **Pueblo Bonito**, **Pueblo Alto**, **Peñasco Blanco**, and **Chetro Ketl** as being more than just the accumulation of daily household refuse. A deep stratigraphic cut in the Pueblo Alto mound revealed deposits that appeared to be periodic, homogenous in content, and of fairly regular thickness. Large quantities of broken pottery were present in these layers. **Chaco Project** archaeologists Wollcot **Toll** and Thomas **Windes** theorized that these trash deposits represented the remains of scheduled feasting events by visitors to the **great house** who gathered for ceremonies that included the ritual destruction of pottery.

Stephen **Lekson** and John **Stein** believe that the mounds functioned as special "earthen architecture" constructed as part of a ritual landscape associated with the great house. These mounds are identified as **berms** at some great houses, particularly **outliers**. Lekson also believes that the two mounds at Pueblo Bonito, and possibly at other great houses, served as **platform mounds**.

Tree-Ring Dating (see *Dendrochronology*)

Tres Huerfanos

(Map 1)

A long mesa crowned with three small buttes located about twenty-five miles due north of **Chaco Canyon**. Visible from throughout the San Juan Basin, it stands as one of the most prominent landmarks on the horizon of the **Chacoan World**. Tres Huerfanos, Spanish for "Three Orphans," is also known as Huerfano Mountain and Huerfano Mesa. In the **Navajo** (Diné) language it is known as "People Encircling Around Mountain," and "Mountain Around Which Moving Was Done." It has a prominent place in Navajo mythology and is said to be one of the homes of First Man and First Woman. Myths also identify it as the place where First Man found the infant Changing Woman. Ruth **Van Dyke** and many other archaeologists believe it was an iconic and sacred landmark for the Chacoan people.

Triangle Bar Triangle Ranch

Richard **Wetherill**'s homesteaded ranch in Chaco Canyon on the west side of **Pueblo Bonito**. Following his work at Pueblo Bonito, Wetherill expanded his trading and ranching businesses, and enlarged the buildings that had served as headquarters for the excavation project. The ranch was sold following Wetherill's death. Most of the buildings were razed by the National Park Service in the 1960s.

Tri-Wall Structure

(Figure 98)

A specialized type of building with two concentric rings of rooms surrounding a large round room. Similar structures with one ring of rooms are called bi-wall structures. About a dozen tri-wall structures have been discovered in the **San Juan Basin**, including one on the west side of **Pueblo del Arroyo** and another at the **Hubbard Site** at the **Aztec Ruins**. Both of these structures are part of a larger building.

All evidence suggests that these tri-wall structures were built after A.D. 1100 and may have cultural ties with the **Mesa Verde** area. Masonry at the Pueblo del Arroyo tri-wall structure is of the **McElmo style**.

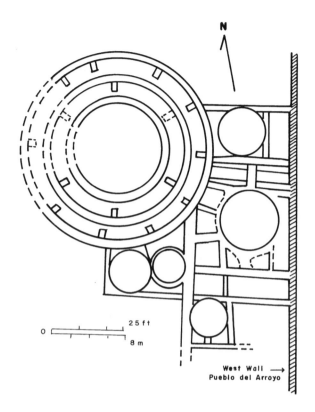

FIGURE 98. Pueblo del Arroyo tri-wall structure and associated rooms and kivas ground plan.

The function of these buildings is unknown, but some have features typical of **kivas,** and most archaeologists agree that they were ritual rather than residential. Some proponents of strong **Meso-american** influence at Chaco suggest that they were **shrines** to the **Toltec** deity Quetzalcoatl. Others believe they served as living quarters and storage places for the ritual items of an emerging priestly class in Chacoan and Mesa Verde culture.

Tseh So

(Map 3; Figure 99)

A **small house site** approximately one-half mile south of **Pueblo Bonito,** also known as Bc50 in the **Bc site** numbering system. It is one of a cluster of small pueblos lying immediately to the east of

FIGURE 99. Tseh So (Bc 50) ground plan. Doorways are not shown.

Casa Rinconada. The rectangular building had twenty-six ground-floor rooms and four **kivas** on the east side (Figure 99). There is some evidence for a few second-story rooms.

Tseh So was apparently occupied in the 900s and 1000s based on ceramics found at the site and a single tree-ring date in the early A.D. 900s. Excavations below the building revealed traces of an earlier **Basketmaker** occupation.

Tseh So and its close neighbor, Bc51, were excavated by the University of New Mexico Archaeological Field School in 1936 and 1937. They became "type sites" for Chacoan small house residences, although with about forty-five ground-floor rooms, Bc51 was very large for this building type. Tseh So is one of several small house sites that has been stabilized and interpreted by the National Park Service.

FIGURE 100. T-shaped doorway, Pueblo Bonito.

T-Shaped Doors

(Figure 100)
Doorways to rooms in Chacoan buildings that have a blocky "T" shape. This type of doorway is common in northern **Puebloan** sites. It first appeared sometime after A.D. 1000, possibly in the Chaco area. A frequent explanation for its form is that it permitted carrying large objects into a room.

T-shaped doors are also common at **Casas Grandes**, Mexico. Stephen **Lekson** suggests that T-shaped doors were visible symbols used to convey a social message. This interpretation is supported by the presence of a T-shaped window in the tower kiva at **Kin Ya'a**. He points out that they are frequently exterior doorways on buildings that would have been highly visible to residents and visitors.

Tsin Kletsin [Navajo for "black wood place" or "charcoal place"]

(Map 3; Figure 101)
A **great house** located two miles south of **Pueblo Bonito** on the **Chacra Mesa**. One of the smallest great houses in the **Chaco Core**, Tsin Kletsin rises to two stories on the north side and contains about

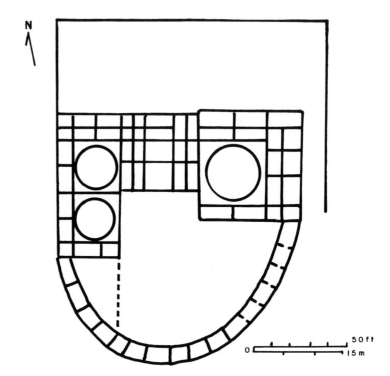

FIGURE 101. Tsin Kletsin great house ground plan. The site has not been excavated; locations of rooms and kivas are based on standing wall and surface evidence. Dashed lines in room arc are estimated rooms. Doorways are not shown.

seventy rooms. It is thought to have been built in the early 1100s based on several tree-ring dates and its **McElmo-style** masonry veneer.

Tsin Kletsin has no associated **great kiva,** but four **kivas** are enclosed within the room block. A large **dam** and reservoir in a short **rincon** to the east of the building probably provided domestic water for its residents.

Tsin Kletsin is unusual in many ways and appears to be transitional in architectural style between the classic D-shaped great houses and the later McElmo style. It has a D-shaped ground plan, but McElmo-style masonry veneer. There is a large rectangular walled enclosure on the north side in addition to an arced plaza on the south.

At least two **roads** enter the site from the north, one of which can be traced to a set of steps cut into the rock on the south cliff face just east of **Casa Rinconada**. This road probably crossed Chaco Canyon to connect with a roadway on the cliff above **Chetro Ketl** that proceeds to **Pueblo Alto**.

The exact positioning of Tsin Kletsin on the Chacra Mesa appears deliberate. Five Chacoan great houses can be seen from the highest part of the building: Pueblo Alto, Peñasco Blanco, Kin Kletso, Bis sa'ani, and Kin Klizhin. If the structure were moved thirty feet in any direction, all five great houses would not be visible.

The site has not been excavated. A National Park Service trail leads to the ruins from the interpretive walk at Casa Rinconada. The rock-cut steps can be seen from a turnout on the National Park Service road just east of Casa Rinconada.

Turquoise

A semiprecious blue, green, or blue-green mineral that was used widely in the prehistoric Southwest for jewelry and ritual items. Turquoise jewelry is still fashionable, and many pieces are produced today by **Puebloan** artists. A number of turquoise mines are found in the Southwest. Those at **Cerrillos**, New Mexico, about a hundred miles from Chaco, were worked in prehistoric times.

Large quantities of turquoise have been recovered from numerous Chacoan sites, both in raw form and as finished products. Perhaps the best-known discovery was a cache of 56,000 pieces, mostly beads and pendants, found by **Wetherill** and **Pepper** in a burial room in **Pueblo Bonito**. Though turquoise is often considered a luxury item associated with **great houses**, many pieces have been recovered from **small house sites**. Joan **Mathien**, an archaeologist with considerable Chacoan field experience, has reported workshops for the production of finished turquoise in both small houses and great houses.

Proponents of strong **Mesoamerican** influence on Chacoan culture believe that turquoise was a major commodity for exchange with *pochteca* traders. Others have suggested that turquoise may have been stockpiled by Chacoans during good times and then used to barter for food when crops failed.

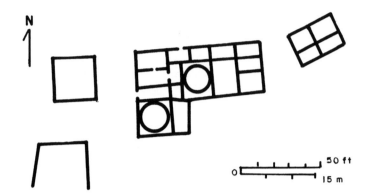

FIGURE 102. Twin Angels Outlier great house ground plan. Structure is largely unexcavated; the locations of most rooms and kivas have been estimated based on standing wall and surface evidence.

Twin Angels Outlier
(Map 1; Figure 102)

A Chacoan **outlier** great house located approximately forty miles north of Chaco Canyon on the western edge of Kutz Canyon, about ten miles southeast of Bloomfield, New Mexico. The one-story, L-shaped building had approximately seventeen ground-floor rooms and two **kivas.** There is no associated **great kiva,** and a small house community for the building has not been defined. However, three rooms near the building may be related to the structure. The **outlier** is about four miles from the point where the **Great North Road** enters Kutz Canyon, and it is presumed that the Twin Angels Outlier was linked to Chaco Canyon via this **road.**

Earl **Morris** excavated seven rooms and one kiva at the site in 1915 for the University of Colorado Museum. The outlier is protected by the Bureau of Land Management.

U

Una Vida [Spanish for "one life"]
(Map 3; Figure 103)

One of the earliest Chacoan **great houses,** located in the **Fajada Gap** area of Chaco Canyon about three miles east of **Pueblo Bonito.** Tree-ring dates from the oldest portion of the building indicate that

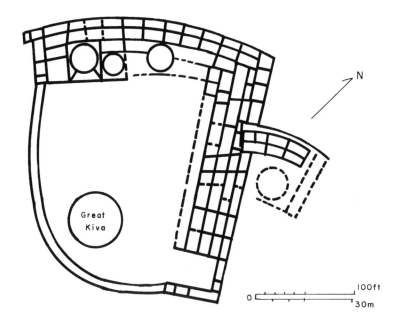

FIGURE 103. Una Vida great house ground plan. Dashed lines represent postulated rooms and kivas not visible from surface evidence. A small portion of the site was excavated and backfilled.

construction was begun in the mid-800s, about the same time as Pueblo Bonito. The structure has a northern core room block and a west wing, but no east wing. The arc of rooms that encloses the plaza on the south continues on to the east side, creating a slightly asymmetrical D-shaped ground plan.

Una Vida is the fifth largest of the canyon great houses with about 160 rooms, including tiered second-story rooms in the west and north room blocks. The largely unexcavated structure has one, and possibly two, **great kivas**. Una Vida may have been closely associated with **Kin Nahasbas**, an early great kiva **community** located west of the great house in an elevated position that provided visual contact with Pueblo Bonito.

Like the other early great houses, **Peñasco Blanco** and Pueblo Bonito, Una Vida was located at the confluence of two major drainages: the **Chaco Wash** and the Fajada Wash. Water for irrigating fields was also diverted from **Gallo Canyon** less than one-half mile to the west of Una Vida.

Limited excavations in the site were carried out by **Gordon Vivian** between 1956 and 1960. This work provided information on early developmental stages of great houses. Before **backfilling** these rooms in 1979, **Chaco Project** staff reexamined them and recorded new information.

Lieutenant **Simpson** recorded the site name in 1849 but provided no explanation for it. The approximate translation of the **Navajo** name for Una Vida is "witchcraft woman's home," a reference to a local Navajo belief that a witch kept prisoners on the top of nearby **Fajada Butte**. Contrary to the usual Navajo practice of avoiding prehistoric sites, several **hogans** and a corral were built on the ruin mound in historic times.

Uto-Aztecan

One of four languages spoken by historic and contemporary **Puebloan** people in the Southwest. The geographic range of the Uto-Aztecan language family is much greater than the other three Puebloan languages, **Tanoan**, **Zuni**, and **Keresan**. At the time of European contact, speakers of Uto-Aztecan languages ranged from the northwestern United States through western Mexico and into Central America.

Today, three groups of Uto-Aztecan speakers are recognized: Shoshonean or Northern Uto-Aztecan in the Great Basin and northern Southwest; Sonoran in the southern Southwest and northern Mexico; and Nahuatl in central Mexico.

The **Hopi** language belongs to the Northern Uto-Aztecan branch. They are the only Uto-Aztecan speakers among modern Puebloan peoples. Their social, political, and religious organization also differs in many ways from other Puebloan groups. Hopi tradition indicates that some of their ancestral clans came from the Chaco area.

V

Van Dyke, Ruth

An archaeologist who has pursued creative new approaches to deciphering the Chaco Phenomenon. Like several of her contemporaries, Van Dyke's research has focused on great house architecture, including great kivas and the interaction of that architecture with the surrounding natural world.

Her early work at the **Andrews Outlier** in the **Red Mesa Valley** and in Chaco-related sites west of **Chaco Canyon** established architectural criteria for identifying Chacoan outliers, paralleling John **Kantner**'s Chaco World studies. She determined that **core-and-veneer** masonry and elevated **kivas** were primary indicators of "Bonito style" architecture. However, the "Chacoan package" in later periods and at greater distances from Chaco Canyon was marked by multiple great kivas and landscape modifications, such as berms. In her subsequent evaluation of McElmo-style architecture, Van Dyke concluded that these distinctive structures were created to reestablish Chaco as a center place in the Late **Bonito Phase** (A.D. 1100–1140).

All of Van Dyke's architectural research is grounded in the broad concept of "lived landscapes" which she evaluates in depth in *The Chaco Experience: Landscape and Ideology at the Center Place*. Van Dyke employs phenomenology, a process grounded in existentialist philosophy, to better understand Chacoan spatial perceptions and the relationship of architecture and the landscape. To insure that these perceptions are not simply her own, she interprets her observations through basic tenets of **Puebloan** world views.

Veneer Styles

(Figure 104)

Different patterns of facing stones laid over the interior core of walls in the **core-and-veneer** masonry used at Chacoan **great houses** and some **small house sites**. Changes through time in the size and placement of these veneer stones allow archaeologists to approximate the date of construction. Both Neil **Judd** and Florence **Hawley** developed veneer typologies. Judd's four-part typology (Types I–IV) is the one most frequently used when describing Chacoan great house architecture.

The earliest veneer style, Type I, was identified in the oldest portion of **Pueblo Bonito,** which was constructed in the mid-800s and early 900s. This wall facing was a true veneer consisting of thousands of small sandstone **spalls**. These stone chips, roughly the size of a matchbook, were set into a mud plaster that covered a core of wide, thin sandstone slabs. Enough examples were found during excavations to suggest that this veneer covered much of the early parts of Pueblo Bonito. Today, the cores of these walls can be seen but little of the spall or chip veneer has survived.

The Type II style, introduced during a building surge at the great houses in the early 1000s, brought a radical change in technique as well as in the type of stones used. The veneer became a load-bearing portion of the wall when the larger facing stones were laid to extend back into the core stones. The irregular courses of these loaf-shaped stones were then surrounded by small sandstone chips, or spalls, set into the mortar. An excellent example of this veneer style can be found on the western half of the curved back wall of Pueblo Bonito.

This banding effect was further emphasized in the Type III veneer style used during much of the middle 1000s. Distinct rows of the larger loaf-shaped stones were now separated by wide bands of small tabular blocks of stone. The sandstone used in Type III veneer was almost always a hard, dark brown form quarried from deposits on the mesa top on the north side of the canyon. Good examples of this style can be seen in several open rooms in the southwestern quadrant of Pueblo Bonito.

The banding effect was almost totally eliminated in Type IV veneer, which consisted of fairly uniform tabular blocks of hard, dark sandstone laid with almost no mortar showing. The style was probably introduced in the mid- to late 1000s and continued in use into the early 1100s. Examples of this style are visible in the eastern portion of Pueblo Bonito and the eastern wing of **Chetro Ketl.**

Judd did not include the **McElmo-style** veneer in his typology, although he was aware of it. The McElmo facing stones continued to be a part of the load-bearing portion of the wall, but the usual dark tabular sandstone was replaced by blocks of soft sandstone

FIGURE 104. Veneer styles of Chacoan masonry:
(A) Type I; (B) Type II; (C) Type III; (D) Type IV;
(E) McElmo style.

gathered from the lower canyon cliffs. Usually these blocks were finished by dimpling, a fairly uniform pecking of the stone surface. The McElmo-style veneer is the predominant type found at the **Kin Kletso** great house and most structures built in the early and middle 1100s in the canyon.

The cultural significance of veneer styles is not known. If the walls of great houses were plastered, as most archaeologists believe, they would not have been seen. Indeed, it is possible that the stone veneers were intended to help hold the soft mud plaster on the walls. The different styles varied through time but cannot provide precise dates of construction. Types III and IV were used at the same time at different great houses. However, the uniformity of veneers among great houses suggests a canyon-wide concept of architecture and may reflect guilds of masons within individual great houses or between great houses.

Vents

(Figure 105)

Small openings in the walls of Chacoan **great houses** that provided for the passage of air. Vents are common features in living rooms and usually appear as one-foot-square openings near the corners of

FIGURE 105. Room vent at Pueblo Bonito.

rooms, about a foot below the ceiling. The vents brought air into **room suites** and may have also drafted smoke from the interior rooms.

Village of the Great Kivas Outlier

(Map 1; Figure 106)

A Chacoan outlier **great house** and associated **great kiva** located approximately seventy-five miles southwest of Chaco Canyon and about twelve miles northeast of Zuni Pueblo. The Chacoan portion of the "village" consists of a rectangular one-story room block containing about eighteen rooms and two **kivas.** A Chacoan great kiva is attached to the front of the room block. There are no tree-ring dates from the Chacoan building, but associated ceramics suggests a date in the late 1000s and possibly the early 1100s.

Later, non-Chacoan additions were made to the room block, and

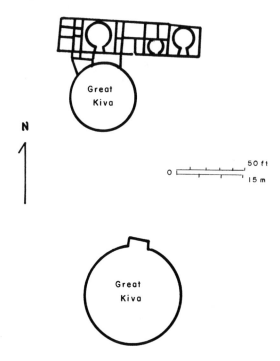

FIGURE 106. Village of the Great Kivas Outlier site plan. Only the Chaco period unit is shown.

a second great kiva was constructed about a hundred feet south of the building. Two other small room blocks built near this great kiva also post-date the Chacoan occupation.

The Chacoan building and great kiva were excavated by Frank **Roberts** Jr. in 1930, and he published a report on his investigations. The site is protected today by the **Zuni** Tribe.

Villages

A word used to refer to Chacoan small houses. The term may have been coined by Edgar **Hewett,** who referenced both "small houses" and "small villages" in discussions of architecture in Chaco Canyon. **Gordon Vivian, Gwinn Vivian,** and others used this term when comparing **great house** and small house architecture. The preferred term is **small house site.**

Vivian, Gordon

A leading Chaco scholar who addressed most of the primary Chacoan research questions during nearly four decades of archaeological work in the canyon. As a high school student in Albuquerque, Vivian bicycled to many archaeological sites in New Mexico, and that exposure to prehistory prompted him to enter Edgar **Hewett**'s Department of Archaeology at the University of New Mexico in 1927. From 1929 to 1935 he served as Hewett's chauffeur, truck driver, and student field assistant, spending his summers at the department's archaeological field schools in the Jemez Mountains and at Chaco. He was a member of the 1929 field school at **Chetro Ketl,** where he and Paul Reiter discovered sealed deposits of turquoise beads and pendants in the Chetro Ketl **great kiva**.

In response to Hewett's desire to investigate numerous great kivas, Vivian was assigned the task of excavating **Casa Rinconada** in 1931. He then stabilized the structure, a job that probably contributed to his lifelong involvement with ruins **stabilization.** He joined the National Park Service in 1937 to organize a ruins stabilization unit with masons drawn almost exclusively from local **Chaco Navajo.** Except for a brief stint with the Army Corps of Engineers in the 1940s, he remained in Chaco until 1958, when he assumed leadership of the National Park Service's Southwest Archaeological Center in Globe, Arizona. This task did not divert him from his work at Chaco, and he continued research there until 1965.

Gordon Vivian's early student involvement with **great house** archaeology continued during his National Park Service employment with small-scale excavation projects at Chetro Ketl, **Pueblo Bonito**, **Pueblo del Arroyo**, **Una Vida**, and the **tri-wall structure** at Pueblo del Arroyo. His most ambitious work in these sites was at **Kin Kletso**, which he completely excavated in 1951.

Vivian also recognized the significance of **small house sites** and excavated a number of the canyon's **Bc sites**, beginning with work at the **Three-C Site**. He investigated the potential for prehistoric **water control** systems in the canyon and used 1930s Soil Conservation Service aerial photography to document the presence of large **canals** at sites in the **Chaco Core**. Conversations with Marietta Wetherill, the widow of Richard **Wetherill**, had made him aware of Chacoan **road** systems, but in some cases he confused roads and canals on aerial photography.

Much of his experience with Chacoan sites and his thinking about Chacoan cultural development were summarized in his last publication, *Kin Kletso: A Pueblo III Community in Chaco Canyon, New Mexico*. In this work, Vivian brought together environmental and cultural data to support his premise that peoples living in Chaco Canyon by the late 1000s were representatives of at least three distinct groups, which he defined as phases of Chacoan culture. This interpretation was based on Clyde Kluckhohn's early suggestion that inhabitants of great houses and small house sites may have represented two ethnic groups who possibly spoke different languages.

Vivian, R. Gwinn

A southwestern archaeologist whose participation in Chacoan archaeology spans more than five decades. The son of **Gordon Vivian**, Gwinn spent much of his boyhood living in **Chaco Canyon** and assisting his father, who provided him with intensive field training. He studied under Florence **Hawley** at the University of New Mexico, where he majored in anthropology with an emphasis in archaeology.

Under his father's direction, he initiated an archaeological survey of the **Chacra Mesa** and used the data collected on early **Navajo** occupation there for his M.A. thesis at the University of New Mexico. His doctoral dissertation at the University of Arizona compared settlement systems of Chacoan **great house** and **small house site** communities, and set the stage for subsequent work in this area.

A commitment to completing his father's work on Chacoan **water control** systems was fulfilled in 1970–71 when he spent a year in Chaco Canyon identifying, testing, and recording canals and water gates in the **Chaco Core**. This work pointed out the early failure of both Gordon and Gwinn Vivian to distinguish **canals** from Chacoan **roads**, a mistake that he corrected during the water control study.

Like his father, Gwinn Vivian has oriented much of his Chacoan research toward defining and clarifying the relationship of great houses and small house sites in Chaco Canyon and the larger **Chacoan World**. In his book *The Chacoan Prehistory of the San Juan Basin*, he elaborated on Gordon's premise of two or more ethnic groups occupying small house sites and great houses.

Vizcarra, José Antonio

Governor of New Mexico (1822–25) during Mexico's administration of the region, and the first known European to see and report on **great houses** in Chaco Canyon. Vizcarra left Santa Fe on June 18, 1823, to enforce a treaty he had established with the **Navajos** the previous year. His route took him through the pueblo of Jemez, and it is likely that he engaged the services of Francisco **Hosta**, who would guide later military and civilian parties through the Chaco area.

On June 25 they arrived at **Pueblo Pintado**, referred to as "Pueblo del Ratón," and probably camped there. The following day they marched through Chaco Canyon, and Vizcarra noted in his diary that "the ruins of several pueblos were found, which were of such antiquity that their inhabitants were not known to Europeans." They camped at "El Peñasco," possibly the confluence of the **Chaco** and **Escavada washes** below the **Peñasco Blanco** great house. On his return, he camped near **Fajada Butte** ("Cerrito Fajado") on August 25 and rested briefly at Pueblo Pintado the following day.

W

Wallace Outlier

(*Figure 107*)

A Chacoan outlier **great house** and **community** located approximately a hundred miles northwest of Chaco Canyon and about five miles northeast of Cortez, Colorado. The ground plan of the bracket-shaped building is similar to the **Wijiji** great house in Chaco Canyon, with two **kivas** on opposite sides of the central room block and two short wings at either end. Unlike Wijiji, however, the plaza at Wallace was enclosed by a wall. The structure had up to fifty ground-floor rooms and rose to three stories in some areas.

Tree-ring dates show that the great house began around A.D. 1060 as a small building with about nine rooms and possibly a kiva. If the A.D. 1060 dates are not from recycled beams, this early room block is older than the nearby **Lowry Ruin Outlier** and could be one of the first Chacoan buildings in southwestern Colorado. A major addition to the structure in the late 1000s or early 1100s surrounded this early unit and created the present ground plan. Masonry veneer, like at Wijiji, was a Late Classic Bonito style using tabular blocks and not the **McElmo-style** veneer. A post-A.D. 1200 occupation at the site is associated with a **Mesa Verde** remodeling and use.

Numerous **small house sites** occur in the vicinity of the Wallace great house and probably formed an outlier community. There is no associated **great kiva**, and no Chacoan **roads** have been traced to the site. Wallace is one of three Chacoan great houses in this im-

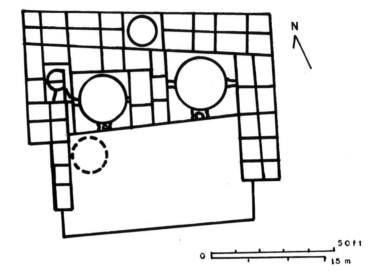

FIGURE 107. Wallace Outlier great house ground plan. The structure has not been completely excavated. Plaza kiva is postulated to be present.

mediate area; the nearby Ida Jean Outlier great house nearly duplicates the Wallace ground plan.

The site is privately owned and has been partially excavated by the owner.

Washington Pass Chert (see *Chert*)

Water Control

(Figure 108)
Methods for capturing, collecting, and delivering water for agricultural use and other purposes. Agricultural water control systems usually include **irrigation** facilities for moving water to the fields (diversion dams, dikes, canals, or channels) as well as improved fields that make more efficient use of the water.

Water control in Chaco Canyon and the **Chaco Core** involved a specialized type of irrigation. Because the canyon has no flowing streams or rivers, runoff from thunderstorms was collected and diverted to the fields from small side canyons and drainages. Large volumes of water that flowed off exposed bedrock on the mesa tops and into gullies leading into the canyon was slowed near the drainage mouth by masonry and earthen diversion **dams**. The water was then channeled into **canals** and run up-canyon to a point near the next drainage, where it was slowed once again behind masonry water gates or within masonry collection boxes with several gates. The water was then channeled to **gridded fields** through smaller ditches.

This process allowed Chacoan farmers to collect and preserve most of the rain that fell on the north side of the canyon and, in addition, to renew the soil in their fields. The silt and mud carried in the water had a high organic content and provided nutrients to the crops.

This type of water control occurs consistently on the north side of the canyon from **Mockingbird Canyon** on the east to the **Escavada Wash** on the west. On the south side of the canyon, only two water control systems have been found: one near **Casa Rinconada** and another below **Peñasco Blanco**. Most of the farming on the south side of the canyon was of the *akchin* type. Water control systems with similar features have also been found at **Kin Bineola** and **Kin Klizhin** south of Chaco Canyon in the Chaco Core. In these systems, water was collected from the Kin Bineola and Kin Klizhin washes and their major tributaries.

Another type of water control system, masonry-walled farming terraces, has been located along the second cliff bench on the mesa behind **Pueblo Bonito** and **Chetro Ketl**. These gardens received water that flowed over the cliff top and down onto the garden plots. The area available for crops was small, and these terrace plots may have been for specialized crops such as tobacco.

Chacoan farmers were probably using some type of **water control** system on the north side of the canyon by the late 800s, but the dams, canals, water gates, and gridded fields that have been found probably date from the 1000s and early 1100s. Their age is estimated on the basis of associated ceramics and masonry **veneer styles** used in some of the water gates and diversion dams.

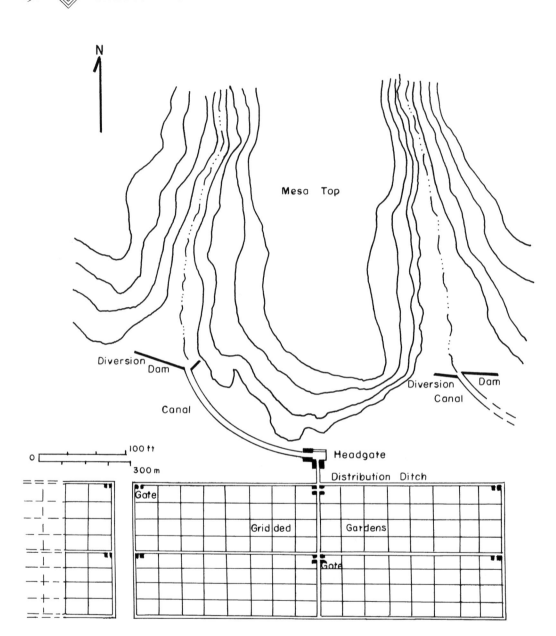

FIGURE 108. Stylized plan of Chacoan water control system.

Wello

A **Navajo** elder who was living in Chaco Canyon when Richard **Wetherill** arrived in 1896. Wello, known also as "Wero," was living in an abandoned ranch building of the LC Cattle Company at the confluence of the **Chaco** and **Escavada washes** as early as the 1880s. He rented a metal stove in the building to Wetherill, who took it to Pueblo Bonito for "the Hyde Kitchen." Wello may have been involved in the excavation of several rooms at **Peñasco Blanco** in search of turquoise in the 1890s. It is not clear if he worked for Wetherill. He may have been a witness to Wetherill's murder, as he was present at the time of the rancher's initial encounter with **Chischilling-begay**.

Wello died in 1926, a year after being interviewed by Neil **Judd**. His descendants and relatives are known as the Wero family, and John Wero worked for the National Park Service for many years. David **Brugge**'s *A History of the Chaco Navajos*, also records information on the Wero family.

Werito, Archie and Cecil

Two members of a **Navajo** family that has a long tradition of work with the National Park Service's Ruins Stabilization Unit. Archie Werito was **Gordon Vivian**'s stabilization foreman and also the park's maintenance foreman for many years. His father had worked for Neil **Judd** at **Pueblo Bonito**. Archie's cousin Cecil spent more than twenty-eight years working in **stabilization** at Chaco and in 1991 received the prestigious Roy Appleman–Henry Judd Award for outstanding service to cultural resources management. For years the Werito family farmed land within Chaco Canyon, including **Werito's Rincon,** and they have lived along the **Escavada Wash** for many generations.

Werito's Rincon

(Map 3)

A large, deep side canyon in the **Chacra Mesa** on the south side of Chaco Canyon that is named for a local **Navajo** family. Situated approximately halfway between **Fajada Gap** and **South Gap,** the mouth of this box canyon is about one and a half miles east of **Pueblo Bonito** and a little more than a half mile southwest of **Hungo Pavi.**

A number of **small house sites** are located on ridges and hills near the mouth of the **rincon,** and several were excavated during **Chaco Center** investigations in the 1970s. Large sand dunes at the back of the canyon would have been ideal locations for prehistoric **dune farming.** Only a thin section of the Chacra Mesa remains at the south end of the rincon, and eventually long-term erosion will create another break, or gap, in the Chacra Mesa.

Wero, Welito

A member of a prominent **Chaco Navajo** family with large land-holdings along the **Escavada Wash.** He worked for Neil **Judd** at **Pueblo Bonito** from 1921 to 1924 and was recognized as one of the principal **Navajo** men in the area. Welito Wero was employed by **Gordon Vivian** in the Ruins Stabilization Unit in the 1940s and 1950s. By 1937 he had moved, or was removed by the National Park Service, from lands within the national monument and shifted to family lands along the **Escavada Wash.** The Wero family still lives along the wash today, and several men—including John Wero, Charlie Welito, and Jimmy Wero—have worked for the National Park Service in Chaco Canyon. Information on the Wero family is recorded in David **Brugge**'s *A History of the Chaco Navajos.*

West Road

(Map 3)

A segment of Chacoan **road** that may have linked **Chaco Canyon** with the Chuska Valley to the west. The road is most visible as a wide depression in the soil where it passes just south of **Peñasco Blanco.** A short spur road links this section of the road with a **great kiva** on the south side of Peñasco Blanco.

From Peñasco Blanco, the West Road has been traced south and west for about a quarter-mile to the cliff edge overlooking the

Chaco Wash just south of its confluence with the **Escavada Wash**. It is assumed that the road continued across the Chaco Wash in a westerly direction toward the **Chuska Valley**.

East of Peñasco Blanco, the road appears to drop down into Chaco Canyon. Rock-cut steps and short road segments on the opposite (east) side of the canyon may be a continuation of the road to the north with possible contact with **Pueblo Alto** or the **Great North Road**. The West Road may have branched and also continued along the canyon floor to **Downtown Chaco.**

The **Ahshislepah Road** has been referred to at times as the West Road, but its route differs from this road.

Wetherill, Richard

A Colorado rancher turned archaeologist who discovered many important southwestern prehistoric sites and conducted the first scientific excavations in Chaco Canyon. Wetherill and a friend discovered Cliff Palace, Spruce Tree House, and Square Tower House at **Mesa Verde** in 1888 while searching for stray cattle. Wetherill then launched a number of trips from the family ranch at Mancos, Colorado, to locate prehistoric sites in the Four Corners area.

To augment income from ranching, Richard and his brothers, Al and Clayton, soon began collecting artifacts from sites at Mesa Verde and other locales, a legal practice at the time and one supported by many museums and historical societies. Wealthy backers were important to such a business, and Wetherill's contact with the Hyde brothers resulted in their sponsorship of several collecting expeditions in the early 1890s to sites in the Grand Gulch, Utah, region.

Wetherill's motives in excavating changed after his contact with Baron Gustaf Eric Adolf Nordenskiold, the son of a Swedish Arctic explorer and scientist. Nordenskiold came to the Wetherill ranch for a brief visit in 1891 but then spent the summer excavating in many of the Mesa Verde cliff dwellings discovered by the Wetherills. His insistence on taking notes, making maps, and photographing archaeological finds impressed Wetherill with the scientific value of their work. This orientation probably accounted for Wetherill's ability to observe and record the differences between **Basketmaker** and **Puebloan** deposits in Grand Gulch and certainly influenced his approach to excavations in Pueblo Bonito.

Wetherill's first visit to Chaco Canyon in 1895 led him to convince the Hyde brothers to shift the operations of their **Hyde Exploring Expedition** to Chaco for the 1896 season. Though George **Pepper** was the official director of the project at **Pueblo Bonito**, Wetherill's long experience with excavation made him the true leader of the project. His career as one of the earliest southwestern archaeologists was cut short through the action of Edgar **Hewett**, who pressured the Hydes to close the Chaco operation in 1901. Wetherill also homesteaded in Chaco Canyon and operated the **Triangle Bar Triangle Ranch** and a trading post. He continued to live at Pueblo Bonito until 1910, when he was shot and killed in a livestock dispute by **Chis-chilling-begay** near **Cly's Canyon**.

White House

(Figure 109)

A possible Chacoan **outlier** great house in Canyon de Chelly, Arizona, approximately eighty-five miles west of Chaco Canyon. Two buildings are present at the site: a cliff dwelling probably occupied in the A.D. 1200s, and a structure on the canyon bottom below the cliff dwelling that has been described as a great house. This rectangular building had between fifty and sixty rooms, and today still rises to three stories. It contains one **kiva** and has at least one **T-shaped doorway**. It is constructed of **core-and-veneer** masonry and has other Chacoan **great house** architectural characteristics. Tree-ring dates are primarily in the A.D. 1070s and 1080s.

An exterior whitewashed wall in the cliff dwelling above the possible **great house** gives the site its name. "White House" is also a place mentioned in the origin stories of several **Puebloan** groups, and they sometimes identify various prehistoric sites or archaeological zones such as Chaco Canyon and **Mesa Verde** as "White House." Other Puebloan peoples believe it is a more general area. The White House in Canyon de Chelly is not directly linked to the more "generic" Puebloan White House.

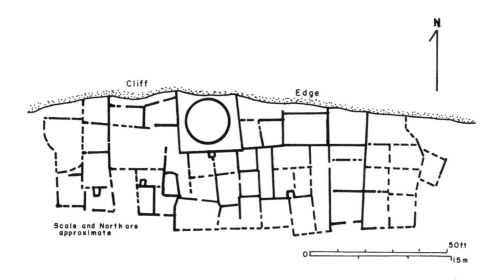

FIGURE 109. White House ground plan.

The canyon-bottom building was partially excavated by Earl **Morris** in the 1920s, but no report was written. White House is within Canyon de Chelly National Monument and is protected by the National Park Service.

Wijiji [Navajo for "black greasewood"]

(Map 3; Figure 110)

A small late Chacoan **great house** about five and a half miles east of **Pueblo Bonito**. With the exception of the **East Community** near the head of Chaco Canyon, Wijiji is the easternmost of the great houses on the canyon floor.

The building stands out in several ways. It appears to be transitional between the Classic **Bonito phase** great houses and those of the later **McElmo style**. The single tree-ring date, in the first decade of the 1100s, places the building in this transitional period. It is bracket-shaped and is constructed with a Bonito phase veneer, but lacks the front enclosing arc of rooms that characterizes the classic D-shaped

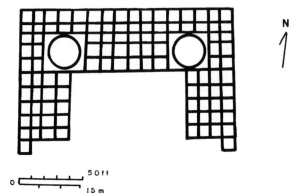

FIGURE 110. Wijiji great house ground plan. Locations of rooms and kivas are based on standing wall. No doorways are shown.

Chacoan great houses. The two **kivas** in the building are placed symmetrically at opposite ends of the northern core room block, reminiscent of its contemporary, the McElmo-style **Kin Kletso**.

It is also small. Although it covers slightly less ground space than Kin Kletso, it has about 60 more rooms (190 total) because they are smaller and more uniform in size than in most great houses.

Archaeologists studying the architecture of Wijiji tend to agree that the building seems to have been erected as one construction event, but the absence of any **trash mounds** near the site and the lack of remodeling raise the question as to whether it was ever occupied after it was built.

Carravahal, Lieutenant **Simpson**'s guide to **Chaco** in 1849, used the name Weje-gi for this great house. This apparently was the only great house visited by Simpson that was given a **Navajo** name, others having Spanish names such as **Pueblo Bonito**, or names of unknown origin such as **Chetro Ketl**. Carravahal did not provide a translation of the name.

Wills, Wirt "Chip"

A **Chaco Project** archaeologist whose work at **Pueblo Alto** stimulated a continuing interest in **great house** architecture and analysis of their **trash mounds**. His interpretation of great houses, particularly the **Chetro Ketl** great house, placed him somewhat at odds with other Chaco Project archaeologists. Rather than subscribing to the more common belief that the buildings represent ritual architecture financed by competitive religious leaders seeking followers, Wills suggested that they were more likely residential complexes whose periodic construction events may have been a type of ritual activity. As evidence, he noted that domestic features were present in great houses, the majority of artifacts from great houses were identical to those from **small house sites**, and evidence from excavated great houses showed continual modification and repair of rooms.

Wills also believed that the **stratigraphy** in trash mounds at **Pueblo Alto** and **Pueblo Bonito** represented small, almost daily deposits of household trash rather than large periodic feasting events as proposed by Wolcott **Toll**. To evaluate this hypothesis and to gain greater knowledge of possible features covered by the mounds, Wills and his wife, Chacoan scholar Patricia **Crown**, obtained National Park Service permission to reopen three trenches Neil **Judd** had cut between and through the two trash mounds fronting Pueblo Bonito. Final analysis of stratigraphic data is still underway, but Crown's discovery of **cacao** residue on **cylinder jar** fragments resulted from this work.

Windes, Thomas

A National Park Service archaeologist and foremost scholar on Chacoan prehistory. As a student of Florence **Hawley Ellis** and a **Chaco Project** staff member in the 1970s, Windes was involved in a number of investigations in Chaco Canyon and throughout the **San Juan Basin**. He played a major role in the excavation of **Pueblo Alto** and was the lead author on the resulting five-volume report on the Pueblo Alto Complex. Work at this and other sites provided him with a broad underpinning on essentially all aspects of Chacoan prehistory.

Among his numerous accomplishments, one of the most important was the reevaluation of the potential for **tree-ring dating** in great houses. By collecting hundreds of new specimens from these sites in the 1990s with park archaeologist Dabney Ford, he not only established more precise chronologies for the great houses but pushed back the date of the earliest construction of **Pueblo Bonito** to the mid-800s.

Following retirement from the National Park Service, Windes has continued his research on multiple aspects of Chacoan culture. These include a comprehensive investigation of early Chacoan development in the **Basketmaker** III and **Pueblo** I periods. His analysis of prehistoric sites on the Lower **Chaco River** and the establishment of great houses in Chaco Canyon is summarized in Stephen **Lekson**'s edited volume, *The Architecture of Chaco Canyon, New Mexico*. (See Selected Annotated References.)

Y

Yellow House (see *Kin Kletso*)

Z

Zuni
(Map 1)
A modern **Puebloan** community in northwestern New Mexico and the language family unique to the Zuni people. The Zuni Indian Reservation is approximately thirty miles south of Gallup, New Mexico, and eighty-five miles southwest of Chaco Canyon. Today the Zuni people live in Halona, or Zuni Pueblo, but at the time of initial Spanish contact in 1540 they were divided among six villages, including Halona. The population concentrated in Halona in the late 1600s, and since then the Zuni people have resided there and in several seasonal farming villages. There are more than 11,000 enrolled tribal members.

The Zuni language differs markedly from the **Tanoan**, **Keresan**, and **Uto-Aztecan** languages spoken by other Puebloan peoples, indicating its distinct linguistic origins. The Zuni social, political, and religious systems are also somewhat different from those of other Puebloans, though they share some aspects, especially with the Western Keresans and the Hopi. The **Hopi** and Zuni peoples have a long tradition of trading and exchanging religious ceremonies.

The Chacoan outlier **Village of the Great Kivas** is within ten miles of Halona, and other prehistoric sites on the Zuni Reservation show some affiliation with Chacoan culture. Several archaeologists believe that a tradition of Chacoan **great houses** and **roads** persisted in the Zuni area after Chaco Canyon was abandoned in the mid- to late 1100s.

Zuni Spotted Chert (see *Chert*)

SELECTED ANNOTATED REFERENCES

Our list of suggested reading material on Chaco has been revised largely as a result of the burgeoning published source material on the subject. Of the twenty-six entries in the first edition we have retained only five. We have not included fourteen technical reports, ten of which were a result of the Chaco Project and were published in relatively limited editions in several series including Reports of the Chaco Center and the Chaco Canyon Series. Many are now out of print. Readers wishing more information on these series should check Mathien's *Culture and Ecology of Chaco Canyon and the San Juan Basin* or consult the staff at Chaco Culture National Historical Park. Four additional technical reports were published in the Smithsonian Miscellaneous Collections and include Kirk Bryan's analysis of the geology of Chaco Canyon and Neil Judd's final reports on excavations at Pueblo Bonito and Pueblo del Arroyo. Full citations for these reports also can be found in Mathien's synthesis volume. A number of more recent general summaries of Chacoan prehistory and history have replaced earlier similar studies.

Cameron, Catherine M.

2009   *Chaco and After in the Northern San Juan: Excavations at the Bluff Great House.* University of Arizona Press, Tucson.
        This source is not only an excellent account of the excavation and analysis of recovered materials from this northern great house but a thorough evaluation of several critical aspects of late Chacoan sites in the northern San Juan region. Cameron and several collaborators review information on great houses and great kivas in

this region, summarize the Chaco and post-Chaco archaeology of the area, and provide the best information to date on earthen architecture. Cameron's final chapter, "Understanding the Bluff Great House," considers in fine detail many of the basic questions about late Chacoan prehistory.

Campbell, John Martin

2007 *The Great Houses of Chaco.* University of New Mexico Press. Albuquerque.

Campbell's black-and-white photography captures not only the essence of Chacoan great house architecture but the country occupied by Chacoans and the material goods they produced. The captions by Katherine Kallestad are rich with information. Thomas C. Windes's introductory chapter, "Chaco and Its Architecture," and David E. Stuart's concluding chapter, "Chacoan Great House Society," provide excellent frames for the photography.

Fagan, Brian

2005 *Chaco Canyon: Archaeologists Explore the Lives of an Ancient Society.* Oxford University Press, Oxford, New York.

Fagan, an internationally known and respected author of multiple popular accounts of archaeological sites and regions, was invited by the Chaco Synthesis group to prepare this volume. He combines a detailed account of a century of archaeological research in Chaco and a highly readable and in-depth analysis of the results of that research in the most recent interpretation of the Chaco Phenomenon.

Frazier, Kendrick

1999 *People of Chaco: A Canyon and Its Culture.* W. W. Norton & Company, New York.

Kendrick's 1999 update of the 1986 publication includes information collected by the Chaco Project, making this book a good general source for the interested layperson.

Kantner, John, and Nancy M. Mahoney, editors

2000 *Great House Communities across the Chacoan Landscape.* Anthropological Papers of the University of Arizona, no. 64. University of Arizona Press, Tucson.

Twelve papers by Chacoan archaeologists that summarize recent theories about the establishment of Chacoan outlier communities. Theoretical scenarios are reinforced by examples from a number of sites. The introductory and closing chapters provide excellent context.

Lekson, Stephen H.

1999 *The Chaco Meridian: Centers of Political Power in the Ancient Southwest.* AltaMira Press, Walnut Creek, California.

Lekson presents a controversial but challenging theory on the multigenerational evolution of Chacoan culture, proposing that it was centered through time in three capitals—Chaco, Aztec, and Paquimé—and united through their location on the same longitudinal meridian.

2009   *A History of the Ancient Southwest.* School for Advanced Research Press, Santa Fe.
Building on the basic premise of a shifting Chacoan capital as presented in *The Chaco Meridian*, Lekson expands his complex geopolitical drama to include the Hohokam region and people. Chapters are divided chronologically into "archaeologies"—scholarly trends and theoretical orientations in the profession—and "histories"—Lekson's accounts of Southwestern prehistories.

Lekson, Stephen H., editor

2006   *The Archaeology of Chaco Canyon: An Eleventh-Century Pueblo Regional Center.* School of American Research Press, Santa Fe.
This "Chaco Synthesis" volume includes summaries of data collected by the Chaco Project on architecture, ecology and economy, production of material goods, and Chacoan communities beyond Chaco Canyon. Other chapters consider alternative interpretations of Chacoan social and political organization, the early roots of Chacoan great houses, comparative analyses of Chaco with regional cultural systems to the north and south of Chaco, and Mesoamerican objects and symbols in Chaco. Lekson provides an introduction, Lynne Sebastian concluding remarks, and Richard Wilshusen and Derek Hamilton place the Chaco Project in historical context.

2007   *The Architecture of Chaco Canyon, New Mexico.* University of Utah Press, Salt Lake City.
Although the title suggests consideration of all Chacoan architecture in the canyon, coverage is limited—with one exception—to great houses, primarily Pueblo Bonito and Chetro Ketl, and great kivas. John Stein and his coauthors reevaluate a number of architectural and natural features in "downtown Chaco" and conclude that they represent a "linescape," a "shamanistic construct," that may date "as early as the fifth century."

Lister, Florence C.

2007   *Chaco's Vanished Past: Hogans, Tents and Ruins.* The Durango Herald Small Press. Durango, Colorado.
An excellent summary of Navajo, Spanish-American, and early Anglo occupation and use of the Chaco area. The Anglo period reviews both Wetherill's and Judd's archaeological investigation

of Pueblo Bonito and commercial trading with the local Navajo conducted by Wetherill and the later Griffin family. Prose sketches of eight local Navajo of historic importance and an edited interview with Richard Wetherill's son "Dick" are valuable additions to the text.

Mathien, Joan

2005   *Culture and Ecology of Chaco Canyon and the San Juan Basin.* Publications in Archeology 18H, Chaco Canyon Studies. U.S. Department of the Interior, Santa Fe.

A thorough, detailed summary of the National Park Service Chaco Project including information on its purpose and organization. The chapters on the environment and natural resources of the Chaco area will certainly remain the most comprehensive subject data source for a decade or more. Mathien organizes site data chronologically including the historic period and also provides valuable commentary on agriculture, the Chacoan people, great house and small house sites, and evidence for ritual, ceremony, and cosmology. Summary chapters on Chacoan outliers and Pueblo social organization build on Project information. A final chapter outlines potential avenues for future research using Project data.

McNitt, Frank

1966   *Richard Wetherill: Anasazi, Pioneer Explorer of Southwestern Ruins.* University of New Mexico Press, Albuquerque.

The revised edition of McNitt's 1957 biography of Richard Wetherill. The meticulous research, comfortable writing style, and superb illustrations continue to make this the primary source on Wetherill and his contributions to Chacoan archaeology.

Neitzel, Jill F., editor

2003   *Pueblo Bonito: Center of the Chacoan World.* Smithsonian Books, Washington, D.C.

An important collection of eleven papers on the best known Chacoan great house. The papers cover a wide range of topics critical to better understanding this and other Chacoan great houses. Topics include architecture, astronomy and ritual, burials, and artifacts as well as consideration of the building siting and great house function. Thomas Windes's paper, "This Old House: Construction and Abandonment at Pueblo Bonito," is a critically important contribution to understanding great houses.

Noble, David G., editor

2004   *In Search of Chaco: New Approaches to an Archaeological Enigma.* School of American Research Press, Santa Fe.

Noble's 1984 edited volume, *New Light on Chaco Canyon,* focused largely on new data from the Chaco Project. Twenty years later some of the same topics such as architecture, artifacts, farming, and outliers in the Chacoan World are considered, but new subjects such as sacred geography are included. Significantly, there are chapters by three Native Americans as well as excellent summaries of the Chaco Navajo, key debates in Chacoan archaeology, Chacoan society, Chaco and Mesa Verde, and Chaco as a potential location of high devotional expression. Florence Lister deftly considers a century of Chacoan archaeology.

Reed, Paul F., editor

2006   *Thirty-five Years of Archaeological Research at Salmon Ruins, New Mexico.* Center for Desert Archaeology, Tucson.

This three-volume publication combines basic elements of Cynthia Irwin-Williams's 1980 report on excavations at the Salmon Ruins with new research in several areas. Many of the original Salmon staff contributed to updating and interpreting site information on one of the most important Chacoan sites in the Totah region. Volume one summarizes architecture and site chronology and presents conclusions drawn from the old and new data. Volume two is devoted to ceramic studies and volume three to archaeobotanical research and other analytical studies.

2008   *Chaco's Northern Prodigies: Salmon, Aztec, and the Ascendancy of the Middle San Juan Region after* A.D. *1100.* The University of Utah Press, Salt Lake City.

Papers prepared for the 2004 Salmon Working Conference organized by Reed to review the past decade of archaeological research in the Middle San Juan region, the Totah. Chapters include comparative studies on ceramic design, sacred landscapes, and the Totah region's relationships with Chaco Canyon, the Bluff Great House region, and the Mesa Verde area.

Sofaer, Anna

2008   *Chaco Astronomy: An Ancient American Cosmology.* Ocean Tree Books, Santa Fe.

A compilation of Sofaer's multiple journal articles and book chapters, some with coauthors, detailing her long-term investigation of Chacoan astronomical phenomena. These are organized in four sections: Light Markings and Petroglyphs on Fajada Butte, Astronomical Expressions in the Major Chacoan Buildings, the Great North Road, and Computer Restoration of the Sun Dagger Site.

Van Dyke, Ruth M.

2007   *The Chaco Experience: Landscape and Ideology at the Center Place.* School for Advanced Research Press, Santa Fe.

Of the varied new approaches to explaining and perhaps understanding Chacoan prehistory, Van Dyke's book offers a unique approach. She argues that landscapes, both natural and culturally modified, provide a means for "seeing" and better understanding ancient worldviews, ideologies, and power relationships. Proceeding from this premise Van Dyke employs phenomenology, an approach grounded in existentialist philosophy, which suggests that because humans share spatial perceptions archaeologists moving through the same landscapes may gain some insights into past worldviews, an argument she supports with her own personal experiences.

Vivian, Gordon, and Paul Reiter

1960 *The Great Kivas of Chaco Canyon and Their Relationships*. Monographs of the School of American Research and the Museum of New Mexico, no. 22. Santa Fe.

Though great kivas are reviewed in several more recent publications, this remains the best summary of great kivas in Chaco Canyon. Comparison with several great kivas outside the canyon is included, though numerous other similar structures have been discovered since this work was published.

ILLUSTRATION CREDITS

FIG. 1: After Michael P. Marshall, John R. Stein, Richard W. Loose, and Judith E. Novotny, *Anasazi Communities of the San Juan Basin*, page 119. Public Service Company of New Mexico, Albuquerque, and State Historic Preservation Office, Santa Fe, 1979.

FIG. 2: Photo by R. Gwinn Vivian.

FIG. 3: After John R. Stein and Peter J. Mc-Kenna, *An Archaeological Reconnaissance of a Late Bonito Phase Occupation near Aztec Ruins National Monument, New Mexico*, report cover page. Southwest Cultural Resources Center, National Park Service, Santa Fe, 1988.

FIG. 4: After Robert P. Powers, William B. Gillespie, and Stephen H. Lekson, *The Outlier Survey: A Regional View of Settlement in the San Juan Basin*, Figure 69. Reports of the Chaco Center, no. 3, National Park Service, Albuquerque, 1983.

FIG. 5: After Powers et al. 1983: Figure 6.

FIG. 6: After Catherine M. Cameron, *Chaco and After in the Northern San Juan: Excavations at the Bluff Great House*, Figure 7.1. University of Arizona Press, 2009.

FIG 7: After Stephen H. Lekson, *Great Pueblo Architecture of Chaco Canyon, New Mexico*, Figure 4.97. University of New Mexico Press, Albuquerque, 1986.

FIG. 8: After Marshall et al. 1979:135.

FIG. 9: Courtesy of the National Park Service.

FIG. 10: After R. Gwinn Vivian, *The Chacoan Prehistory of the San Juan Basin*, Figure 8.34. Academic Press, San Diego, 1990.

FIG. 11: Drawing by R. Gwinn Vivian.

FIG. 12: Drawing by R. Gwinn Vivian.

FIG. 13: Photo by R. Gwinn Vivian.

FIG. 14: After Robert H. Lister and Florence Lister, *Chaco Canyon Archaeology and Archaeologists*, Figure 75. University of New Mexico Press, Albuquerque, 1981; and Lekson 1986: Figure 4.39.

FIG. 15: After Powers et al. 1983: Figure 72.

FIG. 16: Illustration by Bruce Hilpert.

FIG. 17: Photo by R. Gwinn Vivian.

FIG. 18: Arizona State Museum, University of Arizona; Helga Teiwes, photographer.

FIG. 19: After Lekson 1986: Figure 2.5.

FIG. 20: Photo by R. Gwinn Vivian.

FIG. 21: Photo by R. Gwinn Vivian.

FIG. 22: Drawing by R. Gwinn Vivian.

FIG. 23: Drawing by R. Gwinn Vivian.

FIG. 24: Photo by R. Gwinn Vivian.

FIG. 25: Photo by R. Gwinn Vivian.

FIG. 26: After Windes et al., in Kantner and Mahoney 2000, *Great House Communities across the Chacoan Landscape*, Figure 4.6. University of Arizona Press, Tucson, 2000.

FIG. 27: Drawing by R. Gwinn Vivian.

FIG. 28: Photo by R. Gwinn Vivian.

FIG. 29: After Judith A. Hallasi, "Archaeological Excavation at the Escalante Site, Dolores, Colorado, 1975 and 1976," Figure 6, in *The Archaeology and Stabilization of the Dominguez and Escalante Ruins.* Colorado State Office, Bureau of Land Management, Cultural Resource Series 7, Denver, 1979.

FIG. 30: Drawing by R. Gwinn Vivian.

FIG. 31: Photo by R. Gwinn Vivian.

FIG. 32: Photo by R. Gwinn Vivian.

FIG. 33: Drawing by R. Gwinn Vivian.

FIG. 34: After Vivian 1990: Figure 8.20.

FIG. 35: Courtesy of Palace of the Governors Photo Archives, NMHM/DCA, neg. 81714.

FIG. 36: Photo by R. Gwinn Vivian.

FIG. 37: Photo by Limbaugh Engineering and Aerial Surveys, Albuquerque.

FIG. 38: After Durand and Durand, in Kantner and Mahoney 2000: Figure 8.2.

FIG. 39: After Powers et al. 1983: Figure 91.

FIG. 40: After Marshall et al. 1979:242.

FIG. 41: After James H. Simpson, *Journal of a Military Reconnaissance from Santa Fe, New Mexico to the Navajo Country*, Plate 4. Report to the Secretary of War to the 31st Congress, 1st Session, Senate Executive Document 64. Washington, D.C., 1850.

FIG. 42: Photo by Tom Windes. Courtesy of National Park Service, neg. 32289.

FIG. 43: After R. Gordon Vivian, *The Hubbard Site and Other Tri-Wall Structures in New Mexico and Colorado,* Figure 5. Archaeological Research Series no. 5, National Park Service, Washington, D.C., 1959.

FIG. 44: After Lekson 1986: Figure 4.34.

FIG. 45: Photo by R. Gwinn Vivian.

FIG. 46: From Jesse Walter Fewkes, "Hopi Katcinas Drawn by Native Artists," Plate XII, right. In the 21st annual *Report of the Bureau of American Ethnology to the Secretary of the Smithsonian Institution, 1899–1900.* Government Printing Office, Washington, D.C., 1903.

FIG. 47: After Marshall et al. 1979:60.

FIG. 48: After Lekson 1986: Figure 4.86.

FIG. 49: Arizona State Museum, University of Arizona; Helga Teiwes, photographer.

FIG. 50: After Lister and Lister 1981: Figure 79; and Marshall et al. 1979:70.

FIG. 51: After Marshall et al. 1979:202.

FIG. 52: After Neil M. Judd, *The Architecture of Pueblo Bonito*, Figure 22. Smithsonian Miscellaneous Collections, vol. 147, Washington, D.C., 1964.

FIG. 53: After Donald D. Brand et al., *Tseh So: A Small House Ruin, Chaco Canyon, New Mexico,* Figure 2. Preliminary report. University of New Mexico Bulletin, Anthropological Series 2 (2) (1937).

FIG. 54: Drawing by R. Gwinn Vivian.

FIG. 55: After Bertha P. Dutton, *Leyit Kin, A Small House Ruin, Chaco Canyon, New Mexico: Excavation Report*, Figure 1. University of New Mexico Bulletin, Monograph Series 1 (6) (1938).

FIG. 56: After Vivian 1990: Figure 8.14.

FIG. 57: After Powers et al. 1983: Figure 82.

FIG. 58: Photo by R. Gwinn Vivian.

FIG. 59: After Lekson 1986: Figure 2.5.

FIG. 60: Arizona State Museum, University of Arizona; Helga Teiwes, photographer.

FIG. 61: Drawing by R. Gwinn Vivian.

FIG. 62: After Miranda Warburton and Donna K. Graves, "Navajo Springs, Arizona: Frontier Outlier or Autonomous Great House?" Figure 2. *Journal of Field Archaeology* 19 (1) (1992):51–69.

FIG. 63: After Lekson 1986: Figure 4.100.

FIG. 64: Arizona State Museum, University of Arizona.

FIG. 65: After Thomas C. Windes, *The Spadefoot Toad Site: Investigations at 29SJ 629, Chaco*

Canyon, New Mexico, Figure 2.6. Reports of the Chaco Center, no. 12, National Park Service, Santa Fe, 1993.

FIG. 66: After Lekson 1986: Figure 4.8.

FIG. 67: Photo by R. Gwinn Vivian.

FIG. 68: Photo by R. Gwinn Vivian.

FIG. 69: After Powers et al. 1983: Figure 40.

FIG. 70: Drawing by R. Gwinn Vivian.

FIG. 71: Arizona State Museum, University of Arizona; Helga Teiwes, photographer.

FIG. 72: After Jonathan E. Reyman, "Rediscovered Pseudo-cloisonné from Pueblo Bonito: Description and Comparisons," Figure 2. In *Clues to the Past: Papers in Honor of William M. Sundt*, edited by M. S. Duran and D. T. Kirkpatrick. Papers of the Archaeological Society of New Mexico, no. 16, pp. 217–228, Albuquerque, 1990.

FIG. 73: Arizona State Museum, University of Arizona.

FIG. 74: After Lekson 1986: Figure 4.55.

FIG. 75: After Judd 1964: Figure 2.

FIG. 76: After Lekson 1986: Figure 4.63.

FIG. 77: After Marshall et al. 1979:83.

FIG. 78: After Thomas C. Windes, *Investigations at the Pueblo Alto Complex, Chaco Canyon, New Mexico: 1975–1979*, Figure 4-4. Publications in Archeology 18F, Chaco Canyon Studies, U.S. Department of the Interior, Santa Fe, 1987.

FIG. 79: Arizona State Museum, University of Arizona; Helga Teiwes, photographer.

FIG. 80: Drawing by R. Gwinn Vivian.

FIG. 81: Photo by R. Gwinn Vivian.

FIG. 82: Courtesy Paul Reiter/Palace of the Goverors Photo Archives, NMHM/DCA, neg. 66875.

FIG. 83: After Cynthia Irwin-Williams and Phillip H. Shelley, editors, *Investigations at the Salmon Site: The Structure of Chacoan Society in the Northern Southwest* (4 vols.), Figure 4.6. Final Report to Funding Agencies. Eastern New Mexico University Printing Services, Portales, 1980.

FIG. 84: After Frank H. H. Roberts, *Shabik'eshchee Village, a Late Basketmaker Site in the Chaco Canyon, New Mexico*, Plate 1. Bureau of American Ethnology Bulletin 92 (1929).

FIG. 85: Photo by R. Gwinn Vivian.

FIG. 86: After Marshall et al. 1979:112.

FIG. 87: After Powers et al. 1983: Figure 115.

FIG. 88: Photo by R. Gwinn Vivian.

FIG. 89: Photo by R. Gwinn Vivian.

FIG. 90: Drawing by R. Gwinn Vivian.

FIG. 91: After Vivian 1990: Figure 8.19.

FIG. 92: After Kendrick Frazier, "The Anasazi Sun Dagger," *Science 80* 1 (1) (1979): 61.

FIG. 93: Photo by R. Gwinn Vivian.

FIG. 94: After Stephen Lekson, "The Architecture of Talus Unit, Chaco Canyon, New Mexico," Figure 2. In *Prehistory and History of the Southwest: Collected Papers in Honor of Alden C. Hayes*, edited by Nancy Fox. Papers of the Archaeological Society of New Mexico, no. 11, Albuquerque, 1985.

FIG. 95: Courtesy Palace of the Governors Photo Archives, NMHM/DCA, neg. 6153.

FIG. 96: After Gordon Vivian, *The Three-C Site: An Early Pueblo II Ruin in Chaco Canyon, New Mexico*, Figure 2. University of New Mexico Publications in Anthropology 13, Albuquerque, 1965.

FIG. 97: After Marshall et al. 1979:18, 203.

FIG. 98: After Vivian, *The Hubbard Site and Other Tri-Wall Structures in New Mexico and Colorado*, Figure 48.

FIG. 99: After Vivian 1990: Figure 8.12.

FIG. 100: Photo by R. Gwinn Vivian.

FIG. 101: After Lekson 1986: Figure 4.81.

FIG. 102: After Powers et al. 1983: Figure 88.

FIG. 103: Adapted from Lekson 1986: Figure 4.1.

FIG. 104: Photos by R. Gwinn Vivian.

FIG. 105: Photo by R. Gwinn Vivian.

FIG. 106: After Frank H. H. Roberts, *Village of the Great Kivas on the Zuni Reservation, New Mexico,* Plate 1. Bureau of American Ethnology Bulletin 111 (1932).

FIG. 107: After Powers et al. 1983: Figure 75.

FIG. 108: Drawing by R. Gwinn Vivian.

FIG. 109: After Cosmos Mindeleff, "The Cliff Ruins of Canyon de Chelly, Arizona," Figure 14. In the 16th annual *Report of the Bureau of American Ethnology to the Secretary of the Smithsonian Institution, 1894–1895,* pp. 79–198. Government Printing Office, Washington, D.C., 1897.

FIG. 110: After Lekson 1986: Figure 4.75.

MAPS 1–5: Drawn by R. Gwinn Vivian.

Time lines by Bruce Hilpert.

INDEX

ABOUT THE AUTHORS

R. GWINN VIVIAN is a former Curator of Archaeology at the Arizona State Museum, University of Arizona, Tucson. He has carried out research in Chaco Canyon for more than forty years and has published on such topics as prehistoric roads, water control systems, and social organization in the greater Chaco area. He holds a B.A. and M.A. from the University of New Mexico and a Ph.D. in anthropology from the University of Arizona.

BRUCE HILPERT is a former Curator of Public Programs at the Arizona State Museum, University of Arizona, Tucson. For more than twenty years he interpreted the cultural history of the Southwest for the general public through museum exhibits, education programs, classes, and publications. He holds a B.A. and M.A. in anthropology from the University of Arizona.